Advocates for Change

Advocates for Change

How to Overcome Africa's Challenges

EDITED BY

MOELETSI MBEKI

PICADOR AFRICA

First published in 2011 by Picador Africa
an imprint of Pan Macmillan South Africa
Private Bag X19, Northlands
Johannesburg, 2116

www.panmacmillan.co.za

ISBN 978-1-77010-120-3

Editing by Sally Hines
Proofreading by Christopher Merrett
Index by Ethné Clarke
Design and typesetting by Patricia Comrie
Inside graphics by M Design
Cover design by K4
Printed and bound by Ultra Litho

Contents

Foreword

HANNS SEIDEL FOUNDATION

In his recent book, *Architects of Poverty: Why African Capitalism Needs Changing*, Moeletsi Mbeki embarked on a journey through the socio-economic development of Africa's states since independence. He presented a detailed analysis of the most pressing issues hampering growth and preventing the rise of millions of people out of poverty. Among others, he identified the question of leadership as one of the key factors holding African states back. However, if criticism is to be constructive, it must be accompanied by solutions. This is exactly what Mbeki does as the editor of *Advocates for Change: How to Overcome Africa's Challenges*. He has put together hands-on suggestions on how to solve Africa's development challenges.

Mbeki is one of the most outspoken critics of his own continent. Decades of experience all over the world have shown that no external player can replace critical analysis and innovative ideas from the community itself to bring about the transformation of an economy. Sustainable change can only come from within.

However, Mbeki does not pretend to know all the solutions to change Africa's future. On the contrary, in this book Mbeki relies on experts in a wide variety of subjects, such as education, entrepreneurship, economic and social affairs, as well as mining, to describe the solutions they have come up with after years of research and experience. These experts hail from various African countries but through their contributions they all show an unwavering will to contribute to a more prosperous Africa and to a better livelihood for fellow Africans. They are the advocates who promote change.

Advocates for Change complements *Architects of Poverty* perfectly; after laying out the obstacles to development, the focus now shifts to the solutions. Hence the book you hold in your hands contains an urgent call to action – I hope many African readers will feel inspired and motivated to be advocates for change themselves.

Dr Peter Witterauf
CEO, Hanns Seidel Foundation

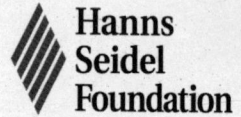

Hanns
Seidel
Foundation

Abbreviations

ACP	African, Caribbean and Pacific
AMTS	Advanced Manufacturing Technology Strategy
ANC	African National Congress
ASEAN	Association of South East Asian Nations
AU	African Union
AZAPO	Azanian People's Organisation
BPO	Business Process Outsourcing
BRIC	Brazil, Russia, India and China
CBO	community-based organisation
CIPRO	Companies and Intellectual Property Registration Office
COPE	Congress of the People
COSATU	Congress of South African Trade Unions
DA	Democratic Alliance
DFI	Development Finance Institution
DRC	Democratic Republic of the Congo
DTI	Department of Trade and Industry
ECOWAS	Economic Community of West African States
EEC	European Economic Community
EPZ	export processing zone
EU	European Union
FAO	Food and Agriculture Organization
FDI	foreign direct investment
GCRO	Gauteng City-Region Observatory

GDP	gross domestic product
GEM	Global Entrepreneurship Monitor
GNP	gross national product
GNU	government of national unity
HDI	Human Development Index
ICT	information and communication technology
IDEA	Initiative for Development in East Asia
IFI	International Finance Institution
IFP	Inkatha Freedom Party
IMF	International Monetary Fund
IMS	Integrated Manufacturing Strategy
ISI	import substitution industrialisation
IT	information technology
JSE	Johannesburg Stock Exchange
MDG	Millennium Development Goal
MMM	Mouvement Militant Mauricien
NARS	National Agriculture Research System
NCR	National Credit Regulator
NEPAD	New Partnership for Africa's Development
NGO	non-governmental organisation
OAU	Organisation of African Unity
OBE	Outcomes Based Education
ODA	Official Development Assistance
OECD	Organization for Economic Cooperation and Development
PAC	Pan-Africanist Congress
R&D	research and development
REC	Regional Economic Community
SACMEQ	Southern and Eastern Africa Consortium for Monitoring Educational Quality
SACP	South African Communist Party
SADTU	South African Democratic Teachers' Union
SAP	structural adjustment programme
SARB	South African Reserve Bank

SARS	South African Revenue Service
SME	small and medium enterprise
SMME	small, medium and micro enterprise
STD	sexually transmitted disease
TB	tuberculosis
TFP	total factor productivity
TIMSS	Trends in International Mathematics and Science Study
UN	United Nations
UNCTAD	United Nations Conference on Trade and Development
UNDP	United Nations Development Programme
UNECA	United Nations Economic Commission for Africa
US	United States
VD	voting district
WHO	World Health Organization

Introduction

MOELETSI MBEKI

In my first book, *Architects of Poverty: Why African Capitalism Needs Changing*, I examined why the African people comprise the majority of the world's bottom billion. There is a generally expressed consensus that Africa lacks a dynamic and innovative political and economic leadership. Africa's second most important deficit is that it lacks power. Africa's governments and its non-governmental institutions, be they for-profit businesses or non-profit organisations, do not really count in the world because they are not powerful. The once-powerful South African mining companies, especially De Beers Consolidated Mines and Anglo American Corporation, are no longer African; the African National Congress (ANC) government sold them off to foreigners for 30 pieces of silver.

'Power', according to a leading American political scientist, Joseph Nye, 'is the ability to attain the outcomes one wants and the resources that produce it vary in different contexts' (p. 2). Africa has no power because it does not have the leaders who are able to mobilise the resources needed to make Africa powerful. But what is a leader?

A leader is someone who identifies political and/or economic opportunities that can lead to the solution of overwhelming social problems or challenges facing his or her community and successfully persuades others to work with him or her to implement those solutions. Leadership therefore requires at least three capabilities:

- capacity to innovate;
- ability to implement by mobilising the required resources; and
- capability to create followers.

Institutions and organisations have a multitude of supervisors and managers. Some of these functionaries and officials see themselves or are seen by the people they oversee as leaders. This is not necessarily the case as most of these managers do not innovate or create a following; they merely see to it that established procedures and processes are followed.

In *Long Walk to Freedom*, Nelson Mandela, one of Africa's great twentieth-century leaders, said: 'There are times when a leader must move out ahead of the flock, go off in a new direction, confident that he is leading his people the right way' (p. 627).

This volume, *Advocates for Change*, brings together specialists from all over Africa who believe that there are solutions to the challenges that Africa faces. From education to politics, from agriculture to mineral resource management, and from foreign intervention to re-industrialisation, entrepreneurship and beyond, this book focuses on how we can solve our continent's most pressing problems.

There is nothing mysterious about why Africa is the least developed continent and why Africans are the poorest and most unhealthy people in the world. Because of its military and technological weakness Africa has been destabilised and plundered for centuries through the slave trade, colonialism, neo-colonialism, the cold war and feeble post-independence leadership. But Africa is not the only continent that has been plundered over the last half a millennium; the indigenous peoples who inhabited the Americas have suffered the same fate, as American scientist Jared M. Diamond describes in *Guns, Germs and Steel: The Fate of Human Societies*.

There cannot be many Africans who do not every day see the causes of their unfortunate situation. These range from corruption in high and low places to inept public officials to a demotivated private sector and parastatal managers and to foreigners helping themselves to Africa's natural resources in return for crumbs for African governments.

This volume, however, is not about focusing on these problems which we are all familiar with. Rather, the chapters that follow are about the *solutions* that will lead to Africa's economic development and political stability as well as to its social development and well-being. The solutions are presented here for those who want to use them in order to develop their countries.

Elites and development

The experience of economic development during the last 500 years since Christopher Columbus reached the Americas and Vasco de Gama reached India via the Cape of Good Hope teaches us that it is the dominant political elite in any given society that determines whether a country develops or does not develop. Entrepreneurs of all descriptions – from pirates to inventors to investment bankers – play a critical role in the economic development process but they can do so only if the dominant political elite allows them to play that role.

There are many reasons why a given political elite promotes or is compelled to promote economic development. When an elite has its power threatened by foreigners who are more powerful than itself, one of the ways it tries to survive is by acquiring the expertise that the foreigners have and in the process developing its country's economy. This was how Japan developed modern industry. Inter-state wars in Europe compelled many of Europe's rulers to develop industries that gave their countries the industrial capacity to withstand these wars and protect their regimes.

The story of why Japan industrialised late is worth retelling in some detail because it holds many lessons for Africa.

European seafarers first appeared in Japan during the mid-sixteenth century, blown off course by a storm. They found a country nominally ruled by an emperor but in reality made up of warring principalities. The guns the Europeans brought were of special value to the warring parties and they soon learnt how to make them. They also learnt from the Europeans how to make clocks and spectacles.

The Europeans, mainly Portuguese, Spaniards and Dutch, brought more than material products; they also brought Christianity, especially Catholicism. Many Japanese people took to that as well. Christianity not only nourished their souls; it also gave them access to Western technology and trade opportunities.

This happy state of affairs came to an end at the beginning of the seventeenth century when the Japanese aristocracy realised that Christianity was going to undermine its hold over its subjects. In addition, having largely overcome internal feuds thanks to guns, the rulers needed to disarm the population and re-assert their authority in traditional ways – with the sword of the horse-mounted samurai. They banned the manufacture of guns, and books from the West were burnt and prohibited. The elite set out to eradicate Christianity by slaughtering its followers in their thousands. Starting in 1616, they banned foreign merchant vessels, except Chinese and Korean ships.

From the beginning of the seventeenth century until well into the nineteenth century, the members of the Japanese aristocracy protected and entrenched the pre-modern feudal society in their country and thus held back economic development for a period of 250 years.

It was only after the revolution of 1867–8, which led to what is known as the Meiji Restoration, that the country started on the road to industrialisation. The revolution of 1867–8 came about as a result of pressure on Japan by Western powers to open up the country to Western merchants. Between 1854 and 1863 the United States, Britain, France and Holland, through gunboat diplomacy, compelled Japan to sign treaties that limited its control over its own foreign trade. As a result, the Japanese realised that if their country was to remain independent it needed to adopt modern science and technology in its production systems. And so began Japan's industrialisation after

250 years of resisting modernisation. Until recently, Japan was the second-largest economy in the world.

While the process of economic development could have been triggered by any number of factors, as the above story on Japan illustrates, once it got going political elites soon realised the advantages that it brought them. Before long one of the objectives of many elites became the economic development of their countries.

Economic development occurs when a population in a given territory applies modern science and technology to drive its production processes. The use of science raises the productivity per worker, which in turn leads to higher standards of living in the society in question. Greater use of science in production also raises the general level of knowledge in a given population. This explains why economic development is not always preferred by some political elites. They see the ramifications of economic development as leading to greater independence of thought in their subjects, which then threatens their power. This is one of the reasons that many countries in Africa have not developed. These weak elites feel threatened by the rising levels of knowledge and skill amongst their citizens.

The story of Japan's feudal aristocracy holding back development for 250 years is replicated to varying degrees by many elites in Africa. One of the striking examples was the apartheid system in South Africa. The new elite that took over at the end of the apartheid era in 1994 has carried forward some of the anti-development features of the past, as we shall see later.

Elites and under-development

The story of South Africa during the last two centuries encapsulates many of the experiences of the African continent today with regard to economic development. South Africa had rulers who feared the rise of knowledge amongst the country's citizens, which led to the introduction of, for example, the restrictive policy of Bantu Education aimed at keeping the 'natives' in their rightful position.

Hendrik Verwoerd, the late infamous prime minister of South Africa, articulated this fear better than anyone when he justified the introduction of the notorious Bantu Education system. In a speech delivered in 1954, which is quoted in David Welsh's book *The Rise and Fall of Apartheid*, Verwoerd said:

> It is the policy of my department that [black] education should have its roots entirely in the Native [black] areas and in the Native environment and Native community. There Bantu education must be able to give itself complete expression and there it will have to perform its real service. The Bantu must be guided to serve his own community in all respects. There is no place for him in the European [white] community above the level of certain forms of labour. Within his own community, however, all doors are open. For that reason it is of no avail for him to receive a training which has as its aim absorption in the European community while he cannot and will not be absorbed there. Up till now he has been subjected to a school system which drew him away from his own community and partially misled him by showing him the green pastures of the European but still did not allow him to graze there (pp. 64–5).

What Verwoerd was describing and was passing off as his original philosophical discovery was, in fact, the enclave economy that had emerged in South Africa with the discovery of diamonds and gold. The mining-based enclave economy has a low labour absorption rate and therefore leaves a large part of the labour force outside the labour market, which then becomes an underclass. The concept of an enclave economy was developed by the Malawian economist Guy Mhone.

There were, however, groups in South Africa that were compelled to promote some economic development of the country in order to reap the benefits of their ownership of the land.

Over the last 200 years South Africa has been ruled by at least four types of political elite:

- indigenous African aristocracy;
- British imperialists;
- Afrikaner landowners; and
- black upper class.

Each of these groups of elites has had its own perspective on economic development. The indigenous aristocracy was completely opposed to the introduction of private property in land. Private property is one of the key pre-conditions to economic development. The indigenous aristocracy was also opposed to many aspects of modern science, especially Western medicine, and it saw Christianity as a force that undermined its rule.

By contrast, during British imperialism's control of South Africa from 1795 to 1910, Britain itself was a leading industrial and military power in the world but saw no need to bring economic development to South Africa. The British objective in South Africa was to control the Cape sea route. It was only when it was realised that South Africa had large deposits of diamonds and gold that the British took an interest in developing the South African economy, but the British imperialist's concept of South Africa's development did not extend beyond extracting these two minerals by building a limited infrastructure to achieve their defined objective.

The Afrikaner nationalist landowners in most of South Africa were largely pastoralists who raised cattle, sheep and horses. There was a small group that grew wheat and grapes for wine making. So until well into the twentieth century, South Africa's agriculture remained under-developed. After this group took power from the British in 1910, it started to promote some economic development in South Africa. The objective of this ruling elite was to make the land it owned more profitable. The Afrikaner landowners' first initiative after coming to power was to establish the Land Bank in 1910. To realise its goals, the Afrikaner nationalist elite had to invest in the building of South Africa's transportation and communication infrastructure. It also had to build the necessary education institutions to provide white citizens with expertise in all aspects of agriculture. Simultaneously, it incentivised others to invest in different sectors of the economy.

As an incentive to investors, this elite group made available a dependable supply of cheap labour from South Africa's black population and its neighbours. All of these efforts culminated in making South Africa the largest economy in Africa today, which produces almost a quarter of the continent's gross domestic product (GDP).

The black upper middle class that became South Africa's dominant political elite in 1994, unlike the previous three political elites, was a class of intellectuals rather than of property owners. Its main objective for acquiring political power was therefore not to protect its property or to develop such property since it did not have any. Instead, its main objective was to bring about equality between the races and to redistribute some of the existing, white-owned wealth to the blacks. To achieve political equality, this elite fought for democracy, which was eventually achieved in 1994. To achieve economic equality, it adopted a policy of wealth redistribution.

There is, however, a downside to an economic strategy that is predominantly driven by wealth redistribution. It diverts resources from investment to consumption. This is already beginning to show with the growing de-industrialisation of the country's economy. The scramble for wealth redistribution has also become a main driver of corruption.

The enclave economy that Verwoerd was so eloquent about is thus perpetuated under the ANC government that came to power in 1994. To maintain its power in a democratic environment that Verwoerd did not have to worry about, the ANC has had to develop welfare programmes that appease the large underclass inherent in an enclave economy.

There is no better positioned organisation on the South African political landscape than the ANC. If its voters remain poor, the ANC wins because they vote for it. In the very unlikely event that they become richer through, for example, 'tenderpreneurship', they will still vote for the ANC because they want to be on the list for the next tender from the ANC government.

Voters for the ANC do not vote for it for ideological reasons or for policy reasons; they vote for it primarily because of their material dependence on the ANC-controlled state. This was brought into sharp focus by a November 2009 study conducted by South Africa's leading market research company, Ipsos Markinor. The study revealed hitherto unknown information about who are the main voters of South Africa's dominant party, the ANC. The study found that two thirds (67%) of people who vote for the ANC do not work. Of the one third that works, 24% work full time and 9% only work part time.

An even more striking revelation by the new study is the education levels of ANC voters:

- only 8% of ANC supporters have higher education qualifications;
- 23% have graduated from high school; and
- 69% either have no education at all or have not completed high school.

What this illustrates is that the primary constituency that votes for the ANC is made up of poor black South Africans.

The solutions
Political stability
The greatest threat facing the people of Africa is the possibility of the failure of their states. There have been many studies undertaken to evaluate the durability of African states, most of which have drawn attention to the weaknesses firstly of Africa's political elites that control these states and secondly to the weaknesses of the states themselves.

There cannot be greater evidence of the weakness of African states than the ongoing instability in Zimbabwe, Kenya, Côte d'Ivoire and Libya. Only a few years ago, these four countries were considered to be amongst the strongest countries on the continent with reasonably diversified economies and high standing in the eyes of most Africans and of the international community. Today these countries are on the edge of disintegration.

In her seminal study of endemic corruption in Kenya, Michela Wrong paints a harrowing picture of how political elites in Kenya and in many other African countries loot, plunder and siphon their ill-gotten gains abroad and therefore curtail economic development. The recent upheavals in North Africa have shone more light on how Africa's ruling elites subsidise the rich world by exporting vast amounts of capital from Africa with the understandable connivance of their partners overseas.

The London-based International Institute for Strategic Studies made the following observation about fragile states:

> There is broad consensus on the general syndrome of state fragility and failure, if not on the specifics of how to measure and weigh each factor. These include weak capacity to provide public security, rule of law and basic social services; low levels of democracy and civil liberties; de-legitimisation and criminalisation of the state; rising factionalism; poor, socially uneven and declining economic performance; inability to manage political conflict; extensive interference by external actors; and, in some but not all cases, outbreaks and armed insurgence.
>
> Secondly, the same set of countries – mainly concentrated in sub-Saharan Africa – tends to appear at the bottom of every ranking related to fragility, poor governance and conflict vulnerability, regardless of methodologies and measurements (pp. 174–5).

There are solutions to Africa's political malaise. In this book, Chapters 3, 7 and 8 analyse the dynamics of democracy in the multi-ethnic, multi-denominational and multi-class environment of African countries. Where societies are reasonably equal, the economy is well managed and elections are free and fair, democracy works in Africa, as can be seen in the case of Mauritius. Even in the highly unequal environment of South Africa, democracy works where elections are free and fair.

The picture becomes more interesting when one moves out of South Africa and Mauritius – sub-Saharan Africa's only middle-income countries – to the rest of sub-Saharan Africa, which, because it is low income, is dependant on donors. The machinations of donors in these aid-dependent countries and the games they play with Africa's fragile and dependent political elites that lead to the creation of pseudo-democracies leave one breathless. This calls for an urgent need to downscale the role of donors in African politics. Africans themselves must finance their freedom and economic development.

Social and economic development
A question frequently asked is what should come first in Africa, democracy or economic and social development? This question is usually inspired by the industrialisation of East Asian countries (South Korea, Taiwan, China, pre-Second World War Japan and Indonesia) that industrialised under authoritarian political systems. Firstly, what Africans overlook is that Asian states are hundreds and even thousands of years old. Secondly, Asian countries are by and large single-ethnic countries and therefore do not have the mega-challenges of ethnic divisions and conflicts that are so prevalent in Africa.

All these attributes of Asia make it possible for Asian dictators to dictate while African dictators merely create mayhem, which in turn makes sustained economic and social development impossible.

Contributions in this book show that Africa's development is possible where conditions of stability obtain.

Conclusion
Many writers on Africa have looked at Africa's challenges and have despaired. Some of the writers have gone so far as to suggest what is

going on in Africa should be accepted as the natural course of events for the continent because, according to them, this is how Africa works. The contributors to this volume are amongst the leading experts in their fields; their message is that Africa's problems are far from intractable. Their second message is that we should not accept what passes as inevitable. There is nothing unavoidable about Africa's political instability; Africa's economic under-performance; Africa's falling health and educational standards; Africa's inability to advance regional integration and to raise the productivity of small-scale agricultural systems. The contributors to this book show that there are practical solutions – as distinct from pie-in-the sky solutions – to Africa's challenges.

Advocates for Change echoes the message that the African people have already arrived at. There is no greater illustration of this message that there are practical solutions to Africa's problems than what has happened in North Africa. In December 2010, 26-year-old unemployed university graduate, Tarek al-Tayyib Muhammad Bouazizi, usually referred to as Mohamed Bouazizi, set himself on fire having been tormented by municipal officials for selling fruit and vegetables without a licence at his home town of Sidi Bouzid in Tunisia. Mohamed Bouazizi's actions resonated with the populations not just of Tunisia but of North Africa and the Middle East.

Bouazizi's actions sent a message that the people had had enough of the arrogance, corruption, ineptitude and incompetence of Africa's ruling elites. The second message Bouazizi sent out was that the people of Africa are ready to take action and to pay the price to rectify 60 years of misrule in Africa.

The response of the South African government to what has happened in North Africa is that it cannot happen here. They argue that South Africa has a democracy which, according to them, shields it from extensive social and political conflict. Ironically, South Africa being a middle-income country like the North African countries is the one country in sub-Saharan Africa that is most likely to experience what has happened in North Africa. Closer examination of events in

South Africa shows that this has already started. South Africa has one of the largest occurrences of social protest against incompetence and corruption at various levels of the public sector. This proves the fallacy that there can be no social and political upheavals in a democracy. One of the largest civil wars of modern times, the American Civil War of 1861 to 1865, took place in what was then and still is the most envied democracy.

MOELETSI MBEKI is a journalist, private business entrepreneur, political commentator and author of the South African bestseller *Architects of Poverty: Why African Capitalism Needs Changing*, published by Picador Africa in 2009.

References and further reading

Berdal, M. and Wennmann, A. (eds.) (2010) *Ending Wars, Consolidating Peace: Economic Perspective* (International Institute for Strategic Studies, London).

Diamond, J.M. (1999) *Guns, Germs, and Steel: The Fates of Human Societies* (W.W. Norton & Company, New York and London).

Ipsos Markinor (2009) *Socio-Political Trends*, Vol. 1, November, Johannesburg.

Landes, D.S. (1998) *The Wealth and Poverty of Nations: Why Some are So Rich and Some So Poor* (Abacus, London).

Mandela, N. (1995) *Long Walk to Freedom* (Macdonald Purnell, London).

Mbeki, M. (2009) *Architects of Poverty: Why African Capitalism Needs Changing* (Picador Africa, Johannesburg).

Mhone, G. (2000) *Enclavity and Constrained Labour Absorptive Capacity in Southern African Countries* (International Labour Organization, Geneva).

Nye, J.S. Jnr (2010) 'The Future of American Power: Dominance and Decline in Perspective' in *Foreign Affairs* Vol. 89, No. 6.

Welsh, D. (2009) *The Rise and Fall of Apartheid* (Jonathan Ball Publishers, Johannesburg and Cape Town).

Wrong, M. (2009) *It's Our Turn to Eat: The Story of a Kenyan Whistleblower* (HarperCollins, London).

1

Negative Trends
in the South African Economy

How Should These be Overcome?

SEERAJ MOHAMED

> The outstanding faults of the economic society in which we
> live are its failure to provide for full employment and its
> arbitrary and inequitable distribution of wealth and incomes.
> — John Maynard Keynes

Introduction

The key negative trends in the South African economy are very high unemployment and inequality. These trends are symptoms of deeper problems, which will be discussed in this chapter. There are strong historical reasons for the negative trends. However, recent behaviour by the private sector and economic policy choices of the government have exacerbated past negative trends and created new economic problems. Further, the South African economy has increased its integration into the global economy and been significantly affected by recent unhealthy global economic trends.

The behaviour of the private sector and government economic policy choices reflect the influence of both domestic factors and global trends on the South African economy. The domestic factors affecting the economy are related to South Africa's specific political and economic history. The evolution of economic institutions and infrastructure occurred during political regimes characterised by colonialism and apartheid. The industrial structure and concentrated character of the South African economy was shaped by the long-standing dominance of mining and minerals processing and the central role of mining-finance groups. The political transition from apartheid to democracy and the recent global economic trends also influenced changes in the South African economy. These global trends were due to increased global economic integration, particularly through liberalisation of trade and financial flows. The consequences of this higher level of economic integration include a huge global economic imbalance, particularly between the United States (US) and China and Japan, and a global financial crisis from the end of 2007–10.

There were similar negative trends in the South African and US economies before the global financial crisis of 2007–10. Both countries experienced economic growth due to debt-driven consumption and increased speculation in financial and real-estate markets. Both countries had rapid growth in financial services sectors, including increasing numbers of highly leveraged financial institutions, such as private equity and hedge funds, and increased use of derivatives, securitised debt and other exotic financial instruments. At the same time, both countries had significant declines in productive industrial sectors, which led them into more dependence on manufactured imports and large trade deficits. The large trade deficits led to increased dependence on foreign capital inflows to maintain their balance of payments. The trends in the South African economy were very different to those witnessed in the high-growth East Asian economies and the Brazil, Russia, India and China (BRIC) group of countries. These countries had growing productive sectors and generally had large increases in exports and trade surpluses. South Africa is better grouped with countries such as Portugal, Ireland, Greece and Spain, which, like the US economy, have large government budget deficits and trade deficits that make them dependent on foreign borrowing and capital inflows.

The nature of recent South African economic growth

Gross domestic product (GDP) growth has conventionally been considered an important measure for assessing the economic performance of a country. French President Nicolas Sarkozy established a Commission for the Measurement of Economic Performance and Social Progress in 2008 as a result of concerns about the adequacy of conventional measures of economic performance, particularly GDP. The commission, chaired by Economics Nobel laureate Joseph Stiglitz, consisted of well-known and respected economists. GDP measures the outputs of production and has been incorrectly equated with well-being. The commission's recommendations included the point that economic performance should take into account well-being rather than production. They suggested that income and consumption should be considered together with wealth and that the distribution of income, consumption and wealth are important for understanding well-being in a society. The authors of the commission's report stressed that well-being is multidimensional. They stated that one's sense of well-being is influenced by material living standards, health, education, personal activities (including work), political voice and governance, social networks and relationships, environment and insecurity (physical and economic). These recommendations and the multidimensional view of well-being highlight the shortcomings of GDP as a measure of well-being and economic performance in a country. The performance of the South African economy is poor when one considers the level of income and wealth inequality and the high levels of poverty and unemployment.

Notwithstanding these many shortcomings of GDP as a measure of economic performance, economic policy-makers and media commentators argued that the South African economy performed well before the global financial crisis of 2007–10 because of GDP growth. There was acknowledgement that unemployment remained too high and that inequality increased but there seemed to be a belief that as long as GDP continued to grow, South African society as whole –

possibly through a trickle-down of wealth from the rich to the poor – would become better off.

The central argument of this chapter is that South Africa experienced the wrong type of economic growth from the end of apartheid and particularly during the five-year period before the global financial crisis. The economic growth achieved was not only associated with high unemployment and growing inequality, it was unsustainable because it required growing private-sector indebtedness and accompanied decline in productive services and manufacturing sectors.

South African GDP grew by close to 5% in 2004 and over 5% from 2005–7. This level of economic growth gives one the impression that the South African economy was strong before the global financial crisis. However, one has to look beyond the aggregate numbers to understand what caused the economic growth. The contribution of manufacturing to GDP growth declined and the contribution of services, particularly financial services, to GDP growth grew. The fact that the services sector is a larger contributor to GDP than the manufacturing sector is not in itself the problem. One has to understand why the services sector has grown and the manufacturing sector has declined.

There was a massive increase in credit extension in South Africa during the 2000s. Most of this credit was extended to the private sector. Figure 1.2 shows that credit extended to the private sector as a percentage of GDP grew by 22% from 2000–8. During that period, private-sector investment as a percentage of GDP grew by only 5%. The question is what happened to the rest of the debt incurred by the private sector in South Africa?

A large part of the increased indebtedness of the private sector was due to increased debt of households. Figure 1.3 shows the huge, rapid growth in household debt to disposable income to a ratio of nearly 80 by 2007. We have to take into account that a large proportion of the South African population does not have bank accounts and an even larger share does not have access to bank credit. Therefore, it is

Figure 1.1   Annual percentage changes in GDP and GDP per capita (2000 prices).

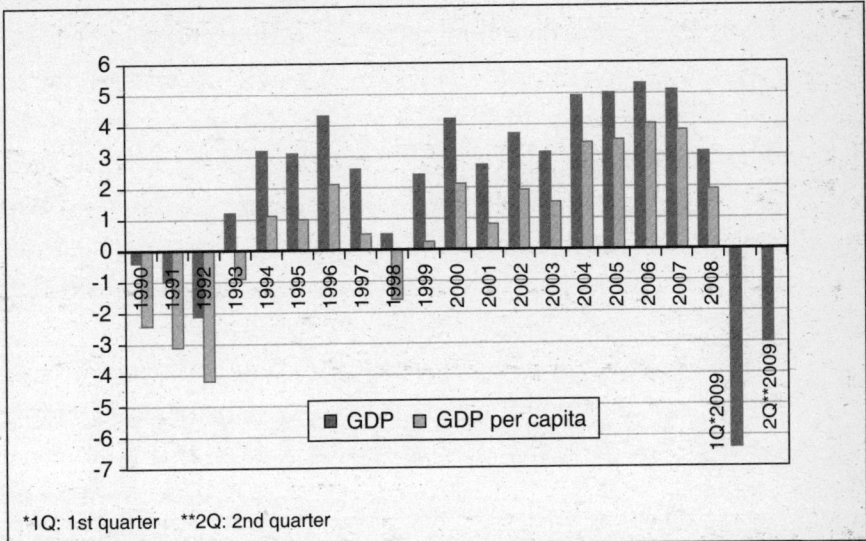

*1Q: 1st quarter   **2Q: 2nd quarter

(Source: SARB)

Figure 1.2   Credit extension and investment as percentages of GDP.

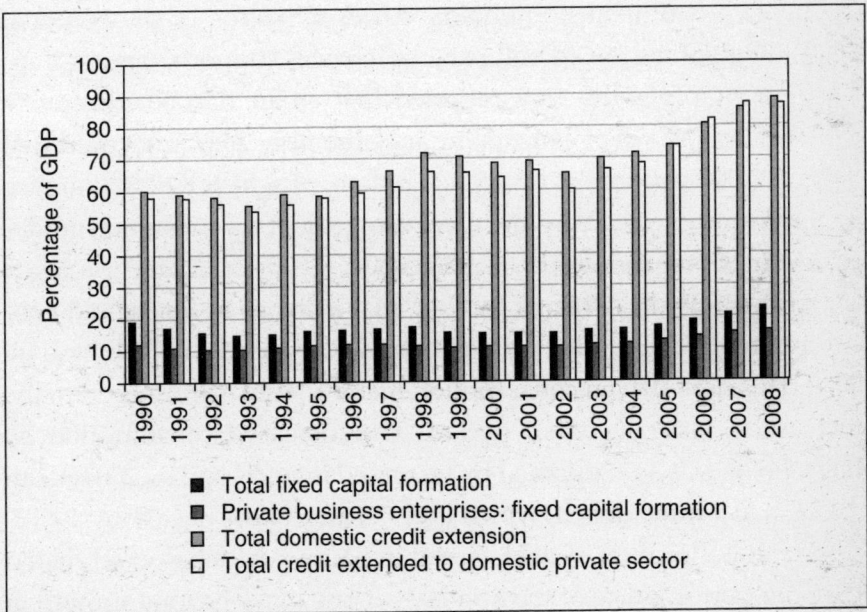

(Source: Calculated using SARB data)

19

Figure 1.3   Household debt to disposable income (ratio).

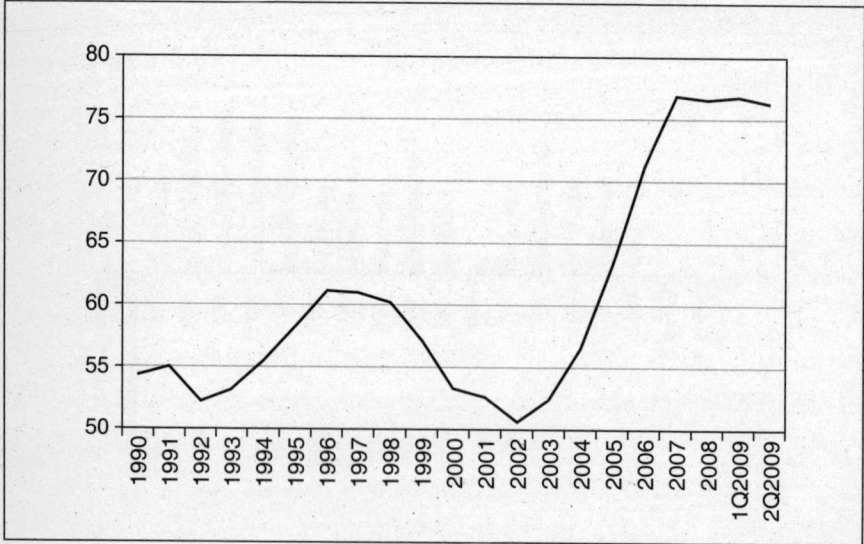

(Source: SARB)

safe to assume that most of the credit extension to households was to the relatively affluent households. An examination of the National Credit Regulator's (NCR) online news updates supports this assumption. For example, the NCR reported that about 100 000 consumers were undergoing debt counselling in September 2009. They said that these 100 000 consumers owed R20 billion, of which R12 billion was in home mortgages. Therefore, the average debt for consumers under review in September 2009 was R200 000.

Affluent South Africans drove a real increase in household consumption up from under R600 billion in 2000 to over R800 billion by 2008. This debt-driven consumption made a large contribution to the increase in GDP over that period. The increased consumption by households was accompanied by increased imports and by 2004 South Africa had a trade deficit, which grew to almost 8% of GDP by 2007.

The misallocation of debt capital in South Africa has exacerbated the poor performance of the economy if one looks beyond growth in GDP to take into account well-being and inequality. Not only was the distribution of wealth and income extraordinarily unequal but allocation of debt caused even greater inequality in consumption. While the affluent spent millions on houses, cars and imported luxury goods, a large proportion of the South African population remained without decent shelter, safe and reliable public transport and struggled to feed themselves and their families. At the same time, private-sector debt was not used to invest in and build industry and create jobs; instead it was used to finance increased speculative activities.

Figure 1.4 shows private-sector credit extension by all monetary institutions from 1990–2008. A large part of the increased extension of credit to the private sector went to mortgages, leasing finance and credit card debt for the affluent South Africans' buying of houses, cars and increased consumption rather than for fixed investment. The increased access to credit drove up house prices and led to

Figure 1.4 Private-sector credit extension by all monetary institutions by type (percentages of total).

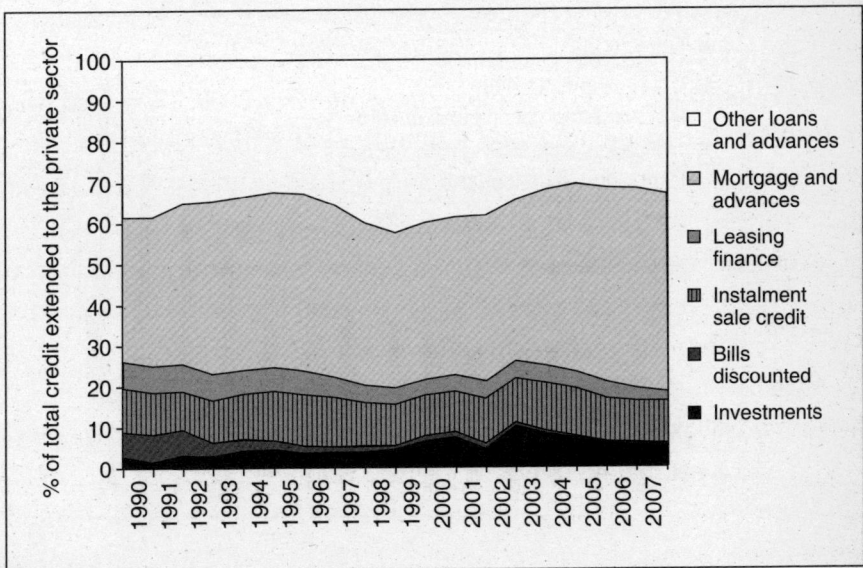

(Source: Calculated using SARB data)

increasing speculation in real-estate markets before the global financial crisis. There was also a large increase in financial speculation during this period. In other words, the private sector used the increased debt extended to them for speculating in financial markets instead of increasing investment in productive activities. Figure 1.4 shows that monetary institutions' provision of credit for investment is less than 10% of their credit extension for the entire period.

Figure 1.5 shows sources and uses of capital by non-financial corporate business enterprises in South Africa from 1992–2007. Except for two years (2004 and 2005), net acquisition of financial assets was higher than net capital formation (fixed investment). The South African corporate business enterprises chose to keep their capital liquid in financial markets rather than invest in the economy. They limited their long-term investment and by consequence employment

Figure 1.5 The main sources and uses of capital in corporate business enterprises, R millions.

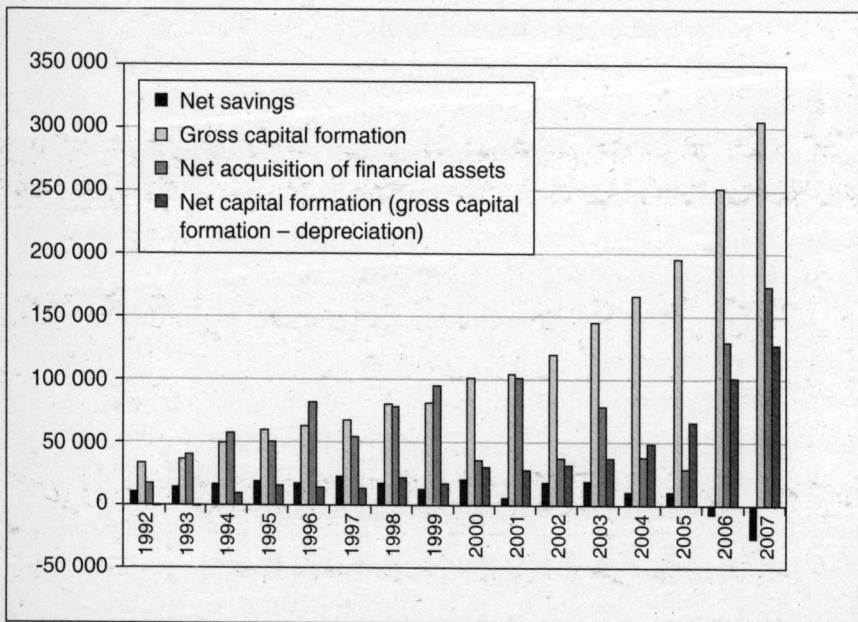

(Source: Calculated from SARB flow of funds data)

opportunities and used their increasing access to credit to speculate in financial markets.

What impact did this behaviour by the private sector have on investment and employment in the economy? The growth in debt-driven consumption and speculation in financial and real-estate markets led to investment and employment in certain services sectors and construction. In other words, the way in which the private sector, particularly finance and corporate businesses, chose to allocate capital in South Africa shaped the economic growth path of the country. By the time of the transition to democracy during the early 1990s, the South African economy was dominated by mining and minerals industries and economic sectors with close links to mining and minerals. The private sector and state-owned enterprises had invested in large-scale, capital and energy-intensive minerals processing projects during the 1970s and 1980s, drawing on the large infrastructure investments in electricity and the low cost of electricity. There were also large state investments in the arms industry, nuclear power and Sasol (oil from coal) in response to growing international economic isolation and resistance to apartheid. By the 1990s, the South African economy was highly concentrated and dominated by six large diversified conglomerates with interests in mining and finance. Economic activity was focused on extracting resource and monopoly rents. The transition to democracy was accompanied by large-scale corporate restructuring and a decline in mining, manufacturing and productive services. The new investment and capital stock was built in areas of the economy fuelled by debt-driven consumption by the affluent and financial speculation.

In 2006, the year before the global financial crisis, services sectors dominated the top ten investment sectors in the economy. The growth in debt-driven consumption and financial speculation supported growth in certain kinds of services sectors, such as finance and insurance, transport and storage and wholesale and retail services. There were only two manufacturing sectors in the top ten investment sectors in 2006. One of these, motor vehicles, parts and accessories

Figure 1.6   Top ten investment sectors for 2006.

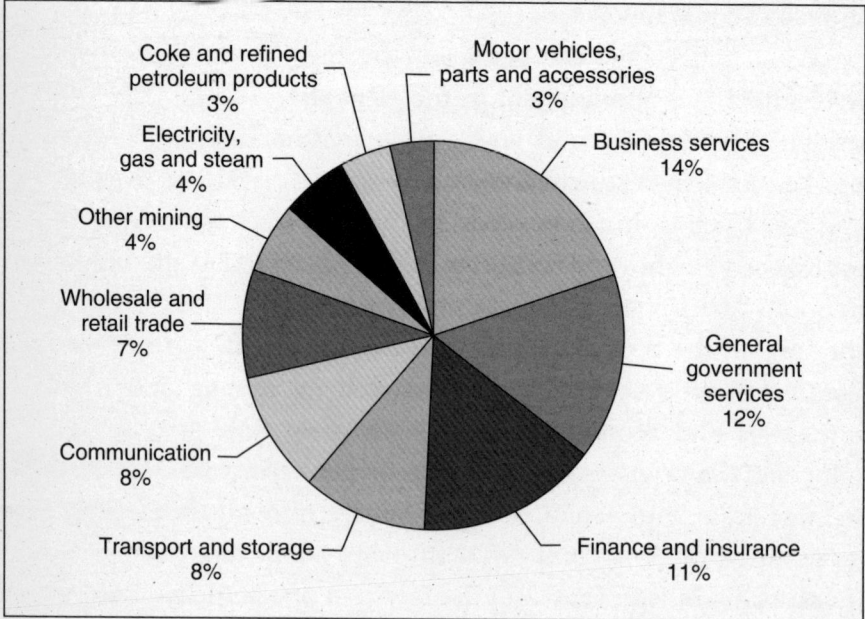

(Source: Quantec)

was a manufacturing sector that was supported by the increased extension of credit to the private sector. Motor vehicles, parts and accessories was also the only industrial sector where government had implemented an industrial policy and clear sector programme since 1994. As a result of the investment pattern, most (17 out of 28) manufacturing sectors had a decline in capital stock for 2000–6. In other words, the economy was losing industrial capacity. Unfortunately, much of this capacity was in manufacturing sectors where unskilled and semi-skilled workers could have been employed.

The consumption and investment behaviour, as well as the problems associated with high unemployment and inequality, influenced employment. On the whole, there was a loss of manufacturing jobs in South Africa over the past decade. Figure 1.7 shows services sector employment from 1991–2008. Over the past decade, there were only two services sectors where there has been significant employment

Figure 1.7   Services employment, 1990–2008.

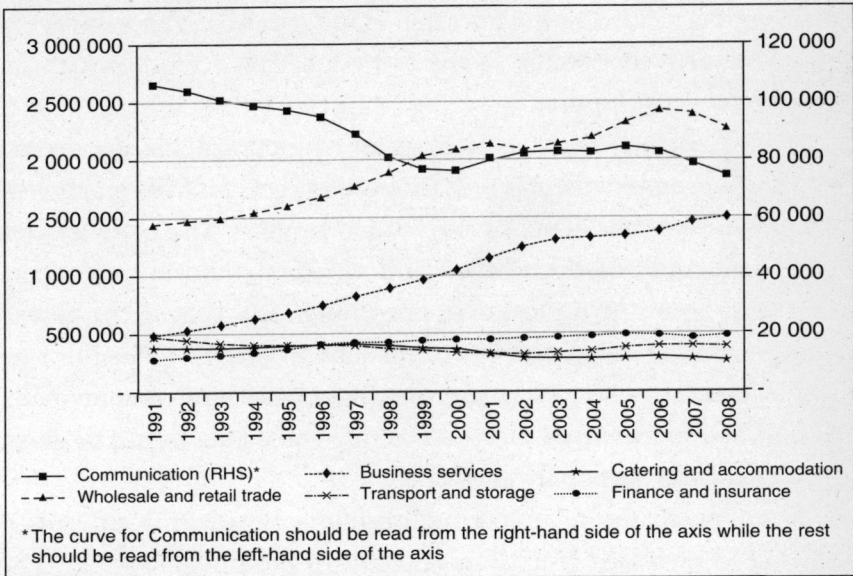

Communication (RHS)*	Business services
Wholesale and retail trade	Transport and storage
	Catering and accommodation
	Finance and insurance

*The curve for Communication should be read from the right-hand side of the axis while the rest should be read from the left-hand side of the axis

(Source: Quantec)

growth: business services and wholesale and retail trade services. The business services sector is interesting because the jobs in this sector are mostly outsourced cleaning jobs and private security workers. In other words, workers that had been employed in manu-facturing and mining have been recategorised as business services workers when cleaning services were outsourced. These workers may have lost jobs that were full-time, better paid and with benefits, for jobs in the services sector that were casual, lower paid and with-out benefits. Further, these outsourced workers may have lost the opportunity to receive on-the-job training and to advance from being cleaners when they were transferred to cleaning companies or labour brokers. The private security industry has grown tremendously in South Africa due to insecurity about crime, unemployment and poverty. As inequality and debt-driven consumption has grown, affluent South Africans have increased their demand for private security services.

The other services sector where there has been growth in employment has been wholesale and retail trade services. The growth in employment in this sector seems to be associated with growth in debt-driven consumption.

The two sectors where services sector employment has grown are sectors where employment is precarious. Workers would be employed on a casual basis and would have limited benefits. These are sectors where jobs could easily be shed and workers could be placed on short-time. South Africa lost over one million jobs during the global financial crisis. A large number of the jobs would have been lost in these two services sectors where there had been large employment creation due to increased access to credit. These jobs would be shed when credit was less easily available.

In summary, the relatively high economic growth from 2004–7 was due to increased extension of credit to the private sector. This increased access to credit led to large increases in household debt and debt-driven consumption. Much of the debt was used for financial speculation and may have contributed to bubbles in financial asset markets, particularly equities markets. This consumption and speculation led to investment and employment predominantly in certain services sectors but these investments would not be sustainable because they depended on continuing easy access to credit. The next section looks at financial markets and how they affected the real economy.

Capital flows and increased access to credit

The developments in South African financial markets and growth in private-sector debt were part of a global trend. There was widespread liberalisation of financial markets from the 1980s. This liberalisation affected financial institutions in domestic markets and led to increased integration of global financial markets. The domestic financial liberalisation led to increased leverage and higher levels of speculation in financial markets. The greater integration of global financial markets meant that cross-border financial flows and speculation in global financial markets became easier. Most cross-border financial flows were between developed economies but there were a few developing countries (or emerging markets) favoured by global financiers. South Africa was one of those countries.

South African economic policy-makers chose to allow relatively uncontrolled movements of capital by non-residents and had a phased liberalisation of exchange controls on residents. The policy-makers believed that a liberal approach to capital controls would attract foreign direct investment (FDI) into South Africa. They were wrong because South Africa has not had large increases in FDI and liberalisation of financial markets caused economic volatility and uncertainty, which negatively affected conditions for investment and employment.

There are three categories of capital flows: foreign direct investment, which is considered to be a longer-term commitment by foreign investors; portfolio capital flows, which are short-term movements of capital into stocks and bonds; and other capital flows, which consist mostly of foreign short-term bank lending. Figure 1.8 shows net (inflows minus outflows) capital flows to South Africa as percentages of GDP for the period 1990 to 2008. The figure shows that these flows were volatile. It shows that South African net FDI was positive for a few years during the period 1990 to 2008. The positive net FDI in 1997 and 2001 was due to offshore listings where the South African assets of corporations that listed offshore were reclassified as foreign assets. The positive net FDI in 2005 and 2008 were due to acquisition of large shares of South Africa's two largest banks by foreign banks. In other words, South Africa's ability to attract net FDI flows has been relatively unsuccessful and the recent FDI has been due to acquisitions in the financial sector.

The main capital flows to South Africa have been portfolio capital flows. Figure 1.8 shows that South Africa's net portfolio flows increased with the end of apartheid and South Africa's economic isolation. Further, there was a surge in global liquidity during the 1990s that led to large increases in portfolio flows to many developing countries. Short-term capital flows are referred to as hot money

Figure 1.8   Net capital flows to South Africa as percentages of GDP.

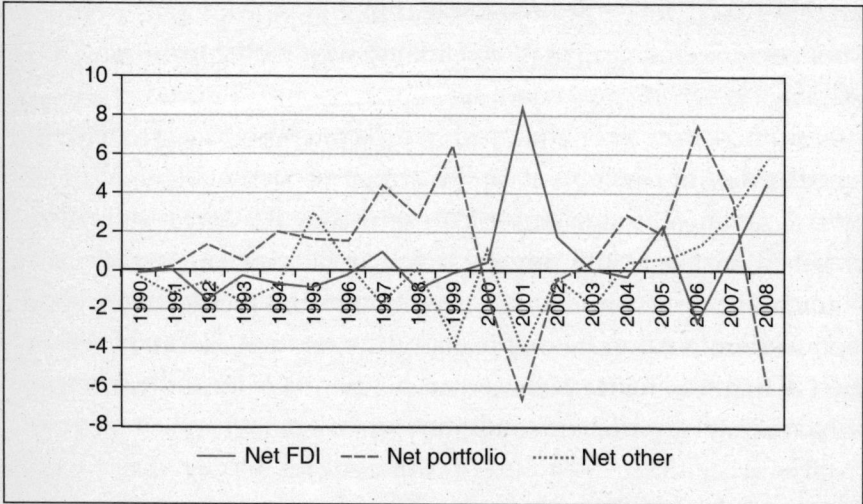

(Source: SARB)

because of the speed at which they can enter and leave economies. Large increases in hot money caused financial fragility and financial crises in many developing countries during the 1990s. These short-term flows usually enter the financial system and increase the amount of available debt. The increased availability of debt in South Africa due to increases in short-term portfolio capital flows during the 1990s and 2000s was associated with increased debt-driven consumption and financial speculation. The hot money flows led to bubbles in real estate and stock markets. These phenomena of increasing levels of leverage and debt, speculation and bubbles in financial and real-estate asset markets are common to most countries that received large hot money flows. These phenomena are associated with increased macroeconomic fragility and vulnerability to financial crises and contagion.

Movement of hot money into and out of an economy leads to changes in macroeconomic variables. Large hot money inflows as experienced in South Africa during the late 1990s and mid-2000s led to massive increases in liquidity and resulted in huge increases in private-sector debt. The surge in hot money flows had the effect of strengthening the rand exchange rate against the US dollar and other currencies, which pushed down inflation and allowed the South African Reserve Bank (SARB) to reduce interest rates. The stronger rand made imported goods more attractive and made exports less attractive. Even though increased hot money flows led to increased credit extension to the private sector, it did not support domestic manufacturing because the stronger rand meant tougher competition from imports and hurt domestic manufacturers and exporters. Further, it will be shown below that internationalisation of large South African corporations caused them to be less interested in increasing domestic fixed investment.

The increased flow of hot money to South Africa from 2003 led to even larger growth in net portfolio flows than during the 1990s. Net portfolio flows were 0.5% of the size of GDP in 2003 and by 2007 they were 7.3% the size of GDP (see Figure 1.8). This massive increase of liquidity into the South African economy set off a boom in stock and derivatives markets and an escalation of debt-driven consumption. The index (where 2005 = 100) for all share prices in South Africa grew from 62 in 2003 to 188 in 2007 (about three times). The outstanding value of futures contracts (a financial derivative) was 63.5% the size of GDP in 2003 and by 2007 it had skyrocketed to 267.2% the size of GDP. The surges in hot money flows of the size experienced after 2003 had a huge impact on leverage and debt in the economy and influenced economic behaviour. In other words, economic decision-making and allocation of capital in the economy would not have responded to actual conditions in the economy; instead increased access to debt, changes in the exchange rate, increased macroeconomic volatility and uncertainty, and bubbles in asset markets would have influenced allocation of capital and economic choices.

On the whole, a liberal regime on cross-border capital flows has not helped to build the productive manufacturing and services sectors in South Africa but has led to macroeconomic volatility where the

29

exchange and interest rates are affected by hot money flows. Macro-economic volatility increased uncertainty for investors who chose to keep their capital liquid in domestic and global financial markets. The hot money surges also caused bubbles in financial markets, which made returns for short-term speculation in financial markets higher than returns in long-term productive investment. The widespread liberalisation of financial markets led to a situation of volatility and speculative possibilities globally. As exchange controls on residents were liberalised, South Africans speculated more and all over the world. The choice by South African non-financial corporate business enterprises to put their capital into financial assets rather than fixed investment can, therefore, be partly explained by the negative impact of uncontrolled hot money flows on the economy.

Economic policy-makers have argued that the reason for low investment levels in South Africa is low household savings. I stress that this argument is incorrect. There has been much capital available for investment in South Africa. Businesspeople have chosen to use that capital for speculation and affluent households have used that capital for consumption. Therefore, policies aimed at pushing up interest rates and reducing capital gains taxes to promote saving are misdirected. The South African economy requires capital controls and other capital management techniques to reduce uncertainty for investors and macroeconomic instability. A stable and weaker exchange rate will support local manufacturers and productive services indus-tries and increased macroeconomic stability will promote investment.

Government policies and corporate structure

The post-apartheid democratic government chose economic policies that it believed would project credibility to foreign investors, global financiers and credit ratings agencies. It chose conservative macro-economic policies geared towards keeping inflation and government deficits low. It adopted inflation targeting. It liberalised trade and financial flows and increased integration of the South African economy into global markets. It voiced support for privatisation of state-owned enterprises. Its concern was to let markets operate with less inter-ference from the state and to improve the overall economic climate.

The first set of industrial policies from the Department of Trade and Industry (DTI) after the 1994 democratic elections were 'supply-side' measures focused on improving conditions for industry as a whole through incentives programmes, skills and technology develop-ment and support for small- and medium-sized businesses (Roberts, 2002; Hanival and Rustomjee, 2010). The DTI's Integrated Manu-facturing Strategy (IMS) of 2001 was focused on building stronger links between sectors by improving conditions within production value chains and improving cross-cutting areas such as skills and technology. The IMS was accompanied by the Department of Science and Technology's Advanced Manufacturing Technology Strategy (AMTS). The focus of the AMTS was to support productivity, innovation and technology in manufacturing.

South African industrial development was centred on heavy, cap-ital intensive resource-based sectors. Ben Fine and Zavareh Rustomjee (1996) provide an excellent discussion of the development of the South African economy and the centrality of mining and minerals to the shape of the economy today. They use the term 'minerals and energy complex' to describe the South African system of accumulation that developed during the apartheid era.

There was a path dependency in the economy as there were existing infrastructure and institutions that had been built to support those sectors. The untargeted approach to industrial policy operated within that existing economic path dependence. As a result, the policies put in place led to continued investment and growth in the resource-based sectors and further entrenched the importance of those sectors in the economy. The increased flows of short-term capital into South Africa supported investments in sectors boosted by debt-driven consumption and real estate and financial speculation and also served to increase imports.

A targeted and more focused approach to industrial policy would have focused on restructuring the economy to develop beyond mining- and minerals-based sectors towards a deeper and more diversified industrial base. There would have been more targeted support for industry sectors and a greater role for the allocation of capital by the state towards its industrial development goals. The failure to implement this kind of industrial policy meant that the infrastructure and institutions of the economy remained focused on the dominant firms and sectors in traditional mining, minerals processing and chemicals and have been built up in sectors linked to debt-driven consumption and financial speculation.

José Antonio Ocampo argues that in addition to institutional requirements (efficient state bureaucracy, non-discretionary legal system and social covenants to secure political stability), specific strategies are required to drive growth and to deal with 'old and new forms of vulnerability' (p. 92). He claims: 'Private spending booms and risky balance sheets tend to accumulate during periods of financial euphoria, indicating that economic agents may underestimate the intertemporal inconsistency that may be involved in their spending and financial strategies.' Ocampo provides three important elements of a strategy to deal with vulnerability: 'macroeconomic policies designed to reduce external vulnerability and facilitate productive investment, productive development strategies aimed at guaranteeing a dynamic restructuring of productive structures, and active social policies' (p. 92). This strategy is consistent with approaches of well-known economists working on industrialisation and economic development, such as Alice Amsden (1989) and Ha-Joon Chang (1997) who have demonstrated that macroeconomic policy has to support industrialisation and the dynamic restructuring of productive sectors.

The macroeconomic, financial and industrial policies of South Africa were very different to the economic policies chosen by the BRIC countries and countries such as South Korea and other Asian economies, which have had industrial growth and created employment over the past decade. An important general difference between South Africa's economic policies and those of the BRIC countries and some Asian economies is that South Africa's economic policies were geared towards appearing credible to attract foreign investment and approval from financial institutions and credit ratings agencies. As a result, these policies have favoured the financial sector at the expense of industry.

Countries such as India, China, Singapore and Taiwan have consciously focused their financial policies to favour industry. Their management (including capital controls and prudential management) of foreign capital flows were designed to promote financial stability and industrialisation, industrial competitiveness and export competitiveness (Epstein, Grabel and Jomo, 2004). These policies restrain their financial institutions and limit their ability to profit from speculation opportunities but they create economic stability and certainty that supports long-term productive investment and employment creation. Therefore, it is not surprising that before the crisis, South Africa did not have the type of industrial development and employment creation success that BRIC and some Asian economies had experienced. Furthermore, these countries with their restrictions on financial institutions and financial flows, which may not get them credibility points from developed country financiers and credit ratings agencies, have had higher levels of FDI than South Africa. It seems that FDI follows economic growth and profit potential, not policies deemed credible by a few hundred financiers working on Wall Street.

Since the global financial crisis, there have been increased hot money flows to developing countries. The inflows have been associated with overvalued exchange rates. These flows threaten the financial and macroeconomic stability of those countries. Many developing countries have put in place measures to attempt to manage the impact of these flows on their economy. South African policymakers have not put in place capital controls to manage the impact of hot money surges. Instead, there has been further liberalisation of exchange controls that may exacerbate macroeconomic volatility and uncertainty. In other words, the now conventionally accepted view that uncontrolled flows of capital can cause macroeconomic instability and uncertainty was not accepted by South African finance and macroeconomic policy-makers (even the IMF has released a position paper that says that the use of capital controls may be justified; see Ostry et al., 2010). The liberal approach to capital flows has huge costs for South Africa in terms of investment, employment and long-term industrial development.

The South African economy remains very concentrated, even though there was widespread corporate restructuring. Some of the largest South African corporations restructured to consolidate their South African businesses and to increase their domination of domestic markets. Many restructured to get their share of the re-apportioned global markets, sometimes through several mergers and acquisitions. Some of the largest corporations, including Anglo American, Old Mutual and Investec, have shifted their primary listings abroad. A perusal of the annual reports of the twenty largest South African listed corporations (by market capitalisation) shows that these corporations have significant international interests and links. Anglo American, Sasol, SABMiller and many of the largest South African corporations have joint listing on the Johannesburg Stock Exchange (JSE) and stock exchanges in other countries. A large proportion of their shares are held by domestic and international institutional investors. As a result, they have been influenced by the shareholder value movement in the US and United Kingdom that has pressured them to focus on their core business.

Andrea Goldstein's interpretation of corporate restructuring in South Africa is illustrated in the following:

> While the refocusing on core business has followed from the need to insure competitiveness against the background of the opening of the domestic economy to world competition and weaker gold and commodity prices, voluntary unbundling has been an expedient strategy to appease the possible rise of nationalization sentiments. In order to build up a black capitalist constituency, it was important to conclude highly visible and large-scale deals. The first such deal was Sanlam's sale of

Metropolitan Life (METLIFE), an insurance company, to New Africa Investment Ltd (NAIL). In 1996 Anglo broke up its majority-owned sub-holding JCI (Johannesburg Consolidated Investment) into platinum (Amplats), a homonymous mining subsidiary, and an industrial arm, Johnnic (p. 15).

Goldstein recognised that global and domestic factors shaped the behaviour of South African big business. Further, Goldstein's research indicated that the boom in merger and acquisitions in South Africa during the 1990s was different to those in other countries. He showed that there were particularly South African characteristics to the mergers and acquisitions. The restructuring in South Africa was more aimed at dismantling pyramid structures than increasing the competitiveness of industrial sectors. According to Goldstein: 'Of the twenty largest South African deals reported in 1992–98, 75% corresponds to the simplification of the corporate structure; 10% to consolidation in the financial industry; 10% to foreign acquisitions; and only one deal – TransNatal's acquisition of Rand Coal to form Ingwe Coal in 1994 – is a "genuine" South African merger' (p. 17). He observed that it was remarkable that South African conglomerates had practically not made any large acquisitions in South Africa. He said that this lack of domestic acquisition did not even happen in sectors such as utilities and Internet-related investments '. . . where family-controlled business groups in OECD [Organization for Economic Cooperation and Development] countries have been active even while refocusing their portfolios on the core business' (p. 17).

The corporate restructuring in the South African economy since the 1990s led to internationalisation of large corporations and a shifting of their capital abroad with relatively little investment in South Africa. These corporations seemed content to extract resource and monopoly rents in South Africa and did not seem interested in supporting further industrial development. The increased influence of the developed country shareholder value movement on South African corporations led not only to a focus on core business but a shift towards high short-term returns at the expense of long-term investment. William Lazonick and Mary O'Sullivan (2000) argue that the predominance of the shareholder value approach to corporate governance has been accompanied by a shift from patient to impatient capital. In other words, the increased influence of financiers and the shareholder value movement over corporate executives caused a shift in management behaviour where investors and management were less concerned with building and nurturing businesses over a long period of time but have become focused on short-term returns.

Conclusion

This chapter not only argues that South Africa has had the wrong kind of economic growth but that the post-apartheid government's economic policy choices have driven the economy towards that wrong kind of economic growth. The policies did not address the structural weaknesses of an economy that developed around mining and minerals where private and state investment was focused on large-scale capital and energy-intensive investments during the 1970s and 1980s. The large corporations that dominated the economy were allowed to extract commodity and monopoly rents and were at liberty to internationalise their businesses while there was no requirement on them to invest in South Africa. In short, the government allowed them to shift capital abroad without increasing domestic investment.

The implications of relatively uncontrolled movements of capital into and out of the South African economy have had a huge impact on the nature of economic growth and have reshaped the South African growth path. Because the South African economy developed around the mining and minerals sectors, the institutions and infrastructure that existed in the country favoured these sectors and other closely linked sectors. The liberalised financial markets and the internationalisation of South African corporations have affected the South African economic growth path since the 1990s. Increased flows of hot money into and out of the economy favoured the growth of services sectors linked to increased debt-driven consumption and financial and real-estate speculation and led to a decline in manufacturing sectors and productive services. However, this growth path is not sustainable because it depends on growing levels of private-sector debt and is associated with industrial decline and continuing high levels of unemployment and inequality.

The solutions offered are that South African economic policies, including macroeconomic and finance policies, should focus on supporting industrial development and employment creation. Industrial policy should be geared to economic transformation that changes the industrial structure of South Africa with the aim of making the economy less dependent on mining and minerals processing and to shift the economic growth path away from debt-driven consumption and speculation towards increasing the competitiveness and productivity of industry and employment creation.

The South African financial system should be reformed to make financial institutions more responsive to the needs of industry and to ensure that capital is allocated towards economic and industrial policy goals. Capital management techniques should be used to ensure macroeconomic stability and certainty and to maintain a stable and appropriate level for the exchange rate. Finally, economic policies should ensure that economic rents, particularly of non-renewable mining products, and in monopoly sectors should be managed by the state to support their economic and industrial policy goals.

SEERAJ MOHAMED is an academic economist and writer with more than twenty years of experience working on economic, industrial and finance development issues. He is the Director of the Corporate Strategy and Industrial Development Research Programme at the University of the Witwatersrand, Johannesburg, and writes a weekly column called 'Global Account' for the business magazine *Engineering News* and the website www.polity.org.za.

References and suggested reading

Amsden, A. (1989) *Asia's Next Giant: South Korea and Late Industrialization* (Oxford University Press, New York).

Chang, H-J. (1997) 'Evaluating the Current Industrial Policy of South Africa'. Prepared for the Trade and Industrial Policy Strategies (TIPS), available at tips.org.za.

——— (ed.) (2003) *Rethinking Development Economics* (Anthem Press, London).

Department of Trade and Industry's National Industrial Policy Framework, available at dti.gov.za/nipf/nipf.htm.

Epstein, G.A. (ed.) (2005) *Financialization and the World Economy* (Edward Elgar Publishing, Northampton, MA).

Epstein, G., Grabel, I. and Jomo, K.S. (2004) 'Capital Management Techniques in Developing Countries: An Assessment of Experiences from the 1990s and Lessons for the Future'. G-24 Discussion Paper No. 27, United Nations, New York and Geneva.

Fine, B. and Rustomjee, Z. (1996) *The Political Economy of South Africa: From Minerals-Energy Complex to Industrialization* (Westview Press, Boulder, CO).

Goldstein, A. (2001) 'Business Governance in Brazil and South Africa: How Much Convergence to the Anglo-Saxon Model?' in *Brazilian Journal of Political Economy* Vol. 21, No. 2, pp. 3–23.

Hanival, S. and Rustomjee, Z. (2010) 'A Review of Industrial Policy, Instruments and Support Programmes, 1998–2008: A Contribution to the Presidency's 15-Year Review of Government Performance', available at tips.org.za/files/industrial_policy_15yr_review_june_2010_sbm20july2010_final_0.pdf.

Keynes, J.M. (1997) *The General Theory of Employment, Interest and Money* (Prometheus Books, Amherst, NY) (First published by Macmillan and Cambridge University Press for Royal Economic Society in 1936).

Lazonick, W. and O'Sullivan, M. (2000) 'Maximizing Shareholder Value: A New Ideology for Corporate Governance' in *Economy and Society* Vol. 29, No. 1, pp. 13–35.

Mohamed, S. (2010) 'The State of the South African Economy' in Daniel, J., Naidoo, P., Pillay, D. and Southall, R. (eds.) *The New South African Review, 2010: Development or Decline* (Wits University Press, Johannesburg).

Ocampo, J.A. (2003) 'Development and the Global Order' in Chang, H-J. (ed.) *Rethinking Development Economics* (Anthem Press, London).

Ostry, J.D., Ghosh, A.R., Habermeier, K., Mahvash, M.C., Qureshi, S. and Reinhardt, D.B.S. (2010) 'Capital Inflows: The Role of Controls'. An International Monetary Fund Staff Position Paper SPN10/04, available at imf.org/external/pubs/ft/spn/2010/spn1004.pdf.

Roberts, S. (2002) 'Manufacturing Competitiveness and Industrial Policy', presented at Trade and Industrial Policy Strategies 2002 Annual Forum, available at tips.org.za/node/1151.

Roberts, S. and Rustomjee, Z. (2010) 'Industrial Policy Under Democracy: Apartheid's Grown-up Infant Industries? Iscor and Sasol' in *Transformation: Critical Perspectives on Southern Africa* No. 71, pp. 50–75.

2

Africa's Mineral Resources
What Must be Done to Make Them Drivers of Development?

PAUL JOURDAN

This chapter outlines how Africa's unique natural resource base could provide its peoples with an important lever to achieve growth and development objectives if the seminal resources linkages industries and clusters are realised. Alternatively, these assets could be squandered under 'free entry' resource regimes, such as the 'free mining' mineral regimes, and a continued 'free market', non-interventionist scenario, which is likely to leave Africa with little more than ghost towns, such as Kabwe, Stilfontein, Yekepa and Welkom, or with exhausted soils and depleted fisheries, forests and other natural endowments.

Africa's natural resources

Africa's natural comparative advantages lie in its natural resources endowment as well as in its potential, particularly in minerals and energy; agriculture and animal husbandry; forestry and biomass; water; fisheries and aquaculture; and tourism.

The continent's energy resources are exceptional, comprising enormous coal reserves, massive hydro-power potential, hydro-carbons, nuclear and potential solar and geothermal energy. Its hydrocarbon and coal reserves could also provide the critical polymer feedstocks essential to industrialisation.

Table 2.1   Africa's natural resources.

Agriculture
    Contributes 40% of African GDP, provides livelihood for 60% of population, but largest user of scarce water
    Enormous unrealised potential (low yields and less than half under cultivation)
    Agri-commodities exported without processing (beneficiation)

Minerals
    World's top producer of numerous mineral commodities
    Has world's greatest resources of many more
    Africa lacks systematic geosurvey: could be greater resources
    But exported as ores, concentrates, metals: need more beneficiation

Energy
    Significant fossil fuels (oil, gas and coal)
    Large biomass and bio-fuels potential (ethanol, bio-diesel)
    Massive hydro-electric potential (Inga 45 GW, Congo River 200 GW)

Forestry
    22% of African land is forested (650 million hectares = 17% of world total)
    Deforestation: Africa's net change is the highest globally = -0.78% per annum
    Huge silviculture potential, but exported as logs/chips: need greater beneficiation

Fishing
    28 000 km coastline (1.28 million km^2 continental shelf) with several oceanic systems
    Decline in catch rate (international poaching and over-harvesting)
    ~70% of marine protected areas under threat
    Aquaculture/mariculture still nascent (large potential)

Tourism
    Major potential (world's greatest diversity: culture, flora, fauna, geomorphology)
    Increasingly important source of livelihood

It has spectacular mineral resources such as the platinum group metals, as well as iron, aluminium, copper, nickel, chromium, vanadium, manganese and cobalt.

Africa is well watered between the tropics, but above and below them its water resources are scarce. Overall, Africa uses less than 4% of its water but water is generally scarce in terms of access with the rivers and lakes in deep valleys or rifts.

Due to its high variety of climatic zones, geology/soils and topography, Africa has almost all the biomes necessary for the production of the bulk of agricultural products, both foodstuffs and industrial feedstocks.

Natural harvesting of sea fisheries has peaked and although Africa's approximate 28 000 km coastline with two oceanic systems could give it a relative mariculture advantage, this industry is still in its infancy. Natural harvesting of forests is in decline but there is enormous potential for plantation forestry, particularly between the tropics.

Africa has huge tourism potential based on its enormous cultural, ecological and geographic diversity. This labour-intensive industry is growing rapidly and could become a major job creator if the natural assets are conserved and effectively managed.

Consequently, Africa's natural resource endowment gives it a potential static *comparative* advantage, albeit a declining advantage in the case of minerals, based on its diminishing mineral resources. A critical endeavour of an Africa development strategy must be to transform this unsustainable comparative minerals advantage into a sustainable *competitive* advantage.

Africa's mineral resources

Africa has the world's largest resources of the platinum group metals as well as aluminium, chromium, gold, manganese (high-grade ore), cobalt and vanadium and large resources of several other minerals. The continent is also a major producer of these minerals (see Table 2.2). In terms of minerals, including hydrocarbons, Africa has virtually all the important minerals for diversified industrialisation, particularly iron/steel and polymers. However, almost all of its mineral wealth is currently exported as ores, concentrates, alloys or metals with very little transformed into fabricated products.

Africa has ample resources of the two most important mineral inputs into manufacturing, namely iron/steel and polymers (from oil, gas and coal). Unfortunately, both are generally supplied into African markets at monopoly prices, severely curtailing potential manufactured exports and job creation.

Table 2.2   Mineral production and reserves in Africa.

Mineral	Production	Rank	Reserves
Platinum group metals	54%	1	60+%
Phosphate	27%	1	66%
Gold	20%	1	42%
Chromium	40%	1	44%
Manganese	28%	2	82%
Vanadium	51%	1	95%
Cobalt	18%	1	55+%
Diamonds	78%	1	88%
Aluminium	4%	7	45%
Also Ti (20%), U (20%), Fe (17%), Cu (13%), etc.			

(Source: USGS 2010)

Critical minerals for agriculture are nitrogen (from natural gas), phosphates and potassium and Africa has considerable reserves of the first two, but needs to import some of its potassium requirements. In terms of infrastructure, the most important materials are cement, construction steel (rebar) and copper. Although Africa has ample resources for their cost-effective production, unfortunately they are undeveloped or production is sold at monopoly prices, significantly raising costs.

Common African markets could make a difference in facilitating greater economies of scale, competition and competitive prices for the essential industrialisation of mineral feedstocks.

Africa's mineral regimes

African mineral regimes are essentially based on the principle of free mining, or 'free entry'. Legal mining expert Barry Barton defines free mining as including:

- a right of free access to lands in which the minerals are in public ownership;
- a right to take possession of them and acquire title by one's own act of staking a claim; and

- a right to proceed to develop and mine the minerals discovered (p. 193).

The mining laws broadly fit into the African mineral regimes re-formulation process initiated and sponsored by the World Bank from the late 1980s until the present and in this regard Professor Bonnie Campbell notes in the *Canadian Journal of Development Studies*:

> ... certain elements of the free mining doctrine that animated the nineteenth-century formulation of mining regimes in the American and British spheres have also guided the liberal-isation process of African mining regimes over the 1980s and 1990s. One of the ways this came about was through the retrenchment of state authority, which in turn contributed to the institutionalisation of asymmetrical relations of power and influence that had important consequences for local political processes, local participation, and community welfare. The approach consequently helps explain some of the social, economic, environmental, or human rights impacts of these regimes, and prompts one to question the extent to which current mining regime reform processes in Africa can transform the asymmetrical power relations that have typified mining activities on the continent in the past (p. 199).

Free mining refers to the mining regimes that were established in the European conquests. Authors Myriam Laforce, Ugo Lapointe and Véronique Lebuis maintain that free mining 'privileges the values and interests of mining companies in contrast to those of Aboriginal groups', and that it was primarily designed to attract European settlers to expropriate the land and minerals and to neutralise the indigenous populations in the Americas, Africa, Oceania and else-where. The mineral regimes of Canada and Australia are modern equivalents of free-mining regimes, which are unsurprisingly strongly favoured by the mining transnational corporations and the World Bank. African mining laws contain many elements of a free-mining regime, particularly the first-come-first-served principle, which dispenses the people's mineral assets gratis, rather than seeking price discovery and the maximisation of the developmental impacts. Fundamentally, according to Ugo Lapointe: 'The free-mining system limits the authority and discretionary powers of governments, and as such, governments' abilities to discharge some of their responsibilities.'

An African growth and development strategy should rather seek to establish a mineral regime that competitively and transparently concessions all 'known' mineral deposits as 25–30 year leases to achieve the optimal resource rents and linkages. Price discovery could include both fiscal criteria (tax rates, such as resource rent tax) and developmental criteria (jobs, infrastructure, product pricing and linkages).

The wholesale handing out of Africa's mineral assets over the last two decades has probably cost several million jobs, including those that could have been catalysed in other sectors. In general, mineral investors will tend to have a much better idea of the value of the state's mineral assets than the state itself, and competitive auctioning (concessions) would be an effective method of achieving fair value and developmental goals. However, where there is little or no geodata, an auction is unlikely to flush out fair value and these terrains should first be thoroughly surveyed by the state (geosurvey departments or contractors) before auctioning via a time-limited mining concession or licence or being opened up for private exploration.

Accordingly, following best practice in the oil and gas sector, this system would divide African states into areas of high risk (low geological data) and areas of low risk over known metallogenic terrains. The former would be reserved for further geosurvey by the respective geosurvey departments, while the latter (known assets) would be auctioned off as blocks with the state tax-take (resource rent share) as the main evaluation criteria (price discovery) in order to flush out the optimal net present value over the life of the concession for the state, as well as developmental criteria such as

jobs, infrastructure, linkages and local capital. With increased investment in resource mapping and geodata acquisition, areas would be
reclassified from high risk to low risk. Unfortunately, the most
geologically prospective parts of the continent have already been
concessioned, usually with no attempt at price discovery or the
maximisation of their growth and development potential. Over 90%
of all new African mines in the last decade were not 'discovered',
but were based on *known* assets, particularly old mines or workings.

Known and unencumbered mineral terrains could be transferred
to a state minerals development vehicle and prepared for competitive
concessions. However, oversight of the auctioning process might be
best undertaken by an adequately resourced dedicated resources
concessions and compliance commission under the respective national
treasuries, which could also carry out the ongoing monitoring and
evaluation of the concession conditions.

However, it remains to be seen whether the juxtaposition of
national and international forces will permit the optimisation of the
developmental impact of Africa's substantial resources endowment.
The resource companies and their international allies (particularly
the Bretton Woods institutions) appear to have prevailed in sub-
verting the first post-colonial developmentalist agenda (particularly
through structural adjustment programmes), but will they prevail
again over a new developmental agenda? The counter-agenda has
arguably been weakened over the last decade by:

- the exit of the main African mining conglomerates (Anglo,
  Lonrho, Union Minière, Gencor and Goldfields): their control
  of African economies, particularly southern Africa, has been
  dramatically reduced through 'unbundling' and a refocus on
  their core competence of mining ('dirt-digging');
- the widespread discrediting of the 'free market' non-
  interventionist ideology by the recent global US toxic debt crisis;
  and
- the increasing success and importance of China and other Asian
  economies in the global balance of power and economic strategies
  (the Beijing Consensus versus the Washington Consensus).

Figure 2.1 Possible mineral resource licensing regime.

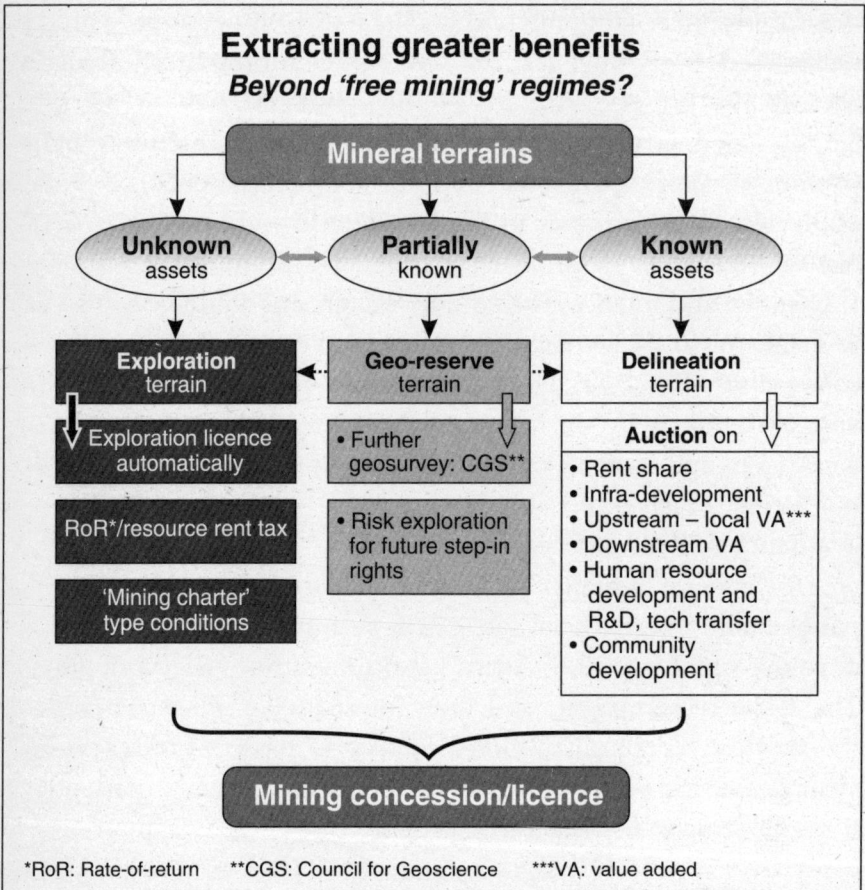

Extracting greater benefits
Beyond 'free mining' regimes?

Mineral terrains

Unknown assets — **Partially** known — **Known** assets

Exploration terrain ← **Geo-reserve** terrain ⟶ **Delineation** terrain

Exploration licence automatically

RoR*/resource rent tax

'Mining charter' type conditions

• Further geosurvey: CGS**

• Risk exploration for future step-in rights

Auction on
• Rent share
• Infra-development
• Upstream – local VA***
• Downstream VA
• Human resource development and R&D, tech transfer
• Community development

Mining concession/licence

*RoR: Rate-of-return   **CGS: Council for Geoscience   ***VA: value added

(Source: Jourdan 2010)

Consequently, the time may be right for establishing a resource-based regional developmental trajectory.

The current crisis and the underlying commodities boom

Any strategy utilising a resource endowment clearly requires a degree of comfort that resources demand will be sustained and that prices will not suddenly collapse as happened in the 1980s and 1990s and in the second half of 2008.

From 2002 to 2008, many developing countries displayed strong growth after several decades of stagnation due to the recent commodities boom, which was provoked by robust demand from China and, to a lesser extent, other emerging economies such as India and Vietnam. Many developing countries have significant potential for commodities production, especially minerals, and consequently foreign direct investment into the majority world has, according to a United Nations Conference on Trade and Development (UNCTAD) World Investment Report, displayed a marked upturn since 2002/3, mainly into the mineral resources and telecommunications sectors. The commodities boom faltered during the second half of 2008 due to the global recession caused by the US sub-prime debt crisis, but most commodity prices have recovered to 2007/8 levels and foreign direct investment is reviving.

Figure 2.2   Foreign direct investment inflows: global and by group of economies, 1980–2008.

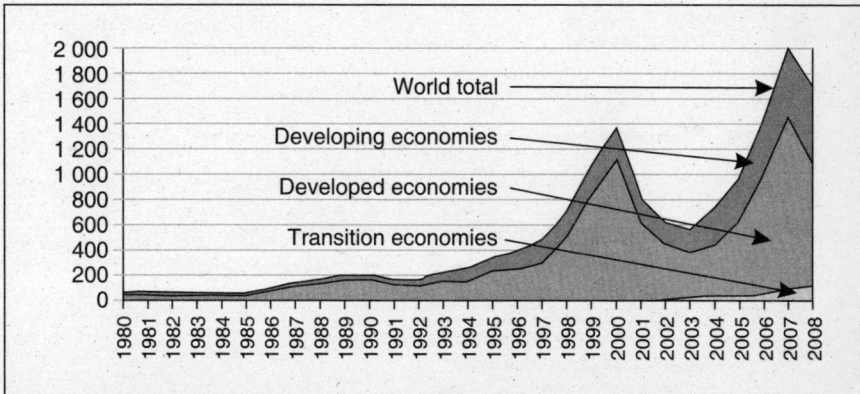

(Source: UNCTAD 2009)

The resources boom took off in 2002/3 with dramatic increases in the prices of minerals, which was followed by agricultural bio-fuels feedstocks in 2006 and other agricultural commodities in 2007. The lag in the price response of agricultural commodities to Asian demand was most probably caused by the price-depressing effects of minority world agro-subsidies, combined with mineral supply inelasticity.

Figure 2.3   Indices of primary commodity prices.

(2005 = 100)1/

1/ indices comprise 60 price series for 44 non-fuel primary commodities. Weights are based on the 2002–4 average of world export earnings.

2/ deflated by US CPI.

(Source: IMF 2009)

Figure 2.4   Commodity price indices (May 1992 – May 2010).

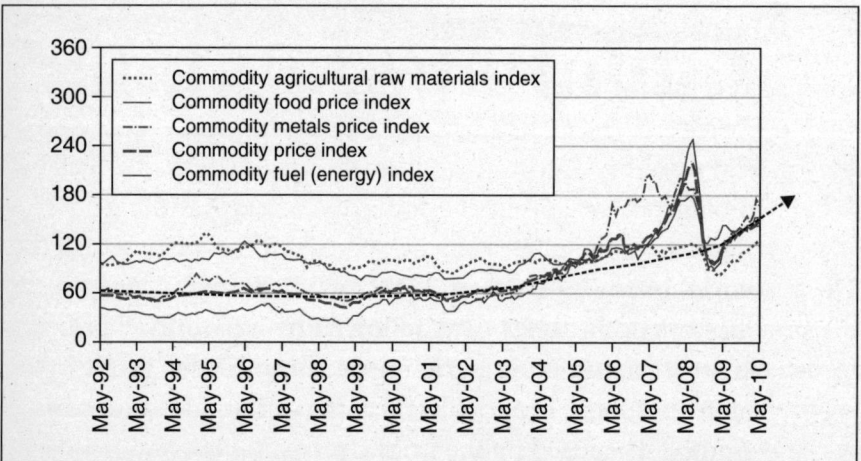

.... Commodity agricultural raw materials index
——— Commodity food price index
–·–·– Commodity metals price index
– – – Commodity price index
——— Commodity fuel (energy) index

(Source: Index Mundi 2010)

Nevertheless, the two seminal questions remain: when will the current global US assets recession abate; and how long will the underlying demand last? Or will it peter out like so many earlier commodity booms?

The underlying driver of mineral demand is the metals intensity of global gross domestic product (GDP) growth. Figure 2.5 displays the global steel intensity, which is a good proxy for metals intensity, per world real GDP per capita.

Figure 2.5   Global steel consumption.

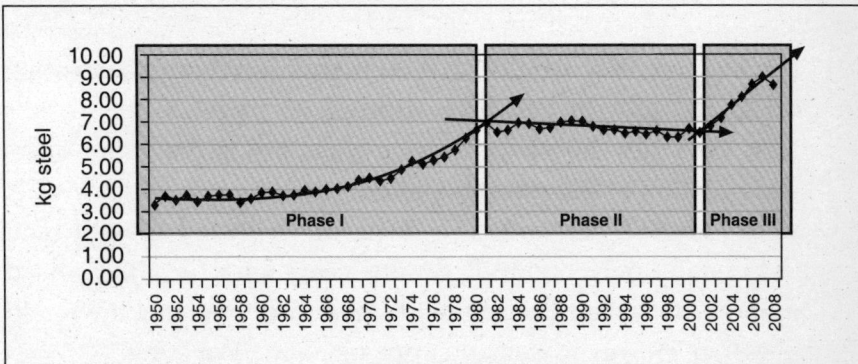

(Source: Jourdan 2008)

The global steel intensity of GDP shows three distinct phases since the Second World War:

- Phase I (1950 to ~1975): high intensity – post-Second World War minority world (first world) reconstruction and increasing buying power within the minority world, resulting in strong minerals demand and prices. Negligible majority world (third world) impact.
- Phase II (1975 to 2000): low intensity – minority world infrastructure installed, move to services (only Asian tigers in high-intensity phase, but too small to impact on global trend). This resulted in over-supply and low prices for most minerals. This gap reflected a failure of continuous global growth due to

49

> minority world hegemony over international trade regimes and widespread use of subsidies.
> - Phase III (2000 to present): high intensity (higher rate than Phase I) as the majority world takes off (Brazil, Russia, India, China – BRIC countries) and trade rules are increasingly revised, reflecting a partial loss of minority world hegemony over global trade systems. Period of high demand and prices, but temporarily stalled due to the extraneous US debt crisis, but by the second half of 2009 demand was already showing signs of recovery through stimulus packages and by 2011 commodity prices had regained pre-crisis levels.

Global metal intensity would have been on a continuous increasing trend if global growth had been diffused to more of the world's people in the 1980s. Instead, diffusion was only to the Asian tigers with a population of less than 80 million, resulting in a minor impact on global minerals demand. The diffusion of global growth (and intensity) finally only occurred twenty years later (in BRIC), but it was temporarily stalled due to the US debt crisis plunging the world into recession. However, demand appears to be recovering.

As is apparent from Phase I of intensity, sustained by minority world growth for any one country, the intensity tends to fall off once the basic national infrastructure is in place and most domestic markets have been developed and penetrated. Growth from then on tends to be in services accompanied by a falling proportion of employment in manufacturing, as evidenced by almost all mature minority world economies (see Figure 2.6).

The country steel intensity per capita data appears to indicate that, at around $16k/capita (2006 US$), the metals intensity of GDP growth falls off, no matter when the initial metals consuming 'lift-off' phase occurred. Given that China is only at about one-third up this high-intensity phase, that India is at about a third that of China and given that they have a combined population approaching three times that of the minority world, it would then be reasonable to assume that the current global high metals intensity phase could

Figure 2.6   Steel intensity per capita.

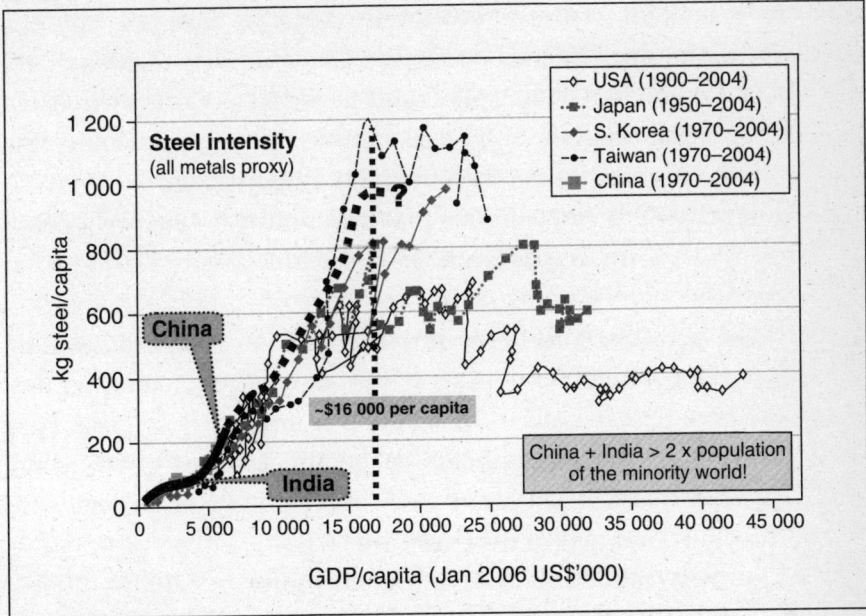

(Source: BHPB 2006)

continue at least as long as Phase I (see Figure 2.6) or roughly 30 years (1950 to 1980). This assumption excludes growing intensity from other emerging economies, such as Brazil, Vietnam and Indonesia, which if included could make this a 30–50 year high-intensity phase.

In concluding this section, it appears safe to assume that despite the recent commodities slump, the underlying boom will be an unprecedented long 'super-cycle', provided that China and India keep up their robust economic growth. This then leaves us with the fundamental question of how can the current commodities-stimulated high prices be transformed into sustainable growth and development in Africa?

A resource-based strategy and the resource curse

The resource curse is a much debated and studied phenomenon, but it is clear that a resource endowment is not always a curse and, if well-managed, can be a blessing as evidenced by strong sustained growth in several resource economies such as Sweden, the US, Norway, Malaysia, Finland, Australia, Canada, New Zealand and Botswana. Researchers Paul Collier and Benedikt Goderis's extensive and illuminating analysis of a large sample of countries refines the impact of the resource curse with the following findings:

- Empirical evidence suggests that commodity booms have positive short-term impacts on growth, but negative long-term impacts on developing countries.
- These adverse long-term impacts are only experienced by exporters of 'high rent' mineral (non-agricultural) commodities.
- The key determinant as to whether a mineral boom will be a blessing or a curse appears to be the level of governance, particularly the existence of sufficiently good institutions.
- The main channels of the curse are:
  — high public and private consumption;
  — low/inefficient investment;
  — overvalued (strong) currency (known as Dutch disease).

What is significant is that all of these channels can be neutralised or ameliorated through appropriate policies and strategies and the resource curse can be turned into a blessing through targeted deployment of the resource rents and opportunities. In this regard, Omano Edigheji also notes in *Constructing a Developmental State in South Africa* that 'what sets developmental states apart from mineral-rich countries is primarily the nature of institutions and consequently state capacity' (p. 12).

Towards a sustainable resource-based African growth and development strategy

Africa's rich and diverse resource base, combined with the strong global resources demand, could underpin a viable resource-based industrialisation strategy that goes beyond supplying raw materials to the world economy. This could be achieved by utilising its extensive resource developmental opportunities to establish the requisite economic infrastructure across the region and to create the crucial resource sector linkages into the local, regional and sub-continental economies.

This 'deepening' of the resources sector though up-, down- and sidestream (infrastructure) industrial linkages could form core industrialisation nuclei for African Regional Economic Communities' economies and will, over time, diversify with increasing human resource development, technology development and skills formation, through the lateral migration of these resource-dependent industrial clusters into resource-independent industrial activities.

In addition to the capture and judicious deployment of resource rents, Africa has a comparative advantage in establishing resource linkage industrial clusters through the following:

- The immediate market offered by the local and regional resource industries' demand for inputs such as plant, equipment, machinery, consumables and services. This market can be relatively large for specialised resource industries' demand, ameliorating economies of scale constraints (for example, the region constitutes three-quarters of the global platinum group metals mining and processing inputs market);
- A potential technological advantage through close proximity to the resource industries' demand for innovation, adaptation and problem solving (these activities often currently take place offshore);
- A feedstock price advantage for downstream resource processing industries, particularly mineral processing (smelting, refining, alloying and fabrication) and agri-processing (food products, leatherwear, meat processing, natural fibres, forestry products, sugar products and biofuels); and
- Opportunities to develop the supplier industries for the extensive resource infrastructure requirements.

Resource linkages industrial clusters
The development of these resource sector linkages slowly builds integrated resource linkages industrial clusters where the different

Table 2.3   Local resource and infrastructure markets.

Resource and resource-based inputs markets
Minerals and mineral processing
Agri-foods and food processing (foods and stimulants)
Livestock and livestock products (leather, meat and fibres)
Sugar and processing (refined, ethanol and lysine)
Agri raw materials and processing (cotton, biofuels and chemicals)
Forestry and wood processing (pulp and paper products and fibre)
Fishing/aquaculture and processing
Energy resources (fossil fuels, hydro-electric power and biomass)
Tourism (hospitality industry, flora/fauna and culture)
Resource infrastructure inputs markets
Construction (cement, ceramics and steel)
Railways (rail, locos, rolling-stock and spares)
Highways, roads (vehicles and trailers)
Ports and airports (capital goods)
Pipelines (gas, fuels and slurries)
Power plants and transmission lines
Water (treatment, pumping, storage and transport)
Telecommunications (transmission)
Knowledge infrastructure (universities and R&D institutions)

(Source: Jourdan 2008)

components reinforce one another and, from initially serving local demand, develop competencies to export goods and services to resource sectors in the region and ultimately globally.

The resource linkages industrial clusters are indirectly anchored on the comparative advantage of the resources sectors and comprise:

- Upstream linkage industries: plant, machinery, consumables (inputs), engineering services, financial services, consultancies;
- Downstream linkage industries: resources processing (value addition) into intermediate products, semi-manufactures, components, sub-assemblies and finished, resource-intensive products. Resource processing usually also produces co-products and by-products, which also constitute potential feedstocks for further downstream linkage industries. These resource beneficiation industries in turn create markets for further upstream industries (capital goods, consumables and services);

- Sidestream linkages: Power generation and supply, construction, process automation, logistics, marketing, transport infrastructure (rail, road and ports), environmental industries, human resource development and skilling entities and other resource sectors that supply inputs into the resource sector (for example, mineral inputs such as fertiliser and conditioners into agriculture, and chemicals into mining). These in turn create new demand for upstream industries.

These linkages are illustrated for the Finnish forestry cluster in Figure 2.7, but similar sector clusters can be developed for Africa's natural comparative advantages.

Figure 2.7   Finland's forestry cluster.

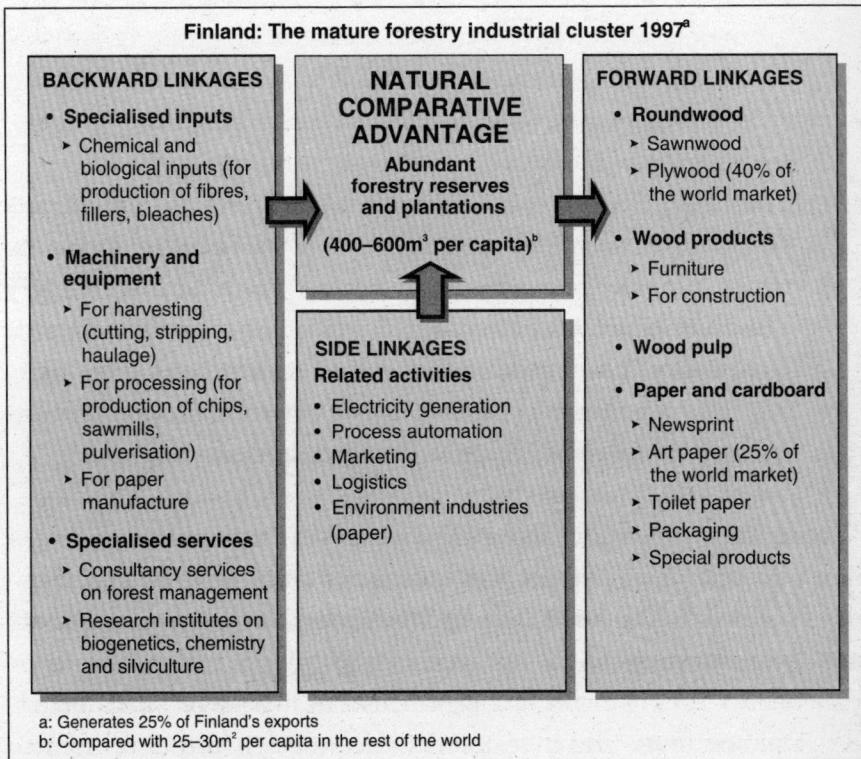

Finland: The mature forestry industrial cluster 1997[a]

BACKWARD LINKAGES

- **Specialised inputs**
  - ➤ Chemical and biological inputs (for production of fibres, fillers, bleaches)

- **Machinery and equipment**
  - ➤ For harvesting (cutting, stripping, haulage)
  - ➤ For processing (for production of chips, sawmills, pulverisation)
  - ➤ For paper manufacture

- **Specialised services**
  - ➤ Consultancy services on forest management
  - ➤ Research institutes on biogenetics, chemistry and silviculture

NATURAL COMPARATIVE ADVANTAGE

Abundant forestry reserves and plantations

(400–600m^3 per capita)[b]

SIDE LINKAGES
Related activities

- Electricity generation
- Process automation
- Marketing
- Logistics
- Environment industries (paper)

FORWARD LINKAGES

- **Roundwood**
  - ➤ Sawnwood
  - ➤ Plywood (40% of the world market)

- **Wood products**
  - ➤ Furniture
  - ➤ For construction

- **Wood pulp**

- **Paper and cardboard**
  - ➤ Newsprint
  - ➤ Art paper (25% of the world market)
  - ➤ Toilet paper
  - ➤ Packaging
  - ➤ Special products

a: Generates 25% of Finland's exports
b: Compared with 25–30m^2 per capita in the rest of the world

(Source: Adapted from Ramos 1998)

According to international economist Joseph Ramos, the evolution of the resource linkage industrial clusters generally goes through the following four phases (p. 112):

- Phase I: Resource extraction with minimum essential local processing (for example, ore concentration, raw cacao beans, roundwood and cotton lint). Almost all the inputs (capital goods, consumables and engineering services) are imported (except for production engineering services) in this phase;

- Phase II: Resource processing and export (for example, wood pulp, agri-processing, mineral smelting and refining) as well as initial import substitution of the lower-technology imported inputs (usually under licence for the local market) and increasing production engineering services;

- Phase III: Initial export of some goods and services established under import substitution in Phase II. The engineering services are increasingly based on local intellectual property and the resources are processed into higher value-added products (for example, fine and special papers, metal alloys, semi-manufactures, packaged agricultural products and textiles);

- Phase IV: Exports of a wide range of resource goods and services of increasing complexity and technology including design engineering services, resource plant and machinery (predominantly based on local intellectual property). Exports of resource-based products of greater variety and complexity and the migration of knowledge-intensive resource services industries, into new, resource-independent sectors.

These phases of resource industrial cluster development are in reality more diverse and complex with some activities moving faster and others slower, but overall there is an increase in product complexity and sophistication (both up- and downstream) that needs to be paralleled with the increasing production of high-level skills (engineers and scientists) and investments into research and development (R&D).

Ultimately, a natural comparative advantage (Phase I) has been transformed into a competitive advantage (Phase IV) with continuous incremental improvements in productivity and design, and the basis has been laid for the migration of hi-tech industries into new, resource-independent (either as a feedstock or market) sectors and generic diversified industrialisation.

There have been several similar linkages studies done for the minerals sector in both South America and southern Africa. A recent study of the South African platinum group metals sector developed the backward linkages diagram in Figure 2.8, which can be considered to be generic to most minerals.

The engineering, procurement, construction management firms are critical to optimising the initial linkages, which also impact on the potential ongoing linkages in terms of the technologies and

Figure 2.8   Backward linkages in the platinum group metals sector.

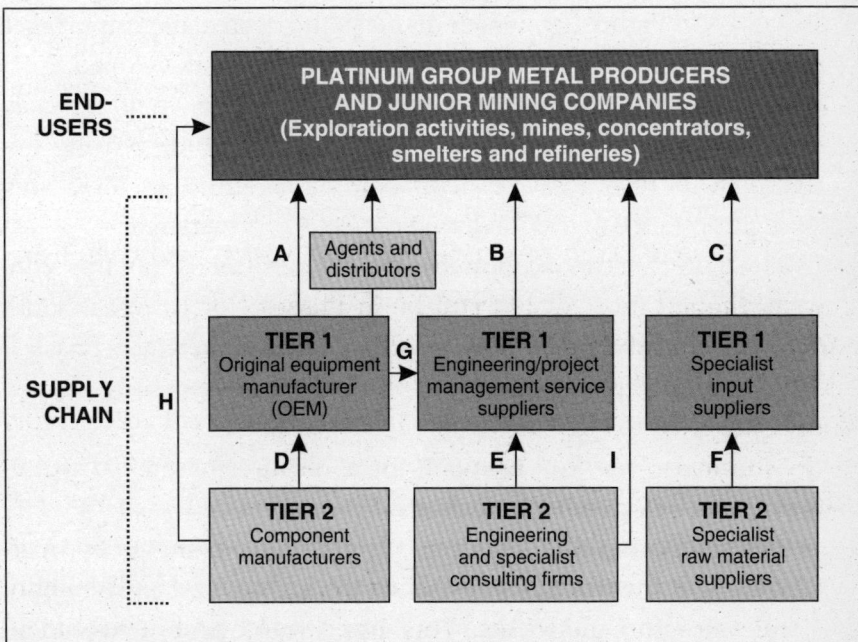

(Source: Lydall 2009)

processes selected. In addition, the Mozal (BHPB) linkages programme has indicated that the configuration of local sub-contracts is important to the success of developing local suppliers. The failure to develop downstream linkages at the Hillside aluminium smelter (Gencor, later BHPB) in Richards Bay is predominantly due to monopoly pricing of the product at import parity price. The stipulation of competitive pricing of all resource products is seminal to any success-ful forward linkages (downstream) strategy.

Nevertheless, the development of regional resources inputs indus-trial clusters is critically constrained by the small national markets of individual states. Even the Southern African Customs Union (Africa's largest market) generally lacks the requisite demand for world-scale viable plants. The establishment of regional common markets would greatly increase the possibility of a successful resource-based development strategy. Other resource-based industrialisation success stories either had larger markets (US) or had access to larger markets (the Nordics: USSR and EU).

A schematic phasing of a resource-based development strategy is presented in Figure 2.9, which displays the decreasing importance of resource exploitation as the resource linkages are developed.

An African resource-based industrialisation strategy would typically go through similar phases of industrialisation, with decreasing im-portance of its resources *comparative* advantage and an increasing relative importance of a skills-based *competitive* advantage.

Almost all African economies can be positioned on this con-tinuum, though most would still be in Phases I or II, while South Africa would probably be positioned somewhere between Phase II and III (though slipping back) and Zimbabwe has possibly slipped from Phase II–III to I–II.

In summary, the key elements of a resource-based industrial-isation and development strategy are:

- The realisation of a resource comparative advantage by over-coming infrastructure constraints through the establishment of infrastructure networks. This has largely been achieved in southern Africa, but not in most other regions of Africa.

Figure 2.9   Schematic resource-based industrialisation phasing.

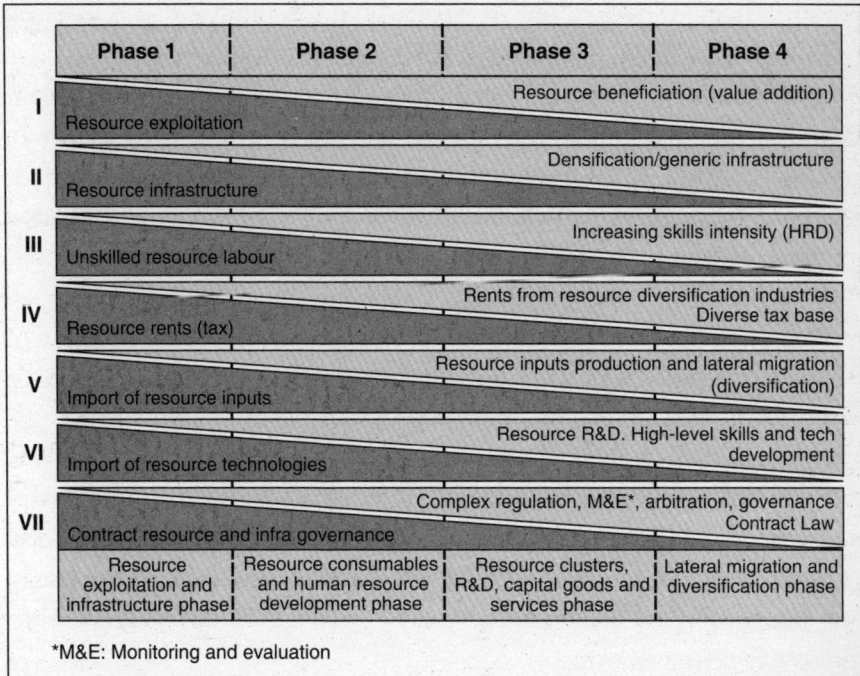

	Phase 1	Phase 2	Phase 3	Phase 4
I	Resource exploitation		Resource beneficiation (value addition)	
II	Resource infrastructure		Densification/generic infrastructure	
III	Unskilled resource labour		Increasing skills intensity (HRD)	
IV	Resource rents (tax)		Rents from resource diversification industries Diverse tax base	
V	Import of resource inputs		Resource inputs production and lateral migration (diversification)	
VI	Import of resource technologies		Resource R&D. High-level skills and tech development	
VII	Contract resource and infra governance		Complex regulation, M&E*, arbitration, governance Contract Law	
	Resource exploitation and infrastructure phase	Resource consumables and human resource development phase	Resource clusters, R&D, capital goods and services phase	Lateral migration and diversification phase

*M&E: Monitoring and evaluation

(Source: Jourdan 2008)

- The 'densification' of the resource-based infrastructure through the establishment of ancillary and feeder infrastructure to enlarge the resources corridor catchments and beneficiary sectors (agriculture, forestry and tourism).
- To deepen the linkages of the mineral sector to the regional economy through beneficiation of these resources and creating supplier and service industries around the minerals sector and developing them into complex resource linkages industrial clusters (up-, side- and downstream industries).
- The capture of resource rents through resource rent taxes and the re-investment of resource rents into human resource development, skills and R&D for technology development to capitalise on the resource linkages opportunities, as well as into long-term infrastructure, for the development of mature

resource industrial clusters and, ultimately, a competitive advantage, independent of resource endowments.

A comprehensive resource-based strategy should develop the labour-intensive resources upstream sectors as well as going further downstream, beyond capital-intensive intermediate goods, into labour-intensive fabrication, which is severely stunted by the widespread practice of monopoly pricing of intermediate industrial feedstocks such as iron/steel and polymers.

A resource-based African industrialisation strategy: Optimising the resource linkages

The key element to a strategy that uses natural resources to catalyse growth and development appears to be, from looking at successful resource-based industrialisation, the maximisation of the concomitant opportunities offered by a natural resources endowment, particularly the 'deepening' of the resources sector through optimising linkages into the local economy.

Resource rents

Resource rents (returns in excess of the expected/average return on capital) should be used to improve the basic physical and knowledge infrastructure of the nation. Generally, the resource rents are not shared with the resource owner (the state/people) and all African states should consider the implementation of a resource rent tax, possibly to be kept offshore to ameliorate currency appreciation and fiscal shocks, and which could be drip-fed back into long-term (ten to twenty year) regional knowledge and physical infrastructure.

Infrastructure

The high-rent resource infrastructure (mainly minerals) should be used to open up other lower rent, resource potential (such as agriculture, forestry and tourism), as per the spatial development initiative methodology in order to access zones of economic potential with lower returns that cannot afford their own requisite infrastructure.

Figure 2.10   Southern African spatial initiatives.

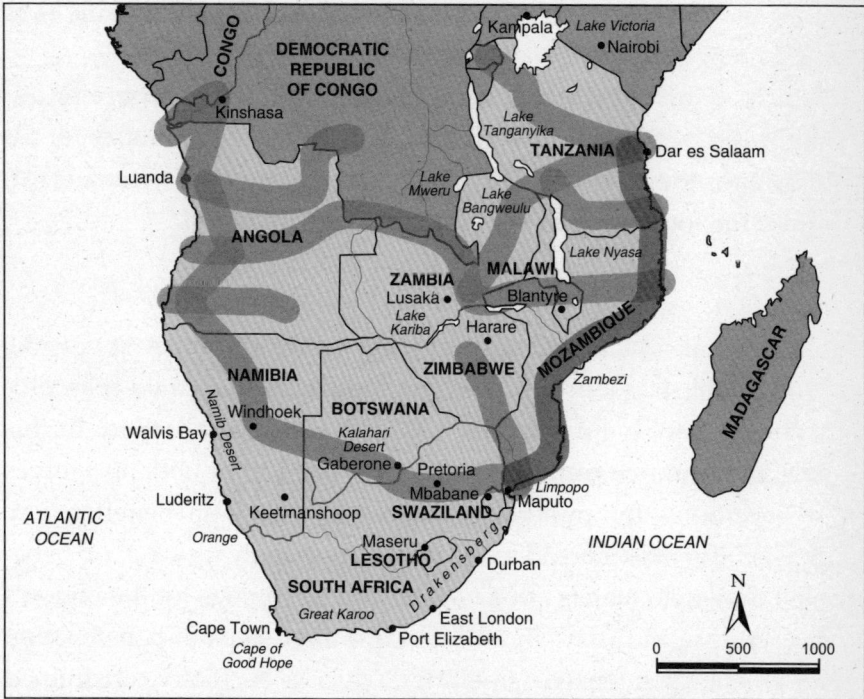

(*Source: Jourdan 2010*)

All resource concessions must include third party access at non-discriminatory user-tariffs to all of the resources infrastructure (transport, power, water and telecommunications), in order to catalyse the resource infrastructure 'hitch-hikers' (such as agriculture), which in general have a much higher socio-economic propulsive impact. This condition needs to be configured into all resource contracts for all resource infrastructure.

Although most of resource-driven infrastructure is in place above and below the tropics, there are still opportunities to link in depressed rural areas: for example, through the coal and platinum group metals resources in South Africa's Limpopo Province and Botswana. However, between the tropics there are numerous

61

opportunities for resource-based infrastructure to catalyse wider growth and development through spatial development initiatives or development corridors.

Resource infrastructure generally relies on state assets (servitudes) or rights (licences) and consequently constitutes a potential lever for encouraging the resource and the infrastructure concessionaires to optimise the local mineral and infrastructure linkages.

Downstream value addition

The locational advantage of producing crude resources should be used to establish resource processing industries that could then provide the feedstocks for manufacturing and industrialisation. In this regard, the resource contracts or licences need to provide incentives or disincentives for mineral resources downstream beneficiation. However, the widespread practice of monopoly pricing of beneficiated minerals/metals often negates this advantage for the region's manufacturing industry. In addition, the first steps of beneficiation are often energy intensive (smelting), which is currently constrained by Africa's power shortages.

Consideration should be given to much greater intra-regional power trade (through, for example, regional power pools), which could be based on potential low cost and sustainable hydro-power from the Congo, Zambezi, Niger, Nile and other rivers between the tropics. However, in many cases, African mining companies have encouraged beneficiation offshore. An example would be Anglo American's divestment from its main platinum group metals downstream beneficiator and technology developer, Johnson Matthey Plc in the 1990s (when it was the major shareholder, at more than 40%), after investing heavily in it, especially in technology development, over the previous 40 years. This was probably due to its increasing focus on 'core competence' (mining) in preparation for its exit and London listing. This appears to indicate that the South African decision to allow Anglo to relist abroad was possibly ill-advised and that the 'unfettered' movement abroad of domestic capital should be curtailed. In this regard, Omano Edighedi correctly argues that 'by virtue of the listing of key South African conglomerates overseas, South Africa's government has lost influence over the conglomerates and stripped itself of resources that it could have used for its developmental purposes' (p. 22). Similarly, the exit of other African resources companies has had the same consequences (Union Minière and Ashanti Gold, for example).

Upstream value addition

The resources sector market should be used to develop the resource supply/inputs sector (for example, capital goods, consumables and services). This often offers a relatively large market for specific inputs for particular resource exploitation. South Africa, Zimbabwe and the Copperbelt (Zambia and the Democratic Republic of the Congo) used to boast a substantial mineral inputs sector, but these have all but disappeared in the latter two and are diminishing in the former. For example, Zambia Engineering Services is long gone and EGM Forrest in Lubumbashi relocated to Europe decades ago.

Africa's mineral capital goods are generally imported and of the few capital goods companies that it had, several have been sold to foreign companies over the last decade, in part due to the refocusing of the old southern African mining houses, which used to invest in a plethora of up- and downstream industries. This was in turn due to their relocation after 1994 to offshore stock exchanges (for example, Anglo American, Gencor, Gold Fields and parts of the former JCI). Academic economist and writer Seeraj Mohamed points out that 'these companies were restructured by shareholder pressure, and while there may have been benefits for shareholders, the South African economy lost influence over large, powerful corporations that could have been part of a developmental project to deepen and diversify the country's industrial base' (p. 161).

Local content milestones need to be built into the resource contracts or licences and a first step could be to base local purchasing milestones (for example, black economic empowerment purchases in the South African mining charter) on local value-added rather than value (this would also curtail destructive local supplier 'fronting' for foreign suppliers).

In an Organization for Economic Cooperation and Development (OECD) Development Centre policy brief, Gøril Havro and Javier Santiso point out that both Norway and Chile experienced:

> direct efforts to diversify their economy and to support industries associated with the natural-resource sector – such as engineering and supply – as well as non-resource sectors. Norwegian policies in the 1970s were markedly interventionist in this regard . . . The legal framework emphasised local content until 1990, to develop the infant petroleum supply industry. Norway also pushed for state participation in the same areas, in spite of reluctance on the part of many of the international companies.

Havro and Santiso further contend:

> local-content requirements could potentially have beneficial effects as well, as seen in Norway, since they would contribute to developing domestic economic activity rather than relying on rents, while at the same time increasing human capital through learning-by-doing and technological spillovers. However, there is a need for good co-operation with the foreign companies to ensure that such requirements are not commercially unviable, and at the same time to ensure that they have a real learning impact and are not just seen as another tax payment by companies. Standardised local-content agreements worked out with experts in the field could be useful in achieving this.

The platinum group metals seams of the Bushveld Complex in South Africa and the Great Dyke in Zimbabwe reportedly constitute the world's largest trackless mining opportunity. However, the requisite capital goods will predominantly be supplied by imports, due to the failure to invest in the development of trackless mining equipment, especially after the demise of the Chamber of Mines Research Organisation (COMRO) in South Africa and the Institute of Mining Research (IMR) in Zimbabwe.

Technology/product development

Resources exploitation technologies generally need to adapt to local conditions (for example, climate, mineralogy and terrain) in order to provide opportunities for the development of niche technological competencies in the resources inputs sector. This sector tends to be knowledge-intensive and accordingly needs 'priming' through investment in human resource development and R&D. However, several studies have shown that it has the capacity to later 'reinvent' itself outside the resources sector to produce new products for other non-resource markets.

African resource exploitation contracts or licences need to facilitate the establishment of a domestic resources R&D capacity, and the requisite human resource development. This type of capacity needs to be rebuilt and resourced across the continent, together with the mining and capital goods sectors to ensure that mineral technology opportunities do not leak away to states such as Sweden and Finland, which offer greater R&D incentives and support. Technology and value addition are central to Norway's 'Oil and Gas for the 21st Century' strategy (OG21). It is primarily based on R&D to increase recovery, extend the resource base, add value to gas resources and to underpin technology exports (see Figure 2.11). There does not appear to be any major constraint to an African development agenda pursuing a similar sustainable strategy for its minerals sector.

Figure 2.11   Norway's OG21 strategy.

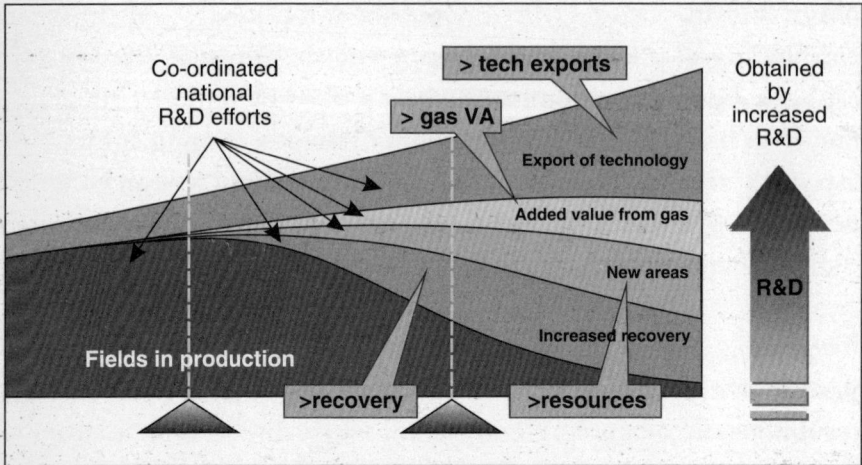

(Source: Jourdan 2010)

Conclusion

The Asian boom and concomitant strong demand for Africa's natural resources could provide a window of opportunity for a regional resource-based development strategy. Such a strategy must optimise the developmental impact of resources by ensuring that the resource economic linkages are made (backward and forward). Investment into technical human resource development and R&D is seminal to the optimisation of the economic linkages.

The African resource regimes (particularly mineral regimes) need to be overhauled to allow for the competitive concessioning of the region's resource endowments (land, minerals, water, fisheries and state rights), to maximise price discovery and developmental objectives. Similarly, the developmental impacts of existing ('first-come-first-served' concessions) need to be maximised through appropriate legislation and/or contract renegotiation. In this regard, investment in systematic geosurvey is fundamental to the identification of mineral assets.

A resource rent tax of 30–50% on all excess profits above a reasonable (expected) return should be imposed on all resource exploitation concessions or licences and should form the basis of offshore regional development funds to finance long-term regional physical and human infrastructure. As virtually none of the African Union member states currently apply this tax, there would be almost no fiscal loss, especially if the resource rent tax was applied after corporate tax deductions. Such a regional development fund could be a major instrument in facilitating equitable regional economic integration and ameliorating industrial polarisation. It would obviously imply a transfer of wealth/rent from resource-rich zones to resource-poor zones, but this wealth/rent is currently untaxed and is generally transferred or remitted to the minority world nations.

Economies of scale and competition would be greatly enhanced by common regional (and, ultimately, continental) markets (customs unions). The success of an African resource-based development strategy would be dramatically compromised without it. A customs union revenue sharing formula could also contribute to the putative regional development funds and thereby facilitate greater equity in the benefits of integration by prioritising investment into depressed areas and new industrial nodes. Consideration could be given to merging the national Development Finance Institutions (DFIs) into single regional DFIs (for example, the Industrial Development Corporation and the Development Bank of Southern Africa in southern Africa) in order to develop and facilitate viable investment projects across the regions.

A first step in regional economic integration could be multi-state co-operation in the establishment of regional development corridors to realise latent economic potential through seamless infrastructure provision, which would provide tangible benefits to all the participating parties.

However, only the future will tell whether the balance of local and international forces will permit the realisation of an African resource-based development strategy, which has the potential to unleash sustainable growth and development and job creation across the continent.

PAUL JOURDAN is an independent development consultant. He is the former Mintek CEO and worked as the Deputy Director-General in the Department of Trade and Industry (DTI). He is the acting Chair of the Coega Development Corporation, a member of the ANC research team into State Intervention in the Minerals Sector and an adviser to the DTI's Regional SDI Programme and the Mozambican Ministry of Transport SDI Unit.

References and further reading

Barton, B.J. (1993) *Canadian Law of Mining* (Canadian Institute of Resources Law, Calgary).

BHPB (2006) 'Where To From Here?'. Paper presented to the Merrill Lynch Global Metals, Mining and Steel Conference, Miami, May, available at bhpbilliton.com/bbContentRepository/Presentations/ 060327CWGML2006ConfMiami.pdf.

Campbell, B. (2010) 'Revisiting the Reform Process of African Mining Regimes' in *Canadian Journal of Development Studies* Vol. 30, Nos. 1–2, pp. 197–217.

Collier, P. and Goderis, B. (2007) 'Commodity Prices, Growth, and the Natural Resource Curse: Reconciling a Conundrum'. CSAE WPS/2007-15, University of Oxford.

Edigheji, O. (ed.) (2010) *Constructing a Democratic Developmental State in South Africa* (HSRC Press, Cape Town).

Havro, G. and Santiso, J. (2008) 'To Benefit from Plenty: Lessons from Chile and Norway'. Policy Brief No. 37, OECD Development Centre.

IMF (2009) 'Primary Commodity Prices', available at imf.org/external/np/res/ commod/index.asp.

Index Mundi (2010) 'Commodity Prices', available at indexmundi.com/ commodities.

Jourdan, P. (2008) 'Plan of Action for African Acceleration of Industrialisation-Promoting Resource-Based Industrialisation: A Way Forward'. Paper prepared for the African Union Commission, Addis Ababa, August.

——— (2010) 'Mining for Development: Towards a Resource-based African Development Strategy?' Presentation, RMG, Stockholm, February.

Laforce, M., Lapointe, U. and Lebuis, V. (2009) 'Mining Sector Regulation in Quebec and Canada: Is a Redefinition of Asymmetrical Relations Possible?' in *Studies in Political Economy* Vol. 84, Fall, pp. 47–78.

Lapointe, U. (2009) 'Origins of Mining Regimes in Canada and the Legacy of the Free Mining System'. Conference on 'Rethinking Extractive Industry: Regulation, Dispossession, and Emerging Claims', Centre for Research on Latin America and the Caribbean (CERLAC) and the Extractive Industries Research Group (EIRG), York University, Toronto.

Lydall, M. (2009) 'Backward Linkage Development in the South African PGM Industry: A Case Study' in *Resources Policy* Vol. 34, No. 3, p. 112–20.

Mohamed, S. (2010). 'The Effect of a Mainstream Approach to Economic and Corporate Governance on Development in South Africa' in Edigheji, O. (ed.), *Constructing a Democratic Developmental State in South Africa* (HSRC Press, Cape Town).

Palma, G. (2005) 'Four Sources of "De-industrialisation" and a New Concept of the "Dutch Disease"' in Ocampo, J.A. (ed.) *Beyond Reforms: Structural Dynamics and Macroeconomic Vulnerability* (Stanford University Press and World Bank, Palo Alto, CA and Washington, D.C.).

Ramos, J. (1998) 'A Development Strategy Founded on Natural Resource-based Production Clusters' in *CEPAL Review*, No. 68, 12/1998, Economic Commission for Latin America and Caribbean.

UNCTAD (2009) 'WIR: World Investment Report', available at unctad.org/en/docs/wir2009_en.pdf.

USGS (2010) 'Mineral Commodity Summaries', available at minerals.usgs.gov/minerals/pubs/mcs/.

Van der Ploeg, Frederick (2007) 'Challenges and Opportunities for Resource Rich Economies'. RSCAS Working Papers, European University Institute.

3

Class Formation and
Rising Inequality in South Africa
What Does this Mean for Future Voting Patterns?

DAVID EVERATT

> Politics is not the art of the possible. It consists in choosing
> between the disastrous and the unpalatable.
>
> — J.K. Galbraith

Introduction

Galbraith's apothegm – being forced to choose between similarly
indigestible alternatives – may apply as much (or more) to voting
(and voters) as to politics. This chapter uses a large baseline survey
conducted immediately prior to the 2009 South African general
election to argue that, while many bemoan the 'single-party dominance' of the African National Congress (ANC) and its apparently
hegemonic dominance of African votes, political pluralism is already
here. This is evident both in the desire for choice and (in 2009) its
translation into the stated (non-ANC) voting intentions, in particular
of younger, better-educated and more affluent African voters.

President Jacob Zuma has argued the reverse, in an interesting
take on theology and politics: 'We shall build this organisation. Even
God expects us to rule this country because we are the only organisation which was blessed by pastors when it was formed. It is even

blessed in Heaven. That is why we will rule until Jesus comes back' (*The Times*, 5 May 2008).

The data used make it clear that divine sanction notwithstanding, the ANC is facing a generational ceiling. The ANC vote is concentrated amongst 'the 76 generation' (and their elders), who kick-started the wave of popular resistance that ended in the 1994 accession to power of the ANC, but did so at great personal, physical, psychological and other costs. According to survey data, young, professional black voters (and better-educated black voters in general) have a far weaker identification with the ANC.

Wikileaks released the following United States (US) cable in January 2011:

> Cable from the United States Embassy in Pretoria to the Secretary of State Washington DC, December 5 2008:
> Subject: STRONG INDICATION OF MBEKI INVOLVEMENT IN COPE
> Classified By: DEPUTY POLITICAL COUNSELOR MADELINE Q. SEIDENSTRICKER FOR REASONS 1.4 (B) AND (D).
> Summary
> 1. (S//NF) Former President Thabo Mbeki reportedly had a hand in drafting a six-page policy document for the newly formed Congress of the People (COPE) and has influence in how COPE is drafting a foreign policy vision, according to prominent University of South Africa professor Dirk Kotze.
> Kotze's comments serve as the strongest indication yet that the former South African leader may be assisting the party formed by many of his longtime allies.
> End Summary.

Whether the contents were true or not, this can be read simply as a clear indication of the success of former President Thabo Mbeki's strategy of building a black, and particularly African, bourgeoisie. This 'class project' was to create a black bourgeoisie that could penetrate the white-controlled upper echelons of the economy, as had already been done with the political structures of the country. Whether or not he wrote the policy documents of the Congress of the People (COPE) does not matter. COPE was launched with much fanfare after the ANC's *broedertwis* (war between brothers) in Polokwane that saw Mbeki's attempt to win a third term as ANC president fail, and leapt from nothing to 7% of the vote (1.3 million voters chose COPE in the national elections and it dislodged the Democratic Alliance [DA] as official opposition in a number of provinces) in 2009. COPE had a ready-made constituency in place and waiting for it. The ANC vote share dropped in seven of nine provinces, with blushes saved primarily by the ethnic identification of Zulu voters with new ANC President Zuma (and the terminal stasis of the Inkatha Freedom Party [IFP]).

The 'class project' so derided by the left, had succeeded. And as the black bourgeoisie grows, the younger generation gets better educated and moves up the employment ladder, so pluralism will deepen. Pluralism, as is argued here, should not be equated with the number of African votes cast for the DA. Pluralism must be measured across the political spectrum as a whole – and when it is, the body politic emerges as considerably more healthy than much commentary would suggest.

Overview and methodology

Moeletsi Mbeki, the editor of this book, has written on the topic discussed in this chapter, and was quoted in an article entitled 'ANC is the party of the middle class' as saying that 'what really lies at the bottom of our economic problems in South Africa is that we have too much . . . one-party dominance . . . we need more competition in our political system . . .' (*Mail & Guardian*, 31 August 2010). This chapter argues that pluralism is already here, although one-party dominance will be with us for a while following the public seppuku of COPE and its decline from drama to farce.

Arguments about 'one-party dominance' come in two forms: those which focus on the dominance of the party in question (the ANC in our case); and others emanating from commentators who adhere to the race-census approach (sometimes dressed up as the 'identity' thesis). In the latter, black voters are an unchanging constant who, because they are black, blindly vote ANC, regardless of whatever calumny the ANC may stand accused. Many of those who have written about 'single-party dominance' have used the notion to reduce states where this occurs to mere 'semi-democratic rule', as R.W. Johnston is quoted on the dust jacket of Hermann Giliomee and Charles Simkins's *The Awkward Embrace*. Such commentators find no 'solution' to the 'problem' because they cannot see beyond race or accept the reality of a black population that is and will remain an overwhelming demographic and electoral majority and whose voting decisions will determine the future course of the country.

As long as blacks keep voting, this logic argues, the ANC will keep winning elections – so the 'solution' to this 'problem' is sought in changing the electoral system or some other form of tinkering with the rules of the game. No other solution seems to be available – certainly not one where black voters change their minds and their votes; and, of course, because when they do, they do not vote for the DA. The 'race census' lies at the heart of much post-colonial ennui, as Adam Habib and Sanusha Naidu noted in their 2006 article in the journal *Africa Development*: 'Since the country's first democratic election, politicians, political scientists and commentators who have explained the voting patterns and behaviour of South Africa's electorate have concluded that South Africa's electoral outcomes are race-based' (p. 81).

The danger, of course, is the pendulum swing – if 'race' is 'bad' as an explanatory variable, then 'class' has been posited as the 'good' that should be used. But race matters, to voters as to commentators. Racial attitudes among black voters are rarely considered, though taken for granted amongst whites. It is as common for pollsters to hear whites stereotyping blacks as the reverse: a common sentiment expressed in focus groups from pre-1994 to the present has been for black voters to note that they would vote for any party led by a black person and never for any party led by a white person. This should be as unsurprising as the frequent excoriation of the ANC and its (black) leaders by white voters in their focus groups.

This is why COPE was so important – it was black led, its leaders had struggle credentials, and it did not threaten a return to white supremacy. It also neatly defined the DA's core problem: while it is widely seen as a good opposition and valued for playing that role, many ANC voters see it as a stalking horse for whites wanting a return to the past. These perceptions will have been confirmed by the building of unwalled toilets and putting in place an all-male provincial Cabinet in the Western Cape. Whatever the merits of either act, both were moments of political infantilism that gifted the ANC with unexpected electoral ammunition and confirmed the worst fears of black voters. Taken with the COPE implosion, the 2011 local election should see a return to the ANC fold by many African voters who left in 2008/9.

Among commentators for whom class is a more appropriate analytic category, few offer any substantive, aggregate class analysis in defence of their argument. It is not uncommon to find voting district (VD) analysis where authors select a few sites whose class compositions they feel they know, and then construct a national argument on the basis of a handful of VDs. In part, this reflects the simple fact that we are data poor: official data do not lend themselves easily to persuasive class analysis, and few polling surveys are made freely available for academics to explore over time (polling surveys are either conducted by political parties and are not released for obvious reasons, or by market research agencies demanding high fees for their data).

That said, the salience of class is often offered as a self-evident truth in rebuttal to the race census. In the hasty rush to disprove the race-census approach, it is equally possible to over-state the role of class without pausing to understand the size, nature, characteristics or behaviours of this or that class – and ask whether it is, indeed, a class at all. Does the much-vaunted black middle class – or 'black diamonds' as the ubiquitous marketers term it – share enough of a social, economic, educational and value base to be called a class? And if they do, are their political behaviours notably different from other classes in society?

Class and voting in post-apartheid South Africa

A class enjoys shared relationships of production and ownership; a legal framework permitting reproduction; family, kinship or broader group membership as well as similar education levels; a more or less common culture and lifestyle that reflect status; and sufficient size to make the class definable and able to act collectively when required. Classes usually adopt ways of behaving, talking, dressing and life-styles and codes (of dress, language and so on) that make them distinctive compared with other classes.

This is a deliberately general definition, not accounting for strati-fication and other common analytic variables. But even in this loose framework, can we really talk of a distinct 'black middle class' in South Africa – or, more pointedly, of an *African* middle class (that is, one that excludes Indian and coloured citizens)? One that is not merely attacked by media and commentators alike for enjoying the conspicuous consumption that the white middle classes did for so long, but that acts coherently to protect its own interests? Do we know how it does so, or are we limited to notions of a 'predatory class' controlling a 'predatory state', as stated by the Congress of South African Trade Unions (COSATU) Secretary General, Zwelinzima Vavi, in the article 'Stop the politicians' feeding frenzy' (*Cape Argus*, 17 August 2010)? And if we do have such a class, which party do they mainly vote for, and why? Why not other parties? Do we know this, at a measurably accurate level, or is it the result of sensationalism and gossip? And, most obviously, have we got our eye on the correct ball – the parties? We watch the voters, but rarely pause to ask difficult questions of the parties themselves, and why they may or may not be attracting votes from different groups, or which class interests they actually represent.

The reason for phrasing the issue in these terms is that a basic assumption in much political science and media commentary seems to be that the interests of a black middle class should be better represented by the pro-business, pro-'equal opportunity society' DA than by the ANC with its on-going talk of pro-poor (tax funded) social grants, nationalisation and a developmental state. We should be more like Britain, in other words, with the Tories pitted against Labour, middle against working class – which we may well be, but commentators may be looking at the issue through the wrong lens.

Political parties are rarely analysed in greater detail than the claims they make on their election posters. Anthony Giddens noted in *Sociology*: '[T]he largest parties are those associated with general political interests . . . There is usually a fairly clear connection between voting patterns and class differences' – and added an appropriate qualification, that this applied in 'most western states' (p. 314). If the ANC says it is the party of the poor, it is assumed that it must then be our Labour Party (the Labour Party of old, that is); if the DA says it supports an equal opportunity post-racial meritocracy driven by unfettered markets, then it must be our Tory party, Helen Zille our Margaret Thatcher. There are two obvious problems: voters are forced into a Manichaean race or class bifurcation, in both of which their behaviour is straitjacketed by the analytic frame being applied; and parties and their class interests are weakly analysed or, worse, reduced to mere pastiche.

Since African voters are self-evidently not flocking in huge numbers to the DA, the logic of this argument goes, it must be because of the race-census theory – because they are voting through racial blinkers. The fact that the ANC may in fact far better protect the interests of the African middle class – whatever it is, however large and in/coherent it may be – is rarely considered. When it is, it usually is an insult thrown at the ANC by its tripartite alliance partners from the South African Communist Party (SACP) or, far more often, from COSATU. But Collette Schulz-Herzenberg's comment on the 2004 general election is even more pertinent now that we are past the

2009 election: '. . . the electorate differ[s] substantially from the one that participated in the 1994 elections in terms of generational experiences and expectations, historical memory, class mobility, poverty levels, education, and political information' (p. 116).

The youngest voters in 2009 would have been born in a world where Mandela was free, would have entered post-apartheid schools, and in 2009 would have been (assuming they were eighteen) about to enter a completely different student or working life from that which older age cohorts had experienced. For the first time in 2009, genuinely 'born frees' got to vote ('born frees' is often used pejoratively to describe young people who did not have to participate in the struggle and – in the eyes of whoever is speaking – insufficiently value both the gains of struggle and the sacrifices of those who took part in the struggle). Despite Schulz-Herzenberg's insistence that South Africa is witnessing a 'silent revolution' via the production of 'floating voters' who evince 'diminishing party loyalties for all parties' (p. 116), the ANC stubbornly keeps winning large majorities. Only 2009 gave the first substantive indication that the weakened party ties she pointed to were finding a new political home, in COPE, rather than sitting on their hands and not voting.

While the ANC does keep winning impressive majorities – long after the halo effect of liberation has faded – it is worth noting that in 2009, when the ANC won 65.9% of the vote, the party actually took a pounding at the polls. The ANC's review of the 2009 elections, 'A Decisive Mandate', argued that the party vote share 'fell back to . . . where it was in 1999', which was both a means of making the result less unappetising and a reminder of the long-term perspective with which the ANC views its own role in the country. It lost ground in seven of nine provinces, notching up small but important gains in Gauteng (where it faced a strong DA campaign) and large gains in KwaZulu-Natal as the IFP campaign was (for a change) marked by torpor rather than temper and the ANC could boast a traditional, rural Zulu president. It received almost a million KwaZulu-Natal votes in return.

The 66% majority should not disguise the fact that the ANC lost vote share and the opposition gained considerably – nor should it obscure the fact that while the DA made some important gains and received 17% of the national vote while smaller opposition parties were wiped out, it was the new kid on the block, COPE, that took 1.3 million votes (7%) and displaced the DA as official opposition in a number of provinces. To leap from 0 to 7% of the vote in a matter of months is a remarkable electoral feat, and indicates the extent of the tensions and differences within the ANC, many of which had burst into the open at Polokwane, but not all of which had been resolved. The year 2010 showed that the tensions that beset COPE were even greater, and the party successfully made itself the political laughing stock of South Africa.

Changing voters, changing parties

Political parties, and the ANC in particular, are not static entities. The parties of today are not the parties they were in 1994, just as the electorate has changed. Parties change, grow and develop. Moreover, their policies are not necessarily the same as their electoral slogans or media sound bites – by some margin, in some instances. As importantly, they continually monitor their own voters, try to understand them, and manipulate voter sentiments via their campaigns, speeches, symbols, images, media (of all types) and so on. This is often neglected by commentators who study voters in great detail, but forget that parties are key players in the electoral arena, continually re-positioning themselves in the electoral marketplace. The electoral fate of the Azanian People's Organisation (AZAPO), the Pan-Africanist Congress (PAC) and other anti-apartheid stalwarts indicates what happens to parties that fail to operate in this dynamic manner.

A similarly static approach often applies when commentators talk of the 'black middle class' as if it is an established entity, a given, with agreed parameters, size and characteristics, when in fact the reverse is true. That South Africa has a black (that is, African, coloured and Indian) and an African middle class is not disputed.

But what it looks like, how big it is, how it behaves and (for our purposes) what its political predilections are, remain unknown or are at best the result of guesstimation. Academics are still battling to find tools and terminology to adequately understand post-apartheid class formation as it occurs around them but the data remain un-helpful. The size and composition of the 'black middle class' is far from established and few, if any, analysts have tried to link class analysis with an assessment of its political behaviour as a class. Some also throw in the notion of a black 'upper class', a concept even more woolly and desperate for analysis and consideration. As former ANC heavyweight, Saki Macozoma, caustically observed of the rush to unearth 'black diamonds' – the apparent post-apartheid black middle class trumpeted by excited marketers but measured at a remarkably low monthly income of R7 000 (and above . . .) – most are 'a cheque away from poverty' (quoted in Marketingweb's 'Black Diamonds Continue to Grow'). A class is more than an income band or occupational category.

The dangers of failing to grapple with the cross-cutting issues of race and class in a context of both changing voters *and* flexible parties, lead to insights such as that offered by a 2009 Institute for Democracy in South Africa (Idasa) election briefing paper that 'racial credentials could also be a code word for class credentials' (p. 4); and in case this inscrutable claim failed to explain why people voted for this or that party, the author helpfully added that 'there are exceptions' (p. 4). Having asserted – as many other authors do – that race and class both matter, the author veered from arguing that the 'emergence of this black upper class and middle class' explained votes seeping away from the ANC to COPE, to the conclusion that 'race and class . . . merely reinforce each other' (p. 7). This kind of pseudo-analysis is widespread and indicates the ease with which complex conceptual language and analytic categories, misapplied, lead to profound confusion.

The ANC, often more self-critical than erstwhile external critics, noted in 'A Decisive Mandate' that the 2009 election witnessed a 'fall in the ANC's share of [the] national vote' which 'resulted from various factors, reflected in mobilisation trends and shifts in support that played themselves out in different ways in different provinces and amongst different sectors'. There are no fixed racial identities here, nor morphing of race and class – rather, shifts, movement, mobilisation and local differences form a key part of the narrative. And they should – they have to be accounted in any decent polling effort.

Methodology

Pollsters – those who take care about everything from design, sampling and fieldwork to data analysis and measurement tools as well as conceptual categories – are usually pretty accurate. For example, polls I have been involved in have consistently predicted actual results for all parties to within 1% or less of what actually occurs come voting day. For all that, let us be clear that it is far easier to predict what people will do on a given (voting) day a few weeks hence than what they may do and how their values and attitudes may (or may not) change months and years into the future as their class positions change. Anyway, trying to measure voting patterns by class, using surveys, is far from easy, as Richard Sennett and Jonathan Cobb remind us: '[It] doesn't mean that poll-takers can't ask profound questions; it does mean they face difficult problems in dealing with the ambiguities, subtleties, and contradictions involved in answers . . .' (p. 44).

The same point can be made about measuring virtually anything using surveys; but Marxists in particular are very edgy about quantitative measurement of class, and no satisfactory and agreed set of variables has been established that measure class to broad satisfaction. All quantitative data carries a 'health warning', precisely because it is about finding generalisable patterns in a large but sampled population where pointed questions are asked of respondents by strangers. The data may suffer from design bias, sample bias and many other possible pitfalls, most of which are well known and for some of which the data can be controlled. This chapter relies heavily on survey data, particularly from a baseline survey that was conducted in Gauteng just before the general election, and whose client (who wishes to remain anonymous) has given permission for the data to be re-analysed for this chapter. Some additional data are taken from a large sample 'Quality of Life' survey commissioned by the Gauteng City-Region Observatory (GCRO), to try to better understand subjective class choices among citizens (and voters) in the Gauteng city-region. The data will be analysed using some key variables that form part of class analysis – income, education, employment status (as well as other variables such as age and sex) – but we do not try to create a proxy set of variables for class.

Both surveys were restricted to Gauteng, the economic power-house of South and southern Africa. The assumption is not that whatever happens in Gauteng will inexorably appear elsewhere, but rather that if we are to find a significant 'black middle class' it is more likely to appear in Gauteng than anywhere else in the country. There is also a frankly utilitarian issue, namely limited access to polling survey data that are recent, accurate in their political findings and have a big enough sample to permit analysis within cohorts.

The 2008 polling survey is particularly important since it allows us to shine a spotlight on a crucial moment in South Africa's post-apartheid political trajectory. Political attitudes – not just voting behaviour – were in a new and exciting political flux, with a deeply divided ruling party having recalled a sitting president and then uniting behind an energetic election campaign, in part fuelled by the split that led to the formation of COPE, a new political party led by former ANC stalwarts which seemed, for the first time, to offer a real choice to black voters in particular. At the same time, an energised DA was effectively mobilising its own supporters, and white voters in particular were highly organised (and far from the stereotypically embittered 'losers' griping from the sidelines while refusing to engage politically). Internationally, the impact of Barack Obama's election campaign and later victory in the US resonated strongly among black voters in South Africa, and led many non-voters to feel that they were wasting their vote and should indeed register and participate in the election. This was a sentiment expressed by multiple focus group participants prior to the election and reflected in registration figures – the proportion of young people registered remained constant between 2004 and 2009, but significant new registrations occurred amongst older cohorts. Registrations also increased markedly in KwaZulu-Natal (across all ages) indicating the ethnic appeal of Jacob Zuma's ANC presidency in this former IFP stronghold.

The state of class

Given the prominence of class analysis during the struggle against apartheid, it is remarkable how rapidly it has almost disappeared from the official post-1994 political and academic lexicon – though even casual observers will find it throughout the literature of social movements, in left discourse and elsewhere. In their book *Class, Race, and Inequality in South Africa*, Jeremy Seekings and Nicoli Nattrass seem unclear whether to weep or whoop the fact that 'class appears to be in danger of falling off the map of South African studies' (p. 29), as they see it. They give a clue when they point the finger of blame at 'scholars who had been at the forefront of Marxist scholarship before they moved into prominent positions advising the post-apartheid state', leaving the field bare barring the work of Seekings and Nattrass, Owen Crankshaw and the barely mentioned outputs of Patrick Bond and Hein Marais – the latter little more, apparently, than a 'rump of radical political economy' (p. 29).

The left, in other words, sold its soul for a few pieces of silver apart from a few 'radicals' (thus labelled, also rendered unworthy of academic attention), leaving a handful of brave academics to stay the course, ploughing a lonely (and poorly paid) furrow. The ongoing work of left scholars, social movement activists, political movements, political and trade union activists and others – traditionally and still the drivers of class analysis – does not warrant a mention.

It is certainly fair to argue that post-apartheid, class analysis has become more complex and messy, and the on-going attempt to match survey-based job occupation categories (as done by Crankshaw, Seekings and Nattrass, Roger Southall and others) with persuasive class positions has had limited success. Much of their work focuses on stratification *within* a not-very-clearly-defined 'black middle class', sometimes within the 'African middle class', often attached to a 'numbers game' (trying to put a figure to the size of the black/ African middle class). Similar confusion occurs when attention is focused on the working class, given the mass of unemployed and the challenges of understanding stratification within the working class. This work, important as it is, only patchily helps us understand how to account – socially, politically – for a workforce that includes a massive unemployed population, racially differentiated wage levels and so on – let alone link this to political or social behaviours, values or attitudes.

Space disallows a review of class-related literature, but it is worth looking briefly at 'the subjective method' – asking people to which class they believe they belong – if only to see the weak purchase of the traditional trichotomy of working, middle and upper class among African South Africans (Giddens, p. 222). This approach – though with 'lower' class rather than 'working' class as an option – was first run by *Fortune* magazine in America in the 1940s, but it was subsequently demonstrated that by adding a fourth option – 'working class' – the results shifted from 80% of Americans describing themselves as middle class to half of respondents choosing 'working class' – they were unhappy being labelled 'lower class' but happy to be called 'working class'.

The GCRO survey had an almost exactly opposite experience. It went into the field offering working, middle and upper class (and the opt-out options of 'don't know' or 'other') – but respondents insisted that fieldworkers amend the instrument to include the option of 'poor', situated below 'working class'. This became the largest single category, with 39.8% of respondents describing themselves as 'poor'. A further 30% of respondents told us they were working class, with 27% selecting middle class and a tiny 2% describing themselves as 'upper class'.

Women (42%) were slightly more likely than men (37%) to call themselves poor. Unsurprisingly, race correlated with class labelling: 46.3% of Africans said they were 'poor' as did 29.7% of coloured respondents – this dropped to 4.4% among whites and 2.6% among Indians. Africans predominated among 'poor' and 'working class' – 29.9% selected the latter as their class descriptor, leaving 20.9% of Africans to describe themselves as middle class, and 0.8% to describe themselves as upper class. (1.4% selected 'don't know' and 0.8% chose 'other'.) Among coloured respondents, 29.7% described themselves as 'poor'; another 36.2% described themselves as working class, 32.1% as middle class and 2% as upper class. Indians were far more concentrated in the non-poor bands: just 2.6% described themselves as 'poor', with 39.7% describing themselves as working class, 52.6% as middle class, and 5.1% describing themselves as upper class. This was similar to white respondents, of whom 4.4% described themselves as poor, a perhaps surprisingly large 31.2% described themselves as working class, 55.3% as middle class and 7.2% as upper class. We now look more closely at African respondents.

Education correlated strongly with self-selected class descriptors. Among African respondents who described themselves as upper class, just one respondent had no formal education, and one other had primary level schooling only, while 30% had completed secondary schooling and 71.4% had tertiary level education. At the other end of the scale, among those African respondents describing themselves as poor, 3.5% had tertiary level education, a surprising finding. So too was the fact that a sizeable 68.3% had completed secondary schooling. Just 6.3% of respondents in this category had no formal education at all, although this was the largest concentration of respondents with no formal education. A fifth (21.9%) had completed primary schooling.

Figure 3.1   Self-selected class descriptor, all races.

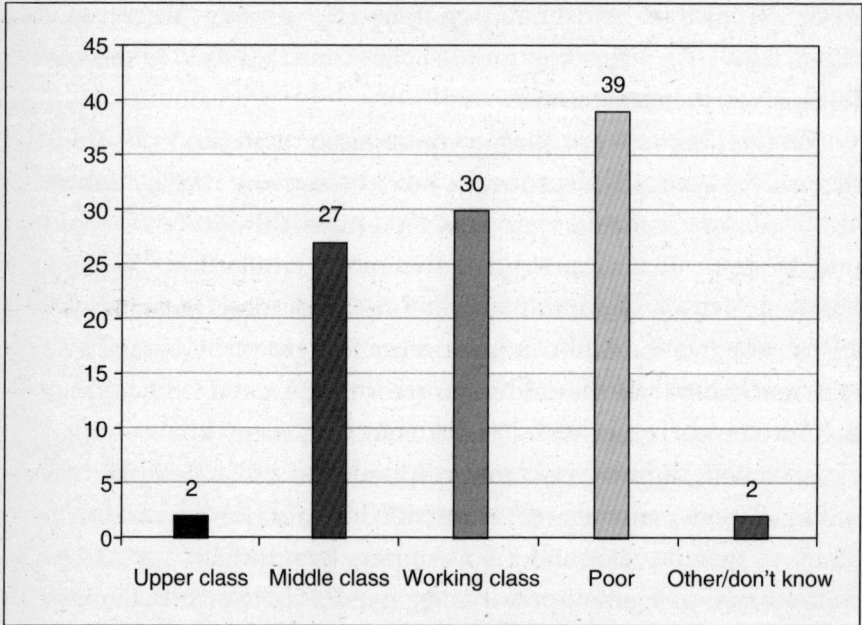

(Source: GCRO 'Quality of Life' baseline survey, 2009)

Employment status also had a strong correlation with class descriptors, though not always in obvious ways. For example, 51.8% of African respondents describing themselves as 'poor' were unemployed, and 23% were not economically active – but 25.2% were employed, so the (self-described) 'poor' are not simply a lumpen underclass of the unemployed and unemployable, they include a substantial number of working poor. Among the self-described working class, the situation reversed itself: 56.4% were employed, 26.5% were unemployed and 17.2% were not economically active. The 'poor' were more likely to live in informal dwellings (25% did so) than those describing themselves as working class (7% did so). While these no doubt fuel the growing 'shack dweller' sensibility, as described for example by Trevor Ngwane, it is notable that the majority in both instances live in formal dwellings – 74.4% in the case of the 'poor' and 92.5% in the case of the working class.

Finally, income is a key variable in class analysis, and one would expect a close correlation between income and self-described class status. In the GCRO survey, 2.9% of respondents told us their household had no regular source of income, 81.3% of whom described themselves as 'poor' and 11.9% as working class – but, oddly, also true of 6.3% who described themselves as middle class. The same pattern is repeated among households with a monthly income between R1 and R400 (that is, households that would qualify as indigent) – 76.9% described themselves as 'poor', 10.4% described themselves as working class, but the same proportion (10.4%) described themselves as middle class. (Not surprisingly, no respondents in this income category described themselves as upper class.)

This pattern becomes more pronounced as we go up the income ladder, but the R801–R1 600 monthly *household* income – scarcely a princely income – seems to be a tipping point as the proportion of 'poor' (66.9%) begins dropping, the self-described working class are rising (16.9%), as are those describing themselves as middle class (13.9%) and for the first time some respondents (admittedly just 0.3%) describing themselves as upper class appear. This pattern continues as income rises. It is worth noting that even in households that should include 'black diamonds' – for example, with a household income between R6 401–R12 800 – 8.9% describe themselves as 'poor', 51.2% as working class, 37.6% as middle class and 1.3% as upper class. In fact, it is only when monthly household incomes reach R51 201 and above that no respondents can be found describing themselves as 'poor' – but of those in the R51 201–R102 400 income band, 34.6% still describe themselves as working class, 50% as middle class and 11.5% as upper class.

So as we look for the black or African middle class, it is worth noting that using the subjective method produces a stratum of society (in Gauteng) that has no gender differential, racially reflects our history (55% of whites call themselves middle class, as do 53% of Indians, 32% of coloureds and 21% of Africans), are most likely to have completed secondary (61.9%) or tertiary (29.6%) education, live in formal dwellings and are in work. But the self-described *African middle class* bears only a passing relationship to income – certainly more African respondents living in households with higher incomes describe themselves as middle class than in lower income bands, but 'middle class' Africans can be found in virtually every income band from bottom to top – as can 'working class' Africans, who disappear only when incomes become extremely high, true also of those describing themselves as 'poor'.

Roger Southall notes in the *Canadian Journal of African Studies* that the prime beneficiary of ANC rule is 'a fairly rapidly growing black (new) middle class' (pp. 521–42), which is benefiting through the affirmative action and procurement policies of the state. The post-apartheid 'democracy dividend' has not been shared equally, the Gini coefficient among Africans has widened, class (and fraction) formation is proceeding apace, but researchers are battling to keep pace with it. This may explain why the notion of 'black diamonds' has found such easy purchase. This group apparently represents almost three million people whose unearthing 'fundamentally changed the way South African marketers approached business', according to the modest claim of the Unilever Institute of Strategic Marketing. The Institute asserted that in the space of fifteen months, 'the new black middle class has grown by an extraordinary 30% and in that time in excess of R50 million has been added to their annual spending power'.

Yet, members of this 'class', while they may enjoy reasonable education and increasingly live in suburbs not townships, have only to earn R7 000 per month to be classified as 'middle class' – so 'middle class' here is less the income of the individual within that class, because it would take a remarkable argument to justify a middle-class wage being set so low. Rather, the mass buying power of a large number of relatively poor people is taken in aggregate and labelled a class. Following this logic through, the Institute claims that the annual 'spend' of 'black diamonds' sits at R180 billion – an impressive figure, but disguising the precariousness of the individuals within this 'class'. How much is debt-financed, how precarious their foothold on the ladder out of poverty, the studies do not discuss; but Macozoma's warning rings loud and clear when a racially defined 'middle class' has an earning threshold set as low as in this instance.

Income and voting behaviour

In Figure 3.2, we look only at the voting behaviour (or self-reported voting intention, to be precise) of African respondents in the 2008 baseline survey, against three broad household income bands that reflect those of Statistics South Africa's Community Survey findings (this 300 000 household survey took the place of what should have been the 2006 Census). It is immediately apparent that the ANC

Figure 3.2   'Which party would you vote for if the election were held tomorrow?' by monthly household income, only showing main parties/categories.

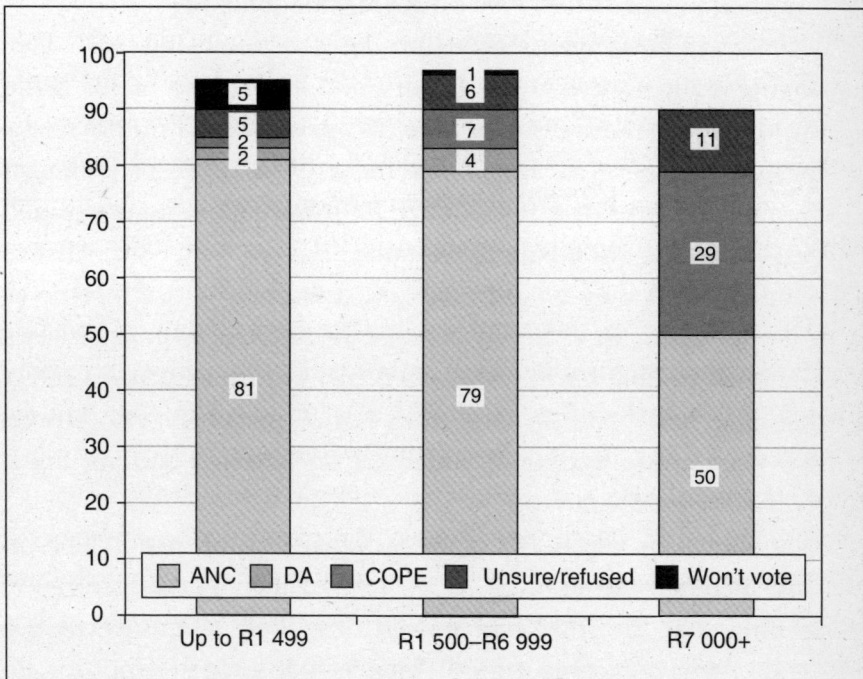

(Source: S&T Gauteng baseline survey, 2008)

continues to draw the overwhelming preponderance of its votes from poorer African voters. Eight in ten African voters from low-income households – which we have seen account for three-quarters of all African households in Gauteng – said they would vote ANC. This is neither new nor surprising.

But higher incomes clearly matter (regardless of how the recipients describe their own class status). Half of the respondents lucky enough to even crawl into the bottom rungs of the 'African middle class' or attain 'black diamond' status (that is, with a monthly *household* income of R7 000 and above) were indeed looking around for an alternative political vehicle. This suggests that there may be some political traction behind the 'black diamond' notion. By itself, these are remarkable results. But it is also notable that those respondents were not looking to the DA, as the logic of race-cum-class might suggest, but at COPE, the new, black-led party – and the child of the 'class project'. The ANC support base among this higher-income cohort was slashed to half as the '1996 class project' hit home.

COPE may have been scolded by the ANC for being 'ANC lite', for laying claim to the ANC's history and symbolism or for being little more than a new home for Mbeki's ousted allies, but that seems to be exactly where its appeal lay for a third (29%) of better-off African respondents. It is notable that a further 11% were undecided who to vote for – but equally notable that *no* better-off African respondents said they would vote DA. If we briefly use income as a proxy for class, then clearly the rise of an African middle class should spell trouble for the ANC – but that in turn assumes a static, unchanging ANC, and an ANC that is not responsive to African middle-class needs, neither of which are uncontested notions. But it spells trouble for the DA too.

Not shown in Figure 3.2 is the fact that 91% of respondents in the top income bracket were 'very sure' of their party preference, suggesting that the ANC had indeed 'lost' half of this small but growing African income cohort. That is not entirely appropriate phrasing, given that only 42% of those who said they would vote

COPE had previously voted ANC – the majority had either not voted before, or had voted for other parties. This is partly reflected in how these respondents ranked what they regarded as priorities for government. Job creation was the top priority across all income groups. For the poorest, the next key issue was housing, with crime coming in third. For the two better-off cohorts, crime was in second place. The R7 000+ cohort had education as its third priority, while poorer groups cited issues such as HIV/AIDS as priorities. There are emerging lines of policy difference that seem to align with income differences, and which deserve sustained attention over time.

Only regular measurements over time can provide a trend analysis, and we should be wary of reading too much into this single snapshot. Nonetheless, it is notable that ANC support was rooted among poor Africans; the DA had very little purchase among Africans generally and none at all among those in the upper-income cohort. If the DA, having consolidated or swallowed most of the smaller party voters in the 1994–2009 period, decides to try to slug it out with the ANC and win poor African voters to its side, it is difficult to see how it will do much more than waste energy and resources. Worryingly for the DA, this is even truer of affluent African voters. Schulz-Herzenberg's 'floating voter' thesis – she identifies a 'silent revolution' among voters as their stated partisanship declines over time – seems to apply less to the electorate in general and more to the recently 'affluent' African voter in Gauteng. Half remain loyal to the ANC (the party that has served them well, as Southall noted), while the other half is looking beyond the ANC for a vehicle that may better serve its interests, which COPE seemed to promise in 2008/9. They are not looking at the DA.

First-time voters

We noted earlier that the combination of factors specific to the 2009 general election – the ANC split, the formation of COPE, the court battles and attendant negative publicity surrounding Jacob Zuma, the very low national mood as the country was buffeted by high interest rates, rising unemployment, high oil prices, electricity black-outs, a murderous outburst of xenophobia, the impact of the Obama victory – all impacted on turnout. In 2009, figures taken from the Independent Electoral Commission show that 23.1 million people registered to vote, representing 75% of those of voting age. Actual turnout was 78%, similar to the 2004 figure (77%) though considerably lower than in 1999. Actual votes cast for the ANC rose from 10.9 million in 2004 to 11.7 million, boosted as the IFP haemorrhaged votes to the ANC in KwaZulu-Natal.

The assumption in much election commentary is that positive responses to COPE were largely responsible for the frisson that ran through the election in 2009, but this may be inaccurate – COPE's formation led to genuine anguish among the ANC faithful (in some pre-election focus groups, ANC-supporting participants were reduced to tears when discussing the new party) and many were mobilised against COPE, not by or for it.

In the 2008 pre-election baseline survey, 14% of respondents were 'first-time voters' – they had not voted in any previous election and stated an intention to vote in 2009. As one would expect, the majority (69%) of these first-time voters were in the youngest age cohort (aged 18 to 25). But what is interesting is that the other 31% of first-time voters had been able to vote previously, but only chose to participate in 2009. Polling at the time (not always welcomed by party leaders) strongly suggested that this in no small part reflected the effect of the Obama campaign and upbeat message.

First-time voters in Gauteng were most likely to be African, residing in Ekurhuleni or Johannesburg, and living in informal dwellings. They were also far more assured of their party preference than the provincial average, with only 6% unsure of who they would vote for or refusing to disclose their preference. When compared with the Gauteng provincial average, Figure 3.3 shows that the largest single proportion (61% in all) were planning to vote for the ANC; the DA (14%) and COPE (11%) were left to fight over the scraps. In other words, COPE did not rouse non-voters from their polling slumber to

Figure 3.3   Party preference among respondents (by first-time voters).

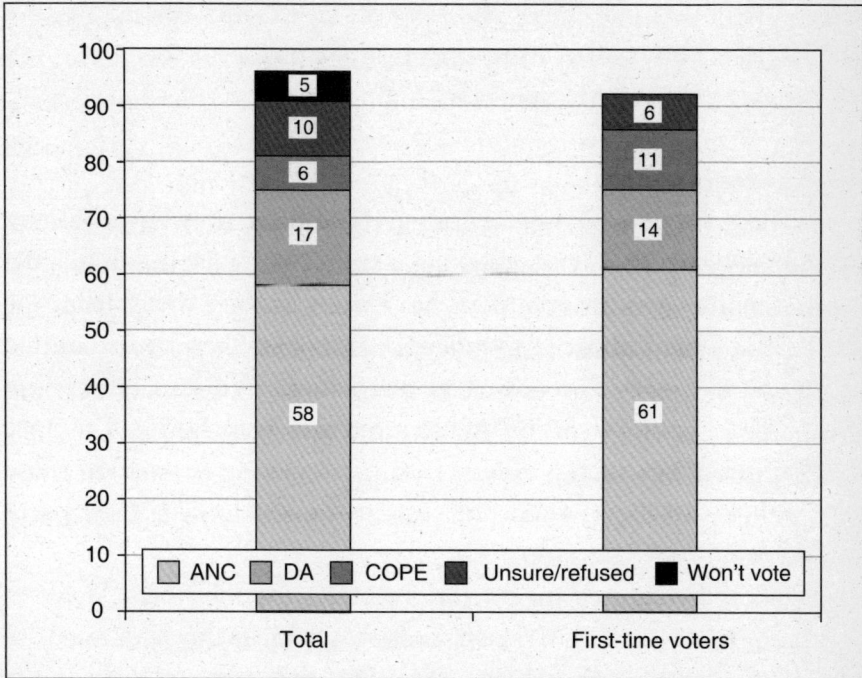

(Source: S&T Gauteng baseline survey, 2008)

vote for it, but against it. It is worth adding that a whopping 90% of these first-time voters were 'very sure' of their party preference and would not consider changing their vote.

While external factors such as Obama's campaign were at play, domestically, COPE's formation did a remarkable job in helping mobilise ANC voters long before the actual ANC campaign began picking up steam. The emergence of COPE mobilised people to vote – *against*, not simply for, a factor not considered in much post-election literature (see, for example, the discussion of the 'COPE effect' in Kate Lefko-Everett, Neeta Misra-Dexter and Justin Sylvester's Idasa article). Moreover, what really marked COPE voters as different from African respondents voting for other parties, was their hostility to the ANC. COPE voters were uncertain of their vote for this new party, with just 61% 'sure' they would vote COPE – but what they were sure of was that if they did not vote COPE, they would also not vote ANC. COPE voters were simply unavailable to the ANC, in a way that DA-voting Africans were not.

Young voters

If first-time voters were not all young, did the age of voters influence their choice of party? It would appear from Figure 3.4 that while the upper-income African vote may have been looking away from the ANC to an extent, those respondents were older than the expanded definition of 'youth' (according to the National Youth Commission Act of 1996, 'youth' in South Africa stretched from 14–35). The ANC had captured 58% of this cohort (not recalculating to exclude those who either said they would not vote or refused to state their party preference).

What these figures meant for the ANC – as they have done in every election – was that registration was vital if the ANC were to realise its potential come voting day, given that many of those in the youngest cohort (18–25) were unregistered. The ANC was the party of choice for the majority of respondents in each of the youth cohorts, and the younger the voters the more 'sure' they were of their vote; but the level of ANC support dropped below the provincial average to 55% amongst those aged 26–30. DA support among African youth is also lower than among older African voters, a further worry for the erstwhile national opposition.

COPE, however, did find purchase among African youth, including the very youngest voters. The high of 12% support for COPE among those aged 26–30 (who were also the least likely of the young cohorts to vote ANC) was twice its provincial average – but when analysed against income, we find that higher proportions of this cohort lived in households that earned more than R7 000 per month, thus reflecting the inroads that COPE was making among young African professionals. However, COPE was still a new voting proposition, so fewer respondents were 'sure' they would vote for COPE

Figure 3.4 'Which party would you vote for if the election were tomorrow?' by age within youth cohort.

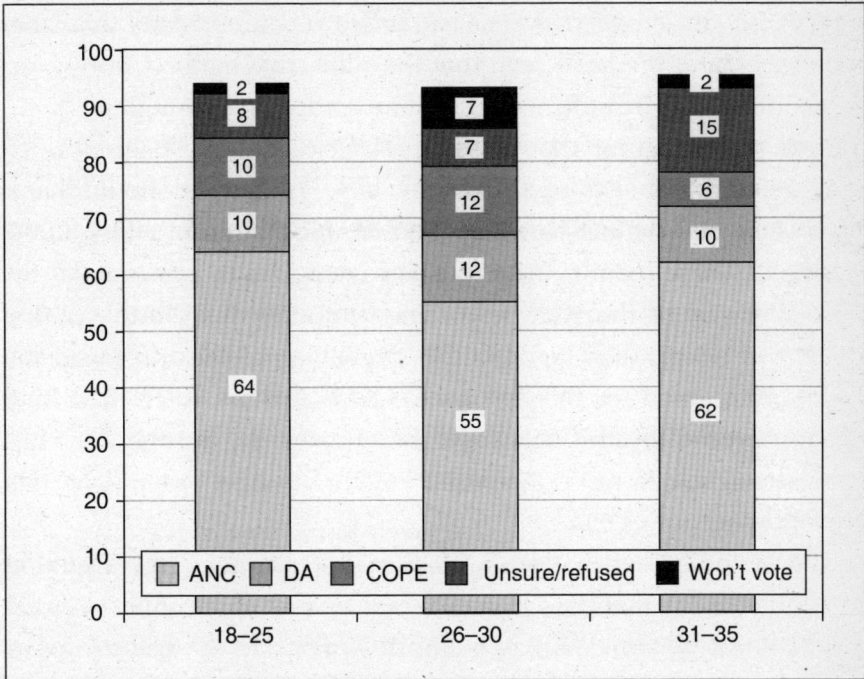

(Source: S&T Gauteng baseline survey, 2008)

than the ANC – but, importantly, those who said they would vote COPE, even if not entirely certain, were indeed certain that they would *not* vote for the ANC. Age thus throws up another aspect of the way in which demographic variables – some pertinent to class analysis – might be at work among African voters. Perhaps not an absolute age-defined cut-off, as I suggested at the beginning; but the ANC's ability to reproduce itself among the young is weakening.

Conclusion

Post-apartheid class formation – notably the African middle class – remains blurry and poorly understood. The 'black middle class' appears in newspapers as often as it does in political commentary, yet there is clearly considerable space and need for work in this area, especially in being able to demonstrate the societal impact and force (let alone size and salience) of a class that clearly exists but equally clearly eludes easy measurement using currently available tools and data. We have seen that the subjective method throws up some interesting insights – but as many confound as enlighten.

The data suggest that class-based cleavages are beginning to become measurable among African voters. For that we should thank both COPE and the messiness of the ANC in 2008, from which COPE emerged. These seem to have pushed young black professionals in particular out of the ANC fold – and simultaneously into politics. Many had never voted before. COPE drew young black professionals into voting, often for the first time. Older African voters had long been 'captured' by the ANC, and they remain so, but the ANC has been struggling to reproduce itself among younger voters, and this created space for COPE.

We noted earlier that while class matters, so does race. Denying this and insisting that class trumps race is to miss much of the electoral and political dynamic at play in South Africa. The DA has struggled to make significant inroads among African voters – not true of coloured and Indian voters – and this in no small part is because it is seen by African voters as a 'white' party (while the ANC is seen as an 'African' party), and there are very strong feelings among significant numbers of African voters that they simply cannot conceive of voting for a white party. In South Africa today, the past is *not* a foreign country, it is merely a memory away. Where this is not true – among young voters, and particularly those who have 'made it' in the new South Africa, the young black professionals – the ANC's grip is weakening.

If the ANC vote remains heavily pegged to a race/age cohort – currently, African voters aged above 35 – the party will hit a ceiling fairly soon. But as we noted above, the ANC is not a static, unchanging entity. It watches its voters carefully. It is facing a challenge that is moving into the territory of class politics as young black professionals seem less attracted to it – they are presumably also less emotionally wedded to it as the party of liberation – and have begun to look around for a vehicle that will better serve their class interests. That challenge has yet to be mounted on a scale that threatens the ANC's national majority, and COPE's implosion has no doubt bought the ANC more time to consider how to respond, but respond it no doubt will. The challenge has not gone; it has merely been postponed.

DAVID EVERATT is the Executive Director of the Gauteng City-Region Observatory (GCRO), a partnership of the University of Johannesburg, the University of the Witwatersrand and the Gauteng Provincial Government. He has served on successive ANC polling teams since 1994.

References and further reading

ANC (2010) 'A Decisive Mandate: Review of the 2009 Elections' in *Umrabulo* No. 34, 3rd quarter, available at anc.org.za/show.php?include=docs/umrabulo/2010/umrabulo34s.html (accessed on 25 September 2010).

Giddens, A. (1989) *Sociology* (Polity Press, Cambridge).

Giliomee, H. and Simkins, C. (eds.) (1999) *The Awkward Embrace: One-party Domination and Democracy* (Tafelberg, Cape Town).

Habib, A. and Naidu, S. (2006) 'Race, Class and Voting Patterns in South Africa's Electoral System: Ten Years of Democracy' in *Africa Development* Vol. XXXI, No. 3.

Lefko-Everett, K., Misra-Dexter, N. and Sylvester, J. (2009) 'Idasa 2009 Election Response' (Idasa, mimeo).

Marketingweb (2007) 'Black Diamonds Continue to Grow', available at marketingweb.co.za/marketingweb/view/marketingweb/en/page71644?oid=83869&sn=Marketingweb%20detail (accessed on 28 October 2010).

Ngwane, T. (2010) 'Bottlebrush Case Study' (mimeo).

Schulz-Herzenberg, C. (2007) 'A Silent Revolution: South African Voters, 1994–2006' in Buhlungu, S., Daniel, J., Southall, R. and Lutchman, A. (eds.) *State of the Nation: South Africa 2007* (HSRC Press, Pretoria).

Seekings, J. and Nattrass, N. (2006) *Class, Race, and Inequality in South Africa* (University of KwaZulu-Natal Press, Pietermaritzburg).

Sennett, R. and Cobb, J. (1993) *The Hidden Injuries of Class* (Faber & Faber, London).

Southall, R. (2004) 'Political Change and the Black Middle Class in Democratic South Africa' in *Canadian Journal of African Studies* Vol. 38, No. 3.

────── (2009) 'Zunami! The Context of the 2009 Election' in Southall, R. and Daniel, J. (eds.) *Zunami! The 2009 South African Elections* (Jacana Media, Johannesburg).

Sylvester, J. (2009) 'Understanding Issues of Race and Class in Election '09' (Idasa, mimeo).

Unilever Institute of Strategic Marketing (2007) 'Black Diamond 2007 on the Move', unileverinstitute.co.za/index.php?option=com_content&task=view&id=72& Itemid=91 (accessed on 11 November 2010).

Wikileaks quoted in News24, 13 January 2011, available at feeds.news24.com/ articles/News24/Wikileaks/rss (accessed on 23 January 2011).

4

South Africa's Education System
How Can it be Made More Productive?

JONATHAN D. JANSEN

Introduction

There are few more frustrating puzzles in continental Africa than the South African education system. The medium-sized pre-tertiary system consists of about 13 million learners, 390 000 teachers and more than 27 000 schools. For some time, education expenditure has taken the largest slice of government spending, hovering around 20%, and growing steadily from R140 billion in 2008/9 to a planned R165 billion in 2010/11.

No other African country spends as much as 5.4% of public expenditure, as a percentage of gross domestic product (GDP), on education. No-fee schools now constitute 64% of all South African schools in which, theoretically, learners do not pay for their education. In 2009 alone, R5.6 million was spent on 18 000 schools where children were fed daily by the state. In higher education, a small system of 23 universities, spending jumped from R7.1 billion in 2001/2 to R15.3 billion in 2008/9 and is expected to stand at R21.3 billion in 2011/12. This multi-pronged, progressive and comprehensive budget for education would be the envy of any developing country.

This is the picture from the side of resource inputs into the education system. But what does South Africa have to show in terms of outcomes or results?

The productivity picture, on its own terms

Despite this substantial investment in education, the evidence is consistent over a number of years that the South African education system is one of the least productive in the southern African region. The most common indicators show a repeat-pattern of low productivity, such as the following. *Enrolments* drop sharply from near-universal attendance through to age fifteen to only 78% for eighteen-year-olds. *Grade repetition* remains high, starting in the very first grade and with more than half the students (51.5%) repeating one or more years in Grades 10–12. A third of all learners repeat a grade at some time during their schooling years. More than 4% of students across grades *miss a year or more of school*. Close to 20% of learners in the senior years of high school are *above the age-grade norms* for their grade. *Drop-out rates* are very high as learners move into high school, with 20% of eighteen-year-olds not in school and not completing Grade 12 (see the recent data made available in a triplet of books on access to education published in 2010 by Social Surveys Africa and the Centre for Applied Legal Studies).

These are measures of efficiency in the school system. The picture looks much bleaker when performance outcomes are taken into account. It must be emphasised that the annual South African spectacle, the Senior Certificate (which used to be called the 'matric exam'), or Grade 12 results, are almost irrelevant as a measure of the effectiveness of the school system.

On the one hand, the Senior Certificate results represent an internal, non-comparative (with other countries) account of the state of the school system measured against one indicator, the national Grade 12 results. It denotes results set in flux, going up and down from year to year, sometimes by large margins that draw public scepticism and demands for greater transparency about how, why and by what degree annual adjustments are made to these results. It is a closed and self-referential system, in other words, and therefore open to the possibility of abuse.

On the other hand, the Grade 12 results are really poor when the comparison is not with previous years' performance, but as an absolute measure of annual performance. Take the 2010 results: 173 030 candidates who wrote the Grade 12 examination failed. Less than a quarter of the candidates (23.5%) qualify, on paper, to do a first degree at university. Fewer students (by a margin of 8 756) passed mathematics than in the previous year. Less than half the students who start Grade 1 make it through the system to reach Grade 12.

What the aggregated results also conceal are the 'racialised in-equalities' in the system; to put it bluntly, if the whites (and middle classes) were taken out of the system, the real inequalities and underperformance for the majority of the population would become evident.

Take, for example, the 2007 data (see Table 4.1) for which detailed analyses are available (courtesy of Professor Servaas van der Berg from the University of Stellenbosch, who has generated and shared the statistical table and figures in this chapter):

Table 4.1   Matriculants by performance, 2007.

	Blacks	Coloureds	Indians	Whites	Total	Black share
Matric-aged cohort	830 720	77 500	21 240	65 720	995 180	83%
Dropped out	325 181	41 370	6 616	22 286	395 453	82%
Pass matric	292 344	27 294	13 266	42 225	377 177	78%
Maths passes	94 818	7 768	7 764	24 501	135 720	70%
Endorsements	50 984	5 392	7 798	22 214	86 993	59%
HG maths passes	9 701	1 226	3 252	10 119	24 549	40%
HG maths: A, B, C or D	6 237	843	2 666	8 239	18 171	34%
A-aggregates	1 303	364	1 696	5 604	9 079	14%

A-aggregates: One in eleven white children, one in 640 black children (half not in historically black schools)

On the other side of government hyperbole, the picture looks very bleak. But judging by government enthusiasm, you would never tell. The government boasts of a rise in performance among candidates who wrote from 60.6% pass rate in 2009 to 67.8% in 2010, and that the students who qualify to do a university degree jumped from 19.9% to 23.5%. In other words, measured against itself, there is progress. But is this a reliable account of school system performance over time given the up-and-down character of the Grade 12 pass rates over time, the concealed processes of upward (and some downward) moderation of raw subject scores and the general public scepticism of the quality of education?

Nowhere is this scepticism more real than among leading universities in South Africa, which routinely adjust their admission requirements upwards as a way of compensating for grade inflation at the terminal or exit levels of the school system, that is, the Grade 12 or Senior Certificate results. This practice, in part informed by a far more reliable account of numeracy and literacy competence among high school graduates – the National Benchmark Test – represents an annual dance between government/school authorities and university authorities that is simply not sustainable.

Still, these results reflect an internal (and of course indirect, since it focuses on individual learner attainment) measure of system performance. What does South Africa's learner performance look like when compared to school systems elsewhere?

The productivity picture in international relief

Every national and regional test of comparison on basic competencies in reading, literacy and numeracy consistently places South Africa at the bottom ends of the performance scales. As far back as 2001, the SACMEQ (Southern and Eastern Africa Consortium for Monitoring Educational Quality) Grade 6 study showed South Africa had the biggest gap in reading scores between rich and poor (Figure 4.1):

Figure 4.1   SACMEQ Grade 6 reading scores by country, 2001: South Africa has the biggest rich-poor gap.

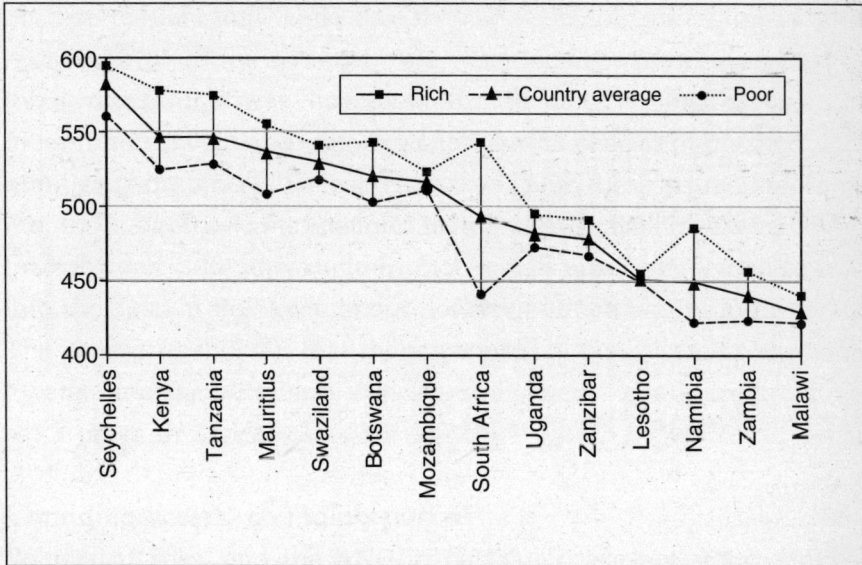

In mathematics, as demonstrated in the TIMSS (Trends in International Mathematics and Science Study) 2003 scores shown in Figure 4.2, South Africa was at the bottom of a comparative table of scores, performing below countries such as the Philippines, Botswana and Ghana.

The percentage of South African students exceeding performance at the 75th percentile of developed countries stands at 10% for literacy and only 6% for mathematics and science as Figure 4.3 shows. This is the number, argue education economists, who would 'make it' economically in developed countries.

And against the international benchmark of 400 points in Progress in International Reading Literacy Study (PIRLS) in 2006, as shown in Figure 4.4, 78% of Grade 5 students in South Africa fall below that level of performance described by the testers as 'very low reading achievers'.

Figure 4.2   Mean maths score in TIMSS, 2003.

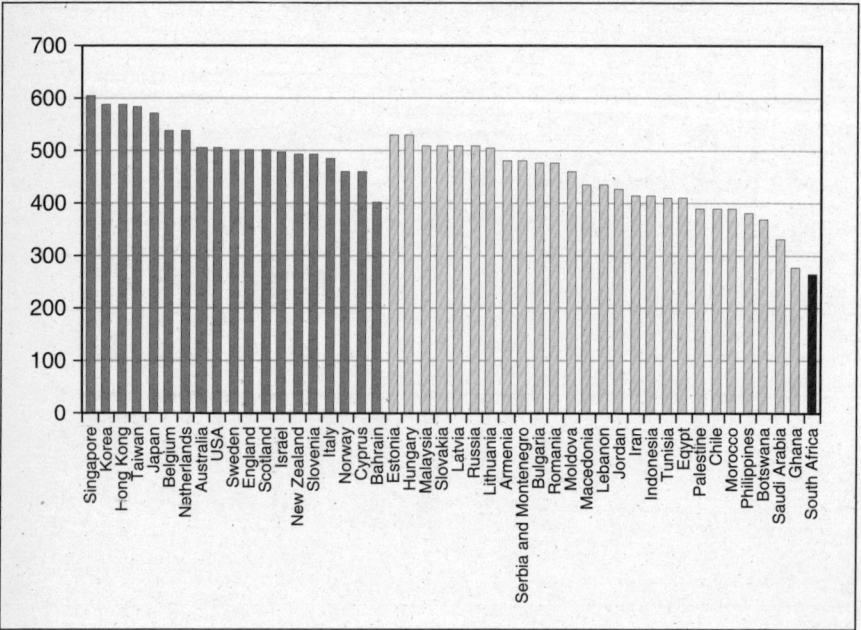

Figure 4.3   Percentage of South African students exceeding performance at 75th percentile of developed countries (who would 'make it' economically in developed countries).

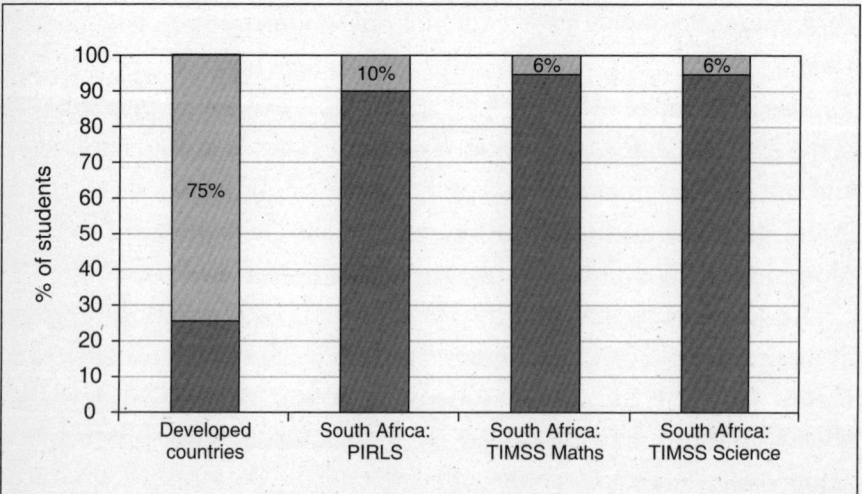

Figure 4.4   Percentage of Grade 4 (or 5 in South Africa) students below
the low international benchmark (400) in PIRLS 2006.

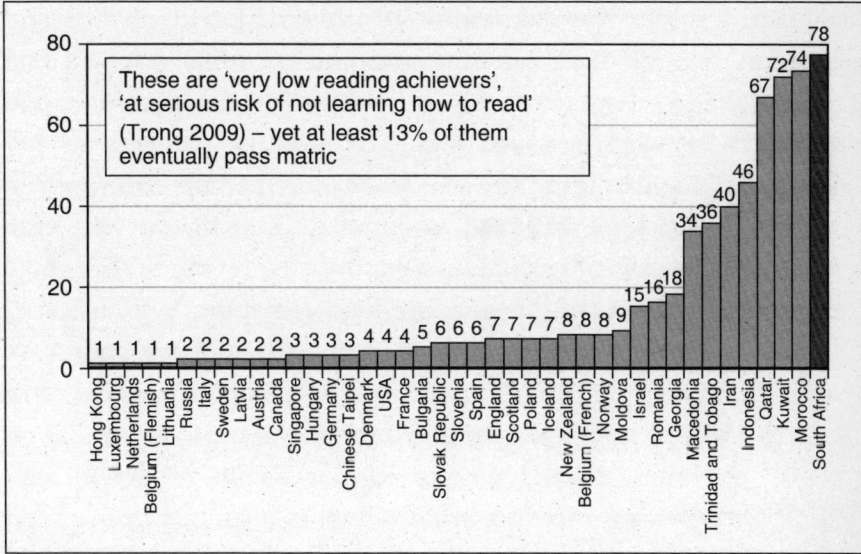

What does all of this mean? It means that when South African learners
are assessed in relation to international standards of achievement in
those competencies regarded as foundational to ongoing learning
and indicative of future economic performance (literacy and numeracy), the volatility and incredulity of the Grade 12 results can be
read in perspective.

We are in serious trouble, and it shows up in the primary education years, which explains also why so few learners even make it
to the final year of schooling.

Explaining low productivity

There are five major reasons that explain the low productivity of the
school system in South Africa.

1. A lack of systematic routines and rituals

The majority of schools do not enjoy the systematic routines and
rituals that account for productive schools anywhere in the world.

There are a small percentage of schools, middle-class white or middle-class integrated, where those routines and rituals have been long-established under the old regime of governance in politics and education. Schools start on time and end on time; teachers and principal are in school every day; class attendance is monitored and reported; homework is issued regularly and on a planned, school-wide basis; regular tests are scheduled and parents informed in advance; feedback on tests and assignments is swift, carrying high formative-value for individual learners over the course of the school year; sports and sporting events are held regularly, with required attendance for non-participating students; disciplinary codes are enforced and disciplinary cultures are not questioned; teachers carry multiple tasks of which teaching is only one; regular reports go to parents; governing bodies receive regular results on school and learner performance. Absence from school is a serious matter, and dutifully recorded and explained by the absentee learner. Individual care is balanced with individual discipline. Schedules are set long in advance. Errant teachers and learners are promptly confronted about their behaviour, and corrective measures put in place. Budgets are carefully planned, and fundraising from outside regularly undertaken. School grounds are clean and broken facilities are quickly repaired. Security is tight. Awards feature prominently in the annual school calendar, and a culture of achievement – from academics to sports to the arts – is instilled in every classroom.

These routines establish productive teaching and learning cultures that explain the significant gap in academic performance between the small minority of outstanding schools and the large majority of underperforming schools. Whatever applies in the comprehensive description of what a productive school looks like in South Africa, the opposite applies in the rest of the schools.

This sharp discrepancy in school cultures of course raises the deeper question of why such emphatic differences exist; more about that towards the end of this chapter.

2. The knowledge problem

The majority of public schools in South Africa have a knowledge problem. That is, teachers and principals lack the various kinds of knowledge required in a professional setting like a school in order to impact on learning and in order to influence change. Note that this is not cast here as a training problem; that is something else. Indeed, many observers make the point that South Africa probably spends more money on teacher and principal training than any other country in Africa. Tens of millions of rand flow into the country, often as part of generous international donor grants for curriculum reconstruction or assessment training for teacher development. The national and provincial governments within their own budgets plan amply for teacher and leadership training. There are credits that accrue through bodies, such as the South African Council for Educators, for teachers to notch up training points on their professional belts.

Training inputs are generous, but they do not address the knowledge problem; typically, such training is geared towards information transfer on a generic basis, rather than according to the knowledge needs of a set of teachers. Here different kinds of knowledge are at play: knowledge of the subject matter (content knowledge); knowledge of teaching (pedagogy); knowledge of learners (psychology); knowledge about knowledge (epistemology); knowledge of communities from which the learners come (anthropology, sociology of learning); knowledge of classroom organisation and discipline (managerial knowledge); and more.

It is especially content knowledge and pedagogical knowledge that remain the major dimensions of what we here call the knowledge problem. Put bluntly – and there is evidence for this in South Africa – if a teacher does not know enough mathematics, he or she would not be able to teach maths effectively, irrespective of the generic training inputs or the individual personality characteristics of that teacher. That is why systematic error often shows up in the Grade 12 assessments of subject scripts of particular schools. The same schools show the same errors, indicative of a teacher knowledge problem in respect of different aspects of the curriculum.

Government knows this, and that is why the President's Office came up with one of the most remarkable interventions to address the problem, that is, treat the teachers as if they were learners in the classroom. This infantilisation of teachers is something for which South Africa will pay a heavy price. How did this happen? Quite simply, the provincial departments of education started to print simple 'how-to' booklets for use by teachers that treated them as if they knew (knowledge) nothing, and needed the most rudimentary texts to instruct their teaching. What was being conceded in this official act is that the teachers who occupy many of South Africa's classrooms as (presumably) trained professionals in fact had little to no knowledge of what was required to teach for gainful learning. In the process, the last vestiges of professional facade among teachers were stripped away.

3. Bureaucratic and administrative ineptitude

Most of the public schools remain in crisis because of the problem of bureaucratic and administrative ineptitude at both the national and the provincial level. At the national level, schools have been overwhelmed by one of the most prolific policy machinery in any African state. There are scores of policies produced and amended for everything from school safety to the minutiae of assessment. The typical problem of 'policy overload' is an extreme case in South Africa. Not only are policies constantly made, they are changed all the time. The worst case, of course, was curriculum policy, represented in what was generally referred to as Outcomes Based Education (OBE). This highly esoteric and unworkable policy collapsed primary schooling in the country in a spectacular mix of curriculum verbosity and impossible expectations for implementation. Even the most ideological of bureaucrats saw this complex curriculum plan falter at the classroom interface: most teachers did not understand it; most schools did not have the resources to implement it; most districts did not have well-learned officials to interpret it; and most senior officials at national level do not have the curriculum expertise to devise simple and sensible plans for a weak and unequal school system.

The attempt to devise weakly conceived, esoteric curriculum plans was made all the more futile by the incapacity to deliver on basic services especially to schools in rural and large provinces. To this day, many schools are unable to start the academic year on time because of the simple administrative incapacity to manage enrolments and develop timetables in advance. Teachers in large numbers still do not get paid on time, and some have not been paid for months and even years in places such as the Eastern Cape. 'Ghost teachers' (teachers who draw salaries without being formally recorded as employees of the state) also remain a problem in some provinces.

Many schools still do not receive textbooks and learning materials on time. The critical skills of leadership, management and administration from national to provincial to regional and to local levels are non-existent in the larger provinces. With the passage of time, the familiar excuses are less convincing: the legacy of apartheid; the lack of resources; and the need for more time for reforms to take effect.

What became clear as a principal explanation for bureaucratic and administrative ineptitude was that South Africa after 1994 placed much more emphasis on policy-making than it did on planning. It was assumed, so it seemed, that merely generating policies would translate smoothly into the realities of planning and practice amongst a docile electorate or, in this case, schools. Of course, the policy literature is clear that in any context, even where there is huge electoral support for the governing authority, policy is never 'implemented'; it is interpreted within the constraints of context by practitioners.

4. Lack of accountability

South Africa has a weak system of accountability in schools. While support to teachers is reasonably strong, and much – as has been indicated – is invested in teacher development, there is a very low level of accountability for performance. This is a tricky subject that can only be understood in historical context. The school uprisings of the 1970s accelerated the end of apartheid but this left in its wake a school system in which resistance and contempt for township schooling remains endemic in such schools. This is a very important and often misdiagnosed problem in township schools, best understood through the following simple and commonsense observation.

Why would a black teacher in a township school take his or her own children and place them in a former white school miles away in the middle-class suburbs? Why would that same teacher disrupt – such as during a public servants' strike – the township school filled with children from the poor communities around that school knowing that his or her own children are safely ensconced in a school where the timetable remains uninterrupted? It does not make sense outside of a theory of contempt for township schools and township children among teachers themselves.

School inspections are frowned upon as political interference in teachers' work. So many principals are unable to take action against errant teachers, such as latecomers or early leavers, for fear of being targeted by a militant teachers' union. Thus, even while school inspection policies were recently produced, they have little purchasing power at the classroom level, especially in provinces such as Gauteng where teacher unionism is very strong. The refrain of the unions? 'Give us more support before you even think of evaluating us.'

Of course, the problem is that in an underperforming school system, it is impossible to increase productivity without being able to impact on performance. Why the current situation is a stalemate between development and accountability, or more broadly between government authority and union control, can only be understood in the context of a political analysis of the state and education, a subject to which I return later in this chapter.

5. A lack of capacity and expertise

The reconstruction of the school system lacks the capacity that comes with the expertise of policy-making, planning and practice reforms in educational contexts. The biggest blunder at the start of the process of rebuilding schools after apartheid was to lose quickly the technical expertise of bureaucrats from the old system and replace them with young comrades who knew nothing about the process of system-level change of complex school systems. To be sure, a host of international expertise was flown into and out of the country to compensate for this loss, but as with all outside expertise, eventually it leaves and nothing but a slim layer of knowledge is left behind.

This kind of dilemma is not, of course, unfamiliar in post-colonial African states. What made this replacement of resident expertise so devastating was the size and complexity of the system left to overhaul in the wake of apartheid. Worse, ideologically excited comrades with a zeal for replacement of every element of the old system embarked on daring changes that anyone with a deep understanding of school change or curriculum theory or teacher pedagogies would have realised was a disaster that would set back an already vulnerable school system. And as indicated earlier, that it exactly what happened in the case of curriculum reforms.

Interestingly, there was much more of a well-developed and well-deployed expertise within the higher education sector, which carefully combined the expertise of previous bureaucrats (especially in areas such as law) with university academic expertise (in areas such as finance) alongside comrades who honed their expertise within higher education studies and university leadership. A small but powerful team of higher education experts remained in place for a long time during the transition to ensure the reform of at least the university sector.

Parenthetically, in recent times (2010/11) that expertise has been lost and replaced with ideological zealots even at senior levels of the bureaucracy who have little expert understanding of, or respect for, higher education systems and the formidable problem of change.

Nowhere is this lack of capacity more evident than in the deployment of comrades to provincial education departments and the districts and circuits which they organise and lead. An ugly racial picture emerges in this context. The more established and especially the former white schools with experienced and qualified teachers are now approached by their seniors from the districts, whom in most cases know less than them about the subject matter, and even less about the organisation and management of schools. The black bureaucrat from the district, invariably a loyal comrade, now has two choices: either enforcing his authority on the former white school principals and teachers as a way of compensating for the knowledge and experience gap between them; or simply allowing the former white schools to continue running their school operations as they always did, and not interfering but rather spending his time with the disadvantaged schools in the same catchment area.

The national government faces an interesting dilemma: it has no authority over schools, since this is a provincial competence, as it is called. It can make allocations from Treasury to provinces, but has little say over how provinces re-allocate central funding, within limits of course, to schools. Policy-making is the national competence. So what does the national Department of Education do with respect to schools? Being impotent to drive school practices at district and school levels, it falls back on simply producing more policies, as one international panel of reviewers observed.

What is to be done?

In the final analysis, the resolution of the crisis of two school systems in South Africa can only be found in a political solution. The large, black, underperforming school system requires the restoration of political authority over schools back where it belongs, in the hands of government and not the teacher unions. It then requires political authority that can effectively hold teachers and principals accountable for re-establishing the rhythms and routines of schooling that have been disrupted for decades: schools that start on time with predictable timetables and uninterrupted teaching schedules alongside the routines of teaching duties, homework assignments, student feedback, school improvement, and the like. Without this 'culture of teaching and learning' firmly established in every province, all policies and innovations will find little traction in the chaos and unpredictability of black urban and rural township schooling after apartheid. It is as simple and complex as that.

This would require a government and a presidency that is prepared to take political risks with especially the South African Democratic Teachers' Union (SADTU), the largest and some would argue most powerful component of the Congress of South African Trade Unions (COSATU), to require the non-interruption of teaching and learning under any circumstances, and the non-interference in the management and administration of schools. The current political calculus would make this difficult, for in a country where party and state are no longer distinguishable in the operations of government, future careers depend on not taking on the very allies whose voice and votes will determine the leadership of the next administration. It would take exceptionally courageous political leaders, including the president, to place the interests of 13 million children before and above the personal and political interests of those currently in power.

In the meantime, the smaller, middle-class and largely white school sub-system will continue to provide the camouflage of an apparently functional education system as it shores up disastrous academic performance with pass rates above 50% and the bulk of the high school graduates who make it into university. In this small group of privilege you find the majority of mathematics and physical science passes, a group of students who annually reproduce the class inequalities of South Africa where a small privileged minority are again destined to rule, economically at least, over the failing (or poorly passing) masses. The face-saving result of this outcome is that the privileged future rulers are no longer whites only.

In other words, until the systemic nature of the schooling crisis is recognised and political intervention directed to re-establishing governmental authority over schools, all other kinds of small-scale, reactive and well-intentioned reforms will change nothing.

PROFESSOR JONATHAN D. JANSEN is the Rector of the University of the Free State. He is an educationalist, a former Dean of Education at the University of Pretoria, who holds a collection of degrees and awards, including the position as President of the South African Institute of Race Relations.

References and further reading

Archer, E., Scherman, V., Coe, R. and Howie, S.J. (2010) 'Finding the Best Fit: The Adaptation and Translation of the Performance Indicators for Primary Schools for the South African Context' in *Perspectives in Education* Vol. 28, No. 1, pp. 77–88.

Fullan, M. (2009) *Motion Leadership: The Skinny on Becoming Change Savvy* (Corwin Press, Thousand Oaks, CA).

Hargreaves, A. and Fullan, M. (2008) *Change Wars* (Solution Tree, Bloomington, IN).

Howie, S.J. (2003) 'Language and Other Background Factors Affecting Secondary Pupils' Performance in Mathematics in South Africa' in *African Journal of Research in Mathematics, Science and Technology Education* Vol. 7, pp. 1–20.

Jansen, J. (2009) 'Can and Should School Change in the Developing World be Guided by Research from the Developed World?' in *Journal of Educational Change* Vol. 10, No. 2/3, pp. 239–43.

Levin, B. (2008) *How to Change 5000 Schools* (Harvard Education Press, Cambridge, MA).

Luke, A., Green, J. and Kelly, G. (2010) 'What Counts as Evidence in Educational Settings? Rethinking Equity, Diversity and Reform in the 21st Century' in *Review of Research in Education* Vol. 34 (full issue).

Meny-Gilbert, S. and Russell, B. (2010) *Treading Water: Enrolment, Delays, and Completion in South African Schools* (Social Surveys Africa and Centre for Applied Legal Studies, Johannesburg).

Strassburg, S., Meny-Gilbert, S. and Russell, B. (2010) *Left Unfinished: Temporary Absence and Drop-out from South African Schools* (Social Surveys Africa and Centre for Applied Legal Studies, Johannesburg).

——— (2010) *More than Getting through the School Gates: Barriers to Participation in Schooling* (Social Surveys Africa and Centre for Applied Legal Studies, Johannesburg).

Van der Berg, S. (2006) 'How Effective are Poor Schools? Poverty and Educational Outcomes in South Africa'. Working Papers 06/2006, Department of Economics, Stellenbosch University.

Van der Berg, S. and Louw, M. (2007) 'Lessons Learnt from SACMEQII: South African Student Performance in Regional Context'. Working Papers 16/2007, Department of Economics, Stellenbosch University.

5

Entrepreneurship
How Can Obstacles be Overcome?

MIKE HERRINGTON

South Africa faces numerous economic, political and social challenges in its new democracy. A major challenge is that of growing unemployment, which is especially evident amongst the country's youth. The expanding body of unemployed and increasingly unemployable young people is placing a considerable burden on a limited government budget that already has to juggle many other demands. The existing formal sector is not likely to absorb the growing labour force and this, coupled with burgeoning youth unemployment, is creating enormous pressures. Unemployment remains a key challenge that needs urgent attention given the impact that it has on poverty, crime, productivity and economic growth.

But unemployment is a complex issue, particularly in a country such as South Africa, where skill levels in large sections of the population are extremely low or do not fit into the new knowledge-based economy. In addition, South Africa's restrictive labour policies and strong unions are limiting the number of lower-skilled individuals that can be absorbed into the workforce. This situation was exacerbated during the latter half of 2008 and 2009 when South Africa, like most other countries around the world, slipped into economic recession. Business failure accelerated with a resultant loss of jobs, and large companies slowed their employment rate of new staff considerably.

South Africa's economy has historically been dominated by large corporations and the public sector. During the apartheid years, there was a conspicuous absence of small businesses, and very little attention was paid to small enterprise promotion in public policy. At this time, black South Africans, except in specially designated areas, were largely prevented from owning property. The result was that they were unable to leverage their property as a form of finance, which in turn impacted on their ability to start new ventures. Following the advent of democracy in 1994, the corporate sector underwent massive restructuring. Jobs were lost in the formal sector, which caused the informal sector to grow rapidly. In spite of this, South Africa's unemployment and poverty levels relative to international standards remain disproportionately high, especially for a country with a relatively high level of per capita income.

Small, medium and micro enterprises (SMMEs) in most developing countries contribute significantly to job creation and to the overall gross domestic product (GDP) of a country. In South Africa, SMMEs contribute over 40% towards the total GDP and provide more than 50% of the employment in the labour force.

Sustaining and growing the number of successful businesses is vitally important to the long-term well-being of the country, in terms of creating employment and in alleviating radical poverty. Employment will also assist in reducing petty crime, which ultimately will boost investor confidence and encourage capital inflow.

SMME development and growth is dependent upon a steady stream of entrepreneurs to drive new business creation and to provide much-needed employment and opportunities, especially for the rapidly growing youth sector of the economy. The word entrepreneur conjures up much debate and interpretation of meaning. 'Entrepreneur' is a French word with its origin dating back to the 1700s and over time has been defined in various ways, most of which relate to starting a new venture from limited resources. Whatever definition is preferred, however, there is little debate that entrepreneurship is vital to any economy and critical in both providing employment and in helping to equalise wealth and standards of living. It is an important force in shaping the changes that take place in the economic environment.

Studies done through the Global Entrepreneurship Monitor (GEM) have played an important role in deepening our understanding of entrepreneurship, not only in South Africa but in many other countries around the world. GEM is a worldwide, multinational, longitudinal study on entrepreneurship and the first reports, involving ten Organization for Economic Cooperation and Development (OECD) countries, were published in 1999. Since then, the study has grown to encompass more than 60 countries and it is now considered to be the most authoritative and comprehensive study of entrepreneurship in the world. GEM seeks to ascertain what factors either inhibit or encourage entrepreneurship in a country and what should be done to promote entrepreneurial activity. Over the years, the study has found that the national economy, in countries with low levels of per capita income, tends to be characterised by the prevalence of very small businesses. As the per capita income increases, industrialisation and economies of scale allow larger and more established organisations to satisfy the increasing demand of growing markets. The large firms provide employment in the form of more stable jobs. These economies are characterised by a reduction in new business start-ups and lower levels of entrepreneurial activity.

GEM research has also shown a consistent association between a country's stage of economic development and its level of entrepreneurial activity. The relationship of GDP per capita and early-stage entrepreneurial rates demonstrates a U-shaped curve. Countries with low GDP per capita tend to show high levels of early-stage entrepreneurial activity as can be seen in Figure 5.1.

This activity decreases as GDP per capita increases, with larger, formal businesses providing the bulk of employment. At the top end of GDP, there is more disposable income which again encourages new business start-ups. South Africa's level of entrepreneurial activity is substantially below that suggested by the line of best fit on the

Figure 5.1   Early-stage entrepreneurial activity rates and per capita GDP, 2009.

AO	Angola	ES Spain	JP Japan	SA Saudi Arabia	
AR	Argentina	FI Finland	KR Korea	SE Sweden	
AU	Australia	FR France	LV Latvia	SI Slovenia	
BA	Bosnia & Herzegovina	GH Ghana	ME Montenegro	SW Switzerland	
BE	Belgium	GR Greece	MK Macedonia	TN Tunisia	
BR	Brazil	GT Guatemala	MX Mexico	TR Turkey	
CL	Chile	HR Croatia	MY Malaysia	TT Trinidad & Tobago	
CN	China	HU Hungary	NL Netherlands	TW Taiwan	
CO	Colombia	IE Ireland	NO Norway	UG Uganda	
CR	Costa Rica	IL Israel	PE Peru	UK United Kingdom	
DE	Germany	IR Iran	PK Pakistan	US United States	
DK	Denmark	IS Iceland	PT Portugal	UY Uruguay	
EC	Ecuador	IT Italy	RO Romania	ZA South Africa	
EG	Egypt	JM Jamaica	RU Russia	ZM Zambia	

$R^2=0.51$

GDP per capita in purchasing power parities ($), in thousands

(Source: GEM global report, 2009)

U-shaped curve. According to the GEM data, a country at South Africa's stage of economic development (ZA) would be expected to have an entrepreneurial rate of almost 13% rather than its 2009 early-stage entrepreneurial activity rate of 5.9%.

South Africa is considered to be a developing economy or, as termed by the Global Competitiveness Report, an efficiency-driven economy similar to countries such as Argentina, Brazil, Chile, Colombia, Indonesia, Mexico, Peru, Russia and Thailand. However, South Africa lags behind other developing countries in promoting early-stage entrepreneurial activity. Its rate of activity has remained within a narrow band of 5.9 to 6.5% (the percentage of the adult population between the ages of 18 years and 64 years who are in the process of starting or who have just started a business), which is significantly lower than the average of 8.3 to 14.9% for other developing and efficiency-driven countries as illustrated in Table 5.1.

Table 5.1 Early-stage entrepreneurial rates (percentage) across efficiency-driven GEM countries.

Efficiency-driven economies (middle to low income)										
Country	2001	2002	2003	2004	2005	2006	2007	2008	2009	2010
Argentina	11.1	14.2	19.7	12.8	9.5	10.2	14.4	16.5	14.7	14.2
Bosnia and Herzegovina								9.0	4.4	7.7
Brazil	12.7	13.5	12.9	13.5	11.3	11.7	12.7	12.0	15.3	17.5
Chile		15.1	16.9		11.1	9.2	13.4	14.1	14.6	16.8
China		12.3	11.6		13.7	16.2	16.4		18.8	14.4
Colombia						22.5	22.7	24.5	22.4	20.6
Croatia		3.6	2.6	3.7	6.1	8.6	7.3	7.6	5.6	5.5
Dominican Republic							16.8	20.4	17.5	
Ecuador				27.2				17.2	15.8	21.3
Hungary	11.4	6.6		4.3	1.9	6.0	6.9	6.6	9.1	7.1
Indonesia						19.3				
Iran								9.2	12.0	12.4
Jordan				18.3					10.2	
Latvia					6.6	6.6	4.5	6.5	10.5	9.7
Macedonia								14.5		8.0
Mexico	20.7	12.4			5.9	5.3		13.1		10.5
Malaysia						11.1			4.4	5.0
Panama									9.6	
Peru				40.3		40.2	25.9	25.6	20.9	27.2
Poland	10.0	4.4		8.8						
Romania							4.0	4.0	5.0	4.3
Russia	6.9	2.5				4.9	2.7	3.5	3.9	3.9
Serbia							8.6	7.6	4.9	
South Africa	9.4	6.5	4.3	5.4	5.1	5.3		7.8	5.9	8.9
Taiwan		4.3								8.4
Thailand		18.9			20.7	15.2	26.9			
Tunisia									9.4	6.1
Turkey						6.1	5.6	6.0		8.6
Uruguay						12.6	12.2	11.9	12.2	11.7
Average	11.7	8.3	11.3	14.9	9.1	12.6	12.3	11.8	11.2	11.4

As South Africa is characterised by a dual economy – both formal and informal – one would expect its entrepreneurial activity to be similar to that of other developing economies with a similar GDP per capita such as Argentina, Chile, Brazil and Peru. However, these Latin American countries tend to have entrepreneurial rates that are at least two times greater than in South Africa.

The Latin American countries show a significantly more positive attitude towards entrepreneurship than in South Africa. Most indicators of entrepreneurial attitudes – including the perception of good business opportunities, individuals displaying entrepreneurial intentions, the belief that successful entrepreneurs have a high status, and individuals' perception that they have the skills necessary to start a business – are all considerably lower for South Africans in comparison to Latin America as observed in Table 5.2.

The large discrepancy in entrepreneurial attitudes and perceptions is likely to contribute to the significant differences between South Africa's entrepreneurial activity and that of its South American counterparts.

What, then, is standing in the way of South Africa increasing its early-stage entrepreneurial activity and bringing it up to that of other equivalent economies?

Education and training
The problem
GEM has shown a consistent link between education and entrepreneurial activity. Individuals with a matric, and more specifically those with a tertiary education, are significantly more likely than those without a matric to own and manage a start-up business. Higher levels of education are also strongly linked to the likelihood that the business will survive beyond the initial start-up phase. Entrepreneurial interest and activity is enhanced when individuals believe in their own entrepreneurial ability. Unfortunately, only 35% of South African adults believe that they have the knowledge, skills

Table 5.2 Entrepreneurial attitudes and perceptions in efficiency-driven economies.

Country	Perceive good business opportunities (%)	Believe they have entrepreneurial capabilities (%)	Have entrepreneurial intentions (%)	See entrepreneurship as a good career choice (%)	Believe successful entrepreneurs have high status (%)
Argentina	44	65	14	68	76
Bosnia and Herzegovina	35	57	17	73	57
Brazil	47	53	21	81	80
Chile	52	66	35	87	70
China	25	35	23	66	77
Colombia	50	64	57	90	74
Croatia	37	59	8	68	49
Dominican Republic	50	78	25	92	88
Ecuador	44	73	31	78	73
Hungary	3	41	13	42	72
Iran	31	58	22	56	78
Jordan	44	57	25	81	84
Latvia	18	50	10	59	66
Malaysia	45	34	5	59	71
Panama	45	62	11	74	67
Peru	61	74	32	88	75
Romania	14	27	6	58	67
Russia	17	24	2	60	63
Serbia	29	72	22	69	56
South Africa	35	35	11	64	64
Tunisia	15	40	54	87	94
Uruguay	46	68	21	65	72
Average	**36**	**53**	**19**	**71**	**70**

(Source: GEM global report, 2009)

and experience required to start a business. This is in stark contrast to Latin America where over 66% believe they have the knowledge, skills and experience to start a business.

Young people often lack the necessary skills experience and expertise to start and successfully sustain a small business. This makes it difficult for them to cope with the numerous challenges facing aspirant entrepreneurs, such as the lack of appropriate financial resources and the inability to accumulate sufficient assets to provide the required collateral.

Over the years, concern has been expressed, not only about the level of entrepreneurial education and training, but, more importantly, about the quality of basic education in South Africa. In a recent GEM report, over 65% of the expert informants interviewed identified problems with education as one of the primary inhibitors of entrepreneurial activity in South Africa. To understand this challenge more fully, one needs to look at the history of education in this country. In 1996 one in four black adults had no access to formal schooling and only 6% of all South Africans had a tertiary qualification. Apartheid education undoubtedly damaged people's confidence and self-esteem, which impacted negatively on their initiative and creative thinking.

According to the Global Competitiveness Index (2009), only 15% of South Africa's population has a tertiary education. Out of the 133 countries reviewed, South Africa ranked 107th in terms of the quality of primary education and 119th for the quality of higher (secondary and tertiary level) education (see Table 5.3). What was of even graver concern was that South Africa ranked last in terms of maths and science education.

Table 5.3　South African indices for 2008, ranking out of 133 countries.

Organised crime	119
Quality of primary education	107
Quality of maths and science education	133
Quality of education system	119
Internet access in schools	100
Tertiary enrolment	94
Hiring and firing practices	125
Pay and productivity	105
Availability of scientists and engineers	123

This finding confirmed the review of South Africa's performance in the 2003 Trends in International Mathematics and Science Study (TIMSS), where South Africa was ranked last of the 50 countries – even coming in behind Botswana and Ghana.

The current education system continues to fail a large proportion of South Africa's youth. According to Azar Jammine, the chief economist at Econometrix, 60% of the pupils who entered the school system twelve years ago never matriculated. Many of these young people have neither the skills nor the knowledge to successfully start a business. The Global Competitive Report of 2009/10 cites South Africa's poorly educated workforce as the second most problematic factor for doing business in the country.

The current educational system in South Africa is therefore not an enabling factor that is able to encourage SMME development. Curriculum 2005 has been singularly unsuccessful and has contributed to a decrease in the literacy and mathematical competency levels of scholars entering university.

The solution

Every government since 1994 has recognised the importance of and the need for improving the quality of education. Education is undoubtedly the key to the success of entrepreneurial development and it is vital that the standard of basic education be improved, with a special emphasis being placed on numeracy and literacy. Teachers, particularly those in marginalised schools, should be retrained and the government should seriously consider re-opening teacher training colleges. Because of the importance of maths and science, special additional payments should be made to teachers in these disciplines in order to encourage them to train to the levels required. At school level, introducing business skills in an accessible and enjoyable way would help to stimulate entrepreneurial interest amongst the youth. Teachers may not feel qualified to do this, however, as the majority have no business experience. Volunteers from the business environment could be utilised to talk to learners, to help with business games and projects, and to stimulate and develop the belief among young people that business is an exciting alternative career option.

Financial literacy and vocational training programmes should target the unemployed, with a focus on an effective apprenticeship system that can provide artisan skills, especially to young people. SMME training programmes need to focus on the entrepreneur's needs. Care needs to be taken that programmes catering predominantly for corporate general managers are not simply repackaged and offered as SMME programmes.

It is also important to ensure that effective technology education is offered in all schools. Too many 'me-too' or 'copycat' businesses are started in which there is very little product/service differentiation. This leads to fierce competition and price slashing, which eventually results in the business becoming economically unviable. Programmes should be geared to ensure that a wider proportion of the population becomes more familiar with technology. South Africa still has far too many schools without computer facilities. In a knowledge-based global economy, these students leave school with an enormous disadvantage.

It is important to ensure that schools are prioritised with regard to physical infrastructure, security, feeding schemes and sufficient textbooks, all of which are vital to create an environment that is conducive to education. Planning and implementation of physical infrastructure needs to be prioritised in a similar manner to the construction of the 2010 soccer stadiums. Textbook ordering and the supply of other school material needs to be well managed to ensure that all schools have the required books prior to the start of the school year.

Corruption within the school tender departments needs to be focused on and a culture of zero tolerance should be encouraged. Teacher absenteeism needs to be addressed. These steps are essential if we are to ensure that all learners are afforded the best opportunity for effective schooling.

Access to finance

The problem

The lack of financial support has been widely cited as the major problem facing entrepreneurs in South Africa. In this South Africa is not unique, however, as GEM has shown that South Africa's financial system is no more reluctant to support entrepreneurs than in other developing countries such as India, Brazil, China, Argentina and Mexico.

Banks and other financial institutions generally require collateral and formal business reports as the main criteria for considering a loan. Many business owners lack the necessary collateral and do not have the training to maintain formal books or accounts. Therefore, they are less likely to be successful when approaching financial institutions.

GEM research conducted in South Africa looked at the financial management practices in black-owned SMMEs and how these practices impacted on their financial health and ability to raise bank finance. Careful management of cash flows is vital for the survival of a young entrepreneurial business. However, a significant number of entrepreneurs from disadvantaged communities indicated a lack of any financial management systems within the business and many did not keep any form of financial records. Given that difficulties were significantly reduced in firms that kept a cash book, kept a record of debtors, actively controlled these debtors and managed their inventory, it is of concern that so few businesses implement these practices. Implementing any of these practices was associated with a substantial reduction in exhausting an overdraft.

Current research has questioned whether lack of access to funding is, in actual fact, the primary barrier to entrepreneurship development. There seems to be growing consensus that the lack of financial management and other business skills may, in fact, be key. Without these skills, wide divergences between the expectation of the entrepreneurs and the sound financial requirements of the lenders will continue to hamper entrepreneurs' ability to raise funding. Many would-be entrepreneurs do not have viable business ideas. The ideas they have are not properly thought through, there has been inadequate research or they are copycat ideas with nothing to differentiate their product or service offering from what is already out in the marketplace.

Where business plans are completed, they are often prepared by inadequately trained service providers using standardised templates. The entrepreneur is not involved in the process so has little idea as to how the business plan was constructed. The entrepreneur is therefore unable to answer questions relating to the plan. Consequently, the financial institution, which is lending money to the entrepreneur and not to the service provider, is likely to be reluctant to offer the loan.

True venture capital is virtually non-existent in South Africa when compared to developed countries, where this type of funding is relatively accessible to business start-ups. In South Africa, preference with respect to funding is given to businesses that already have an established product or service, have a revenue stream and can show a successful track record. South Africa has a lack of seed funding options that cater specifically for small start-ups. A priority should be to increase the number of micro-finance initiatives, along the lines of initiatives in developing countries such as Kenya, India and Bangladesh where highly efficient micro-finance structures allow lending institutions to successfully manage the risk of default and yet still provide thousands of loans to small-scale entrepreneurs.

Unlike these micro-finance initiatives, banks are reluctant to lend to risky ventures, particularly if the idea is not a viable one. Traditionally, banks have made their financing decisions more on asset-based calculations and less on the cash flows of the business and the background, experience and qualifications of the entrepreneurs. It has been easier and more profitable for the banks to lend to large corporations and not to relatively risky start-ups.

The solution

Many would-be entrepreneurs lack the knowledge of where to go for funding for their particular venture. There is currently no single source of funding information, and websites for funders are often outdated and contain incorrect information. A comprehensive small business website should be constructed where all institutions that offer funding to SMMEs can list. The site, which must be kept up to date, should provide contact information, what funds are on offer and for what purpose, as well as details regarding the criteria for successfully applying for funds. The application processes should be simplified to accommodate the levels of education and the standards of proficiency in English found amongst the majority of potential South African entrepreneurs.

Many of the entrepreneurs involved in start-up ventures lack the skills, knowledge and experience required to ensure the survival and growth of a business. Mentorship support is essential in promoting the sustainability of many small businesses. The provision of start-up funding therefore needs to be coupled with ongoing mentorship, training and access to adequate support services. South Africa needs to create a national mentorship index, managed by competent and experienced people with a proven track record in small business support and development. This index could include retirees with particular information and communication technology (ICT), legal, accounting or other professional skills.

Investec, via The Business Place, is attempting to address this problem by establishing a series of 'one-stop shop' offices throughout major centres in South Africa where potential entrepreneurs can seek help. This initiative is excellent, but is inconsistent in its quality of service depending on its location.

Many government agencies that have been mandated to provide financial support to the SMME sector have been unsuccessful. The organisations have been poorly managed, are inefficient and are run by political appointees rather than by experienced professionals.

Unsuccessful agencies should be closed or where possible, partnered with successful private organisations. Business Partners has proved to be efficient and extremely well managed and is a successful lending model. This business model should be replicated to ensure that the millions of rands the government has made available for SMME funding is used efficiently. This decision will need to be coupled with the decision to remove all political appointees who have little or no business experience from key positions in the new organisation.

Government policies and regulations

The problem

A study by the independent private sector development and research company, SBP, in 2004 showed that compliance costs in small businesses with a turnover of less than R1 million per annum represented a staggering 8.3% of turnover. It also calculated that these compliance costs in South Africa amounted to approximately R72 billion or 6.5% of GDP. This is prohibitive and these costs act as a serious restraint to business. Excessive bureaucracy and cumbersome application processes, offices that are only open on weekdays, and protracted, inefficient decision-making has compounded the issue. Although the government has repeatedly acknowledged the impact these constraints have on SMME development, little has been done to ease the regulations and costs. In 2007 nine procedures were required to start a business in South Africa, taking on average 35 days. By 2009 this had been reduced to six procedures taking 22 days. Although this is an improvement, South Africa still lags behind a number of other African countries.

In Mauritius, by comparison, starting a business involves five simple procedures and takes a mere six days. Egypt, one of the top African performing countries, has simplified its regulations in order to improve the ease of doing business in the country, requiring five procedures for business start-ups, taking a total of seven days.

The solution

Of all the obstacles and challenges facing entrepreneurship in South Africa, the area of regulations is both easy and quick to fix. Policies should be introduced to reduce the cost of doing business in South Africa. For example, set-up costs could be dramatically reduced in areas such as licensing and onerous statutory requirements, which are costly to comply with, take extraordinary amounts of time and are inefficient.

Registration procedures for businesses should be simplified to, for example, a single form of maximum three pages for banks or tax and the Companies and Intellectual Property Registration Office (CIPRO) plus the provision of business online facilities similar to those used by the South African Revenue Service (SARS). Tax regulations for business start-ups should be dramatically simplified. Long and time-consuming queues at SARS offices discourage registration and compliance by many small businesses.

The World Competitiveness Report of 2009–10 showed that 'inefficient government bureaucracy' had deteriorated in ratings from 2002 to 2008 (see Table 5.4).

In addition, the percentage of South African experts (in the 2009 GEM survey) that cited government policies as a key constraining factor has increased significantly from 40% in 2008 to 61% in 2009.

Table 5.4   Most problematic areas for doing business in South Africa, 2002 versus 2008.

	2002	2008
Inadequately educated workforce	1 (21%)	2 (16%)
Crime and theft	2 (19%)	1 (19%)
Restrictive labour regulations	3 (17%)	4 (12%)
Poor work ethic in national labour force	4 (10%)	7 (5%)
Inefficient government bureaucracy	5 (7%)	3 (14%)
Access to financing	6 (6%)	5 (9%)
Corruption	10 (2%)	6 (7%)
Inadequate supply of infrastructure	13 (2%)	8 (4%)

(Source: World Competitive Report 2009–10)

The 2008 GEM report noted that South Africa's restrictive employment laws are one of the biggest regulatory obstacles limiting business
growth. This was confirmed by the Global Competitiveness Report
which cited labour regulations as the second most problematic factor
for doing business in South Africa (see Table 5.3). Out of 133 countries
reviewed, South Africa ranked 90th in labour marketing efficiency,
125th with respect to inflexible hiring and firing practices, 123rd in
the lack of flexibility in wage determination and 121st in poor labour-
employer relationships. Labour inflexibility does not create a climate
that is conducive to entrepreneurial activity and does not foster a
spirit of competitiveness. Inflexible labour practices hamper innovation and can breed a culture of entitlement. GEM has shown that
strict employment protection laws, especially in terms of hiring and
firing, reduce the attractiveness of entrepreneurship, especially for
high-potential individuals. These individuals are generally more
mobile and may decide to set up their business in countries with less
restrictive practices. This is of particular concern in a country like
South Africa, as high-potential individuals are more likely to set up
businesses with good employment prospects.

GEM has found that government support for small businesses in
South Africa is severely lacking. There are few support centres
targeted towards the informal sector, and government initiatives
directed towards the formal sector are largely too generic and
have had little tangible success. This finding was supported by a
WorldWideWorx small and medium enterprise (SME) survey that
showed that government efforts to promote small businesses were
not highly regarded by small and medium companies. Many of the
companies surveyed were not aware of the different support agencies,
and of the few that had heard of them only a small percentage had
actually used them. What was of even greater concern was that of
the small percentage who had made use of the services offered, a
large proportion was not satisfied with the outcome. A number of
the agencies that were started in early 2000 were disbanded due to
ineffectiveness. These have been replaced by new organisations;

however, it remains to be seen whether these new organisations will be more effective than the organisations they replaced. Unless these organisations are better staffed, hire professional management teams and are driven by economics, rather than political will, it is questionable whether they will be significantly more successful.

Finally, many government agencies are concentrated in urban areas. The need for proactive programmes is often more critical in less developed provinces, so government policy should ensure that these provinces are not sidelined.

Telecommunications, particularly the use of mobile networks, are still prohibitively expensive when compared to both the rest of Africa and global costs. It was hoped that the advent of a third mobile operator would encourage strict competition, but this was not forth-coming. Given the poor landline infrastructure, more and more people, especially in smaller towns and rural areas, are reliant on mobile phones to conduct business. While new and simplified packages which make use of mobile telephony and which will enable very small enterprises to conduct business in a simpler and more streamlined manner are being developed, they are still in the infancy stage. However, unless government ensures that the cost of telecommunications is comparable to countries that display high levels of entrepreneurial activity, these benefits will not have widespread appeal.

Government should aggressively incentivise entrepreneurship through greater development of specialised economic zones. This could include providing tax breaks for businesses below certain revenue thresholds and lower barriers to entry in certain selected industries. Key industries in each province should be targeted to encourage business start-ups and incubators by utilising current sector strengths, for example pharmaceuticals, information technology (IT) and boat building in the Western Cape. Less entrepreneurial provinces such as the Eastern Cape, Mpumalanga, North West and Northern Cape should be offered export processing zones with tax-free incentives in order to encourage industries to relocate or overseas businesses to establish operations in these provinces. This was done very effectively in Mauritius in the 1980s. However, unless labour relations improve, it is doubtful that many overseas businesses will see South Africa as an attractive relocation option.

To promote competitiveness, South Africa should take steps to liberalise the labour market. This should be in the form of a two-tier labour market with increased flexibility for smaller companies. Differentials in minimum wages – particularly for the youth – have been mooted. This would have the dual benefit of increasing wage flexibility and offering employment possibilities to more young people. South Africa's restrictive labour laws discourage start-ups and reduce the attractiveness of business expansion. It is extremely onerous to remove poorly performing individuals and this, coupled with the cost of downsizing when business climates dictate, is prohibitive. Businesses are therefore less likely to increase their staff complement unless absolutely necessary.

Cultural and social norms
The problem
In the past, very little was reported on and celebrated in the public press with respect to entrepreneurship. Although sporting heroes and politicians are revered and receive considerable coverage and respect, there have been few role models for aspiring entrepreneurs, particularly in the black African community.

Fear of failure is also a barrier inhibiting entrepreneurial behaviour. South African society is hard on those legitimate businesses that fail as people tend to lose not only their money, but also their social respect. Our society has created an environment where it is believed that it is better to get a job in order to be secure. There is a sense of entitlement and an expectation that big businesses, government and others should create jobs, rather than creating one's own employment.

Research seems to indicate that South Africa has a noticeable lack of 'can-do' attitude, which was partly attributed to low levels of entrepreneurial experience and informal learning opportunities. In addition, South Africa lacks a co-operative entrepreneurial culture as people are reluctant to share skills and facilities in order to foster the possible success of entrepreneurial ventures.

The solution

A societal ethos of self-sufficiency rather than state-dependency should be inculcated into the youth from primary school level. Starting your own business and providing employment should be part of the norm rather than the exception. The youth should be encouraged to think freely through focused entrepreneurial education in primary and secondary schools, which should inculcate a positive and vibrant attitude towards entrepreneurship as a viable employment option.

Interventions aimed at increasing female participation in the SMME sector are an important strategy for economic development as women are still under-represented in opportunity-orientated businesses and show a lower interest in starting a business. Recent research indicates that the majority of women do not want to have a business employing a number of people. They want flexibility in working times to allow for domestic duties and do not want the responsibility of having to look after a labour force. Practical assistance from government in the form of affordable childcare facilities will go a long way in overcoming this hurdle. The Business Partners Women's Fund is playing an important role in encouraging women in business. They have found women to be better business risks than men, with a significantly lower rate of failure.

Entrepreneurship is not seen as a legitimate or desirable career choice, as corporate or professional careers represent the pinnacle of achievement. This attitude is especially seen amongst the youth of South Africa, the majority of whom aspire to be politicians.

Solutions have been put forward for the main four factors influencing entrepreneurial development in South Africa. However, there are a number of other initiatives that could also be undertaken to promote business start-ups.

Science parks and incubators for hi-tech and research and development orientated start-ups should be developed, possibly through public-private partnerships. In addition, general business clusters or incubators should be created that include entrepreneurs as well as commercial and professional support structures. This would mean that start-ups can be assisted in a more proactive and supportive environment. Such an initiative would be particularly important in rural and semi-rural areas, where poor infrastructure, both physical and commercial, is a major barrier to small businesses. It is in these marginalised areas that the most sustained help is needed.

South Africa is undoubtedly at a crossroads in its history. It is facing a major dilemma in that it is attempting to right the wrongs of the past by trying to eradicate the depth of poverty that exists, and by trying to equalise the huge income discrepancy between the rich and the poor while at the same time attempting to boost the economy, provide jobs and decrease unemployment. Poverty cannot be reduced without high and sustained rates of economic growth. This growth is necessary to provide the funding government requires in an attempt to address income inequality. However, such redistributive spending reduces public and private expenditure on infrastructure. This, coupled with an often inefficient government sector, compounds the problem and increases the dependency of the poor and uneducated on government support thereby creating a culture of dependency and entitlement. This does not encourage entrepreneurial activity.

The final solution, although not a quick fix, is to improve education and training systems, including vocational training for those in school and for those who have already left school.

According to an article by the Centre for Development and Enterprise, the current redistributive model is unsustainable and often the money has gone into redistributing resources to people that are not poor. Maybe South Africa should follow the example of Brazil and adopt a modest increase in welfare expenditure, but spend most of what is available on encouraging rapid economic growth through improved education, easier access to finance and reducing the amount of legislative 'red tape' and make starting a business easier.

Considerable good work is being carried out by a variety of well-meaning organisations in both the public and private sectors. Numerous large corporations are doing admirable work in a variety of different areas to help promote entrepreneurial activity and SMME development. However, it is fragmented and still not enough. Unemployment is not decreasing. A concerted, singly focused strategy is required with specific objectives, strategies and plans. It is certainly not an easy task, but South Africa could well learn from the tangible success in other developing countries. The eradication of corruption, nepotism and entitlement must start at the top and permeate down into all levels of society.

MIKE HERRINGTON is the founder and Director of the University of Cape Town (UCT) Centre for Innovation and Entrepreneurship at the Graduate School of Business.

References and further reading

Global Competitive Report 2003–2004 and 2009–2010, World Economic Forum.

Herrington, M.D., Kew, J. and Kew, P. (2008) *Global Entrepreneurship Monitor: 2008 South African Report* (Graduate School of Business, University of Cape Town).

Herrington, M.D., Kew, J. and Kew, P. (2010) *Tracking Entrepreneurship in South Africa: A GEM Perspective* (Graduate School of Business, University of Cape Town).

World Bank (2008) 'Youth and Employment in Africa: The Potential, the Problem, the Promise', siteresources.worldbank.org / INTAFRICA / Resources / ADI_youth_Employment_summary.pdf (accessed on 1 October 2010).

6

Health in Africa
How Can the Situation be Improved?

FRANCOIS VENTER and HELEN REES

Introduction

The world has made huge gains in life expectancy in the last 50 years, including historically 'poor' countries. Countries such as India, Brazil and Mexico are enjoying lifespans that are starting to approximate those in the United States (US) or Spain. Remarkable gains have been closely correlated with economic improvement, reflected by country-specific gross domestic product (GDP).

Africa is the big exception. While there have been some gains in most African countries, these have been slower than anywhere else on the globe, with the Congo having a life expectancy not much different from 100 years ago. In addition, the correlation between economic improvement and life expectancy is not as strong in Africa as elsewhere. Rich African countries, such as South Africa and Botswana, have not mirrored their Asian or South American counterparts in their health gains. The lack of gain in life expectancy is also a proxy marker for poorer quality of life; for example, a child who dies of diarrhoea pushes down overall life expectancy, and leaves behind a traumatised family who have been further impoverished due to medical expenses and time out of work.

It is unclear why African health should lag in this way. Economists and public health experts have advanced a range of reasons, from corruption, war and poor health systems, to the rise of AIDS and tuberculosis (TB). It is likely that the HIV epidemic has had a profound impact on many sub-Saharan countries, but this still does not explain many other poor health outcomes. Africa is a huge and disparate continent, and is not alone in experiencing corruption, war and poor health systems, but suffers disproportionately poor health. The African continent is characterised by a changing demographic. While in most countries total fertility rates remain high, some have seen a decline in numbers of children, more so in urban than rural settings. Migration from rural to urban settings is the norm and the resulting slum settlements characterise all major sub-Saharan African cities. While rural life predisposes many people to diseases of poverty, urbanisation has increased lifestyle diseases, violence and trauma and has created a new context for infectious diseases. Beyond unscientific Afro-pessimism speculation, an all-encompassing convincing theory to explain the disparity in health outcomes between Africa and the rest of the world is not forthcoming.

Country-level poverty, as discussed below, is often seen as a priority in the fight for better health. However, recent studies suggest that there are now more extremely poor people living in middle-income countries than in poor ones. This is partly because large countries, including China, India and Brazil, have grown quickly to become middle-income countries, and yet have large segments of their population that have not benefited from the economic boom. Health research indicates that the Gini coefficient, a measure of the difference in income distribution between rich and poor within a country, is related to health outcomes. In addition, quality of life has been correlated strongly with the index. Africa has more countries with this level of severe inequality than any other continent. In many African countries, people are so poor that they cannot afford the most basic co-payments towards their care, and often are burdened with the hidden costs of transport and time off work. The link between poverty, economic opportunity and health outcomes is clear: better opportunities for employment and increased benefits may make the biggest impact on health. Wiser choices regarding resource allocation and economic policy could make African populations healthier and happier.

But what makes Africans sick, or injures them? And what can we do about it?

The answers to the first question are well studied; the answers to the second are complex. The United Nations (UN), through the widely accepted and politically powerful eight Millennium Development Goals (MDGs), has tried to provide guidance to governments as to what to focus on for development, with disease prevention and mitigation forming a large part of the interventions. Significant progress measured against the MDGs has been made in many parts of the world, including developing countries in Asia, South and Central America. However, progress in Africa, specifically sub-Saharan Africa, has been slow, with indications that many health goals will not be achieved by the stated 2015 deadline.

Health systems failure

Much of the challenge of good health care is simply the delivery of the service, an issue that bedevils everything from vaccinations to clean water. A recent provocative chapter in a book called *False Economy: A Surprising Economic History of the World* asked the question why Africa is not a major exporter of illegal drugs, like Latin and South America. The slightly tongue-in-cheek conclusion was that the poor reliability of systems of transport, and ambiguous legal frameworks around border controls, commerce and communication, meant that drug lords preferred more trustworthy suppliers.

Health is the same. Delivery systems, frequently constructed during colonialism, often have not been updated to deal with modern realities. Intermittent, poorly designed, inaccessible and under-performing primary clinics do little to inspire confidence in poorer populations, who may have alternatives in the form of home remedies, traditional healers and the private sector. This may be compounded by inadequate and under-motivated health-care staff, unreliable medication and diagnostic supply chains, poor prioritisation and lack of accountable management systems.

The fact that health outcomes seem weakly related to resource investment (South Africa's poorly performing but relatively well-funded primary care service is a good example) suggests that gains can be made with existing infrastructure. Delivering services is not impossible in Africa. Soft drinks, commercially manufactured beer, lottery tickets and cell phone services are available in even the most remote areas, despite significant logistical problems. Organisations like the Clinton Foundation have started to tackle what they call the 'non-sexy' issue of supply-chain management and systems repair. Other organisations, such as the Institute for Healthcare Improvement, have made it their mission to dramatically improve the quantity and quality of delivery using existing resources, utilising a mixture of meaningful engagement with health-care deliverers, intelligent local problem solving and target setting, with some notable results in Malawi, South Africa and Ghana.

Health-care professionals

There is some correlation between health staffing levels and health outcomes, although this is not as simple as it may seem. Africa has the lowest number of doctors, nurses, pharmacists and other health-care professionals per capita in the world. The World Health Organization (WHO) has identified 57 countries globally with 'critical health-care shortages', where there are insufficient medical staff to yield the most basic provision of care. Of these, 37 countries are in Africa. However, within the continent there is very wide disparity, with countries such as Botswana, Namibia and South Africa not figuring in the 'critical' list, yet performing as poorly against some health indicators as these 'critical' countries.

Health-care migration is a continued and vexing issue, with the WHO estimating that a quarter of all doctors trained in Africa now work in developed countries, mainly in Europe and the US. This migration is difficult to counter, as higher salaries, professional opportunities and much better working conditions are present in these countries, although legislation and improved salary structures appear to have had some effect. At the same time, organisations like Médicins Sans Frontières have demonstrated that health professionals from the developed world are prepared and willing to work in developing countries.

Better management of health-care practitioners in Africa is possible. Coupling improved retention strategies with using these professionals more effectively in health-care environments would show immediate gains. Opening more medical schools and nursing colleges is an expensive and long-term strategy, and, while necessary, a critical review of the requirements of health care may mean that other health-care tiers could be trained and recruited at less cost. Facilitating a cadre of international health-care workers to work in poor countries, even for limited periods, would certainly help with the skills shortage.

Water

Much of Africa is very dry. Access to safe and adequate water remains a huge challenge throughout Africa, with less than half the overall population enjoying potable water. Humans are required to ingest several litres a day, depending on activity and ambient temperature, posing a huge continued risk to individuals where water access is inconsistent and unsafe. Water-borne diseases account for a large percentage of illness, especially in poor communities, with children being particularly vulnerable. Diarrhoeal illness accounts for up to 18% of deaths of younger children and significantly compounds malnutrition problems in survivors. Bacteria and parasites account for the majority of health problems, although increasingly industrial contamination with chemicals and heavy metals has also become an issue.

In general, almost all water requires some form of water purification treatment, even water that is relatively uncontaminated. Freshwater sources are few and precious, and are threatened by sewage, industry and climate change. Provision of large-scale potable water requires significant capital infrastructure in the form of treatment plants and pipes to homes or access points. Maintenance of the system is required to prevent water loss through leaks. Governments of poorer countries have been unable or unwilling to prioritise spending in this area, especially in rural areas, and many poorer households spend a significant percentage of their income and women's time on accessing water, thus compounding their poverty trap.

Recognising the key link between safe water, health and poverty, access to clean water has become a MDG, with indications that this will be met at a global level. This is not the case in Africa, with sub-Saharan Africa making particularly little progress in meeting the goal of halving the number of people who do not have access to clean water. With the creep of desertification, affected communities and countries are facing emerging problems of drought and crop failure, and tribal and regional wars are beginning to be fought over water resources and the shrinking areas of arable land that accompanies this problem. It is imperative that all African governments should prioritise water management and develop regional water agreements, as rivers know no country borders.

Other forms of pollution

The term 'pollution' has become a catchphrase from the forms with health implications such as water and air pollution. Contaminants in the air, often a by-product of industry and mining, car exhausts and wood fires, contribute to pollution, and many large African city populations have poorer respiratory health as a result. Industrial air pollution, especially where coal is mined, such as in South Africa, may contribute to acid rain. Land pollution, due to chemical leaks and poor management of waste disposal, may contaminate food and water supplies. Johannesburg, the 'Egoli' of South Africa, currently faces an imminent crisis of water pollution produced by years of mining with inadequate water management systems.

Poor monitoring, lack of recognition of risk and lack of enforcement of laws contribute to the vulnerability of African populations. Several public scandals involving the dumping of radioactive and industrial waste from developed countries has highlighted the possibility of preventable environmental pollution.

Natural and humanitarian disasters

In 2010 the world experienced some 373 natural disasters, including floods, earthquakes and weather-related events, making this the worst year for such events for the past two decades. The UN predicts that climate change and changing weather patterns, together with the overcrowding occurring with rapid urbanisation and the unregulated environmental degradation seen in many poor countries, will combine to worsen the impact of natural disasters. Whenever events such as the Mozambique floods of 2007 occur, it is the poorest people who are the most vulnerable, with no means of escape, limited emergency assistance and loss of possessions, crops and lives pushing them further into poverty. But Africa also experiences humanitarian crises resulting from wars and political instability as seen in Sudan, Sierra Leone and Zimbabwe. Whatever the cause of the crisis, what has become clear is that countries are poorly prepared to respond. While we can predict that disease outbreaks will occur in these circumstances, there are no guidelines on the use of vaccines in different emergency scenarios, and the WHO is about to produce global guidance on this topic. The WHO keeps a roster of experts that it can call upon in the event of global public health emergencies (International Health Regulations) but in most poor countries effective plans for emergencies are either weak in conception, and if in place have so far proved hard to implement. The recent threat of pandemic H1N1 influenza showed that while the rich world could respond with plans for national vaccine stockpiles and population immunisation campaigns, this was not the case for Africa despite the mortality of H1N1 influenza being much higher in the African region than in any other part of the world. Countries and regions should develop disaster response plans that anticipate the health threats from a likely disaster or pandemic and which allow countries to co-ordinate their own efforts with those of international agencies.

Nutrition

Despite huge improvements in the per capita food production in the world, almost a third of Africa goes hungry, accounting for a UN estimated quarter of the global hunger burden. The first MDG calls for the halving of starvation by 2015. For growing children, under-nutrition impacts on growth, mental development and resistance to infections, and may prime the individual for a range of diseases in adulthood, including diabetes. For adults, hunger and starvation are linked to multiple poor health outcomes such as vulnerability to TB and other infections. Many African communities live in rural areas and rely on local agriculture. Water insecurity, unsophisticated irrigation and water retention strategies and the impact of climate change make these communities extremely vulnerable to water problems, with resulting starvation.

Communities within Africa have developed strategies to cope with famine, at the cost of stunting and high mortality rates but allowing them to survive and thrive during times of plenty. However, the toll of famine appears to be higher recently in HIV-affected areas, leading some researchers to speculate that 'AIDS variant famine' leads to a situation where the fittest individuals within a community are being struck down by HIV, when previously they could be relied upon to implement strategies that would benefit the entire com-munity, as well as look after more vulnerable or ill members.

Heath policy-makers often explain away food insecurity as the product of poverty, poor climate or poor individual choices. Star-vation and famine are deeply political issues, with economist and Nobel Prize winner Amartya Sen observing that famine does not occur in functioning democracies, as governments respond more efficiently to the desperate circumstances that starvation induces. Priority of urban food security over rural needs, ignoring poorer and smaller farmers and the use of food aid as a weapon in internal conflict, has been a feature of many undemocratic governments and dictatorships. In Africa, one of the starkest examples has been the destruction of Zimbabwe's ability to produce food. Previously the 'breadbasket of Africa', the country has become an importer of food, with hunger and food riots present in the country for the last decade.

Paradoxically, under-nutrition is not the only food problem in Africa. An explosion in obesity has occurred in the last 50 years throughout the world, with the rise of easily obtainable, relatively cheap foods with high caloric values and increasingly sedentary lifestyles. As in other developing countries, such as Mexico, Brazil and China, increasing affluence seen in some urbanised African settings has been accompanied by a rapid increase in average weight. In many African urban settings, female obesity rates are now in excess of 30%, higher than rates seen in many developed countries. Cheap, high calorie foods, together with limited access to the nutritional food required in childhood, sometimes results in the paradoxical situation of households with obese adults and yet with undernourished children. Cultural views on what is over- or underweight appear to play significant roles in stigma and motivation around obesity, and in some communities becoming fatter may be seen as a sign of health and affluence. Being overweight is linked to substantial health problems, including high blood pressure, diabetes, heart disease and poorer surgical outcomes. Dealing with established weight gain is very difficult. While diets and exercise may help with short-term weight loss, it is rarely sustained. Governments will need to tackle this problem at the source with the same approach used for alcohol and cigarettes. Higher taxation on fast foods and on sugar-laden carbonated drinks, with tax breaks on healthier foods, together with increased community education about healthy eating and exercise need to be recognised by politicians as priority interventions.

HIV and AIDS

HIV has decimated large parts of sub-Saharan Africa. HIV and its co-traveller TB account for almost half of all South African and Botswana adult deaths, with around 15–20% of the adult population infected with the virus at any one time. While figures are less reliable in countries such as Zimbabwe, Namibia, Zambia, Swaziland and Lesotho, it is likely that a similar situation exists, with many countries in central, East and West Africa having lower but significant rates of infection. The disease, while disproportionally affecting young women, cuts readily across all social, racial and age strata, depleting certain professional classes, such as teachers and nurses, and has placed a huge burden on the health system.

HIV is largely sexually transmitted. The virus, once established, results in a steady decrease in immunity. Antiretroviral treatments stop virus production, allowing the immune system to recover. Young women in the 18–25 year age group in southern Africa are the most at risk for contracting the virus. Men tend to start catching up as they get older, and older women similarly remain at risk throughout their lives. In South Africa, well-funded education campaigns by public health communication organisations have targeted the highest risk groups, but the effect has been modest at best. Most African countries are deeply conservative, making public health sex-linked education interventions very difficult to win support for. In addition, the rise of evangelical churches, often with explicit support from US-based religious organisations, has allowed for effective mobilisation against condoms, gay men and sex worker legislation and programmes within many African communities.

Pregnant women are at higher risk of contracting HIV as they have recently had unsafe sex, and the physiology of pregnancy makes them more vulnerable to infection. Without antiretrovirals, a third of women will transmit HIV to their uninfected infant. Once infected, children are at risk of early death if not treated and of growth stunting if antiretroviral therapy is not instituted timeously. HIV-infected adolescents, a growing population in the region, face a complex world. Their sexual debut occurs with the knowledge that they have a deadly infectious disease and they are frequently without parents to support them.

Antiretroviral therapy has had the same revolutionary impact on HIV that penicillin has had for bacterial infections and insulin has had for diabetes. Highly effective, affordable and safe, the same 'first-line' drugs used in New York or London are available in many African state health sectors. Life expectancy for those on anti-retrovirals has been increased by decades and may approach near normal levels. Quality of life is dramatically improved much like diabetes or asthma with effective treatment. Effective early treatment for pregnant women stops transmission to their infants in almost all cases.

Unfortunately, people have to access this treatment to benefit from it, which has been a major challenge for the system for the last few years. Although coverage has improved steadily throughout Africa, treatment is usually initiated very late, when immune systems are severely affected and patients require complex and expensive treatments of various opportunistic infections and cancers. This late presentation is probably largely a product of two things: patient stigma and fear, and inappropriate health system service provision. Due to its sexual transmission, its link to death and the fact that the drugs for treatment were stigmatised, HIV testing has remained low. Health systems have, however, not been able to respond appropriately when testing has been improved. Healthy HIV-infected patients, when not requiring antiretrovirals, see little reason to attend clinical services that are busy, often chaotic and unfriendly, and that require access during precious work hours. This means that proper monitoring, with the institution of appropriate antiretroviral therapy prior to falling ill, rarely happens, even in people fully aware of their HIV status.

Although HIV services are costly, health systems have vested interest in getting eligible people on to antiretroviral therapy as soon as possible, as it is a very effective mechanism to reduce expensive and unnecessary hospitalisation and clinic visits.

Large donor-driven programmes arose during the early 2000s to support AIDS treatment programmes, and unprecedented amounts of money were invested in many African countries. However, this commitment has wavered as the global recession took hold. A combination of the recession with resultant trimmed budgets, along with a level of AIDS fatigue and frustration with multiple failed HIV-prevention programmes, has meant that the global appetite for continued funding may be a wanting issue in future. Should funding diminish, difficult moral questions will be raised about stopping the provision of antiretroviral drugs.

South Africa may have the only sustainable African antiretroviral programme on the continent at present with over 80% of the costs of the programme currently coming from government coffers.

The failure of HIV prevention

HIV prevention in adults has been a failure by any measure, particularly in Africa. However, it is debatable that we have had a useful model to work off for prevention. The prevention 'toolkit', a list of largely non-evidence based recommendations, has proved to be a failure in southern Africa. Countries with strong leadership (Botswana), documented behaviour change (Uganda), high levels of knowledge (South Africa), high condom use (South Africa) and high HIV testing rates (Botswana and South Africa), all remained frustratingly hyperendemic despite implementation. 'Success stories', where HIV prevalence dropped, proved transitory (Uganda) or unsatisfyingly explained (Zimbabwe, Kenya), offering little evidence to guide policy-makers. HIV prevalence rates in South Africa, for example, have risen steadily during the last two decades, although they appear to be plateauing or possibly even decreasing slightly, albeit at very high levels. This steady increase is despite widespread and relatively well-funded HIV education programmes, high levels of basic knowledge about HIV in the general population and broad access to condoms.

Coupled with all this is the fact that prevention programmes have had poor science to inform them. Behaviour change science has been subject to much recent criticism for making broad statements regarding the impact of different transmission behaviours without proper research to back it up. In addition, the biological transmission during sex has been more complex than previously realised, with vastly different levels of infectiousness during different phases of the disease. The explosive nature of the epidemic in sub-Saharan Africa, the fact that some populations seem significantly more vulnerable to infection than their near neighbours, and the complexity of the interaction with other sexually transmitted diseases (STDs), challenged conventional wisdom as additional data was accumulated.

For Africa, it is clear that current prevention efforts are failing. However, alternatives for action are difficult to suggest. The biggest potential game-changing prevention technology would be an effective HIV vaccine but we are at best decades away from a marketable product. While antiretrovirals as either tablets or microbicides are beginning to show promise, the challenge will be to market a partially effective prevention product. However, even if these interventions occur, mathematical models show that the prevention impact will only be felt at a population level a decade later.

But there are some sensible measures that can be implemented immediately with relatively limited resources that could affect HIV rates, although they will take a while. Medical male circumcision, which is highly effective in stopping HIV acquisition, should be accelerated. Routine neonatal circumcision offered to male children at delivery will ensure a generation is protected. Circumcision also lends itself to concurrent education programmes focusing on men – a group who are frequently ignored in such programmes. Evidence exists that interventions making men aware of the consequences of gender violence leads to less violence against their partners. Further education about the consequence of alcohol use and risk inhibitions is also appropriate.

Male and female condoms work well at an individual level, and have increasing acceptability across communities, especially among the youth. Condom programmes need to be strengthened as presently only between two to eight condoms are apportioned per sexually active man per year in African country programmes. Wider distribution and promotion of the female condom, together with bold new programmes introducing condoms into schools, should be considered notwithstanding that condom distribution is currently forbidden in schools in most countries.

Schools themselves present as potential targets for HIV-prevention interventions, as girls in that age group who remain in high school seem to be protected from HIV. Innovative programmes, such as incentivising girls through free uniforms or social grants to stay in school, need to be explored. It is a worthwhile investment to deliver reproductive health services to this group in order to prevent problems such as teenage pregnancy.

Behaviour change presents a major difficulty. The behaviour-change lobby – mindful of the low amounts spent on these prevention programmes when compared to the amounts spent on HIV treatment – has argued that commitments to these programmes need to be improved. Controversial campaigns with explicit messages, famously pioneered in South Africa by loveLife, were watered down in the face of furious public opinion. An expert group should prioritise sexual and other behaviours and the country should support such targets with meaningful interventions and evaluation. An important component of behaviour change is to ensure that the messages and actions of politicians and social commentators are consistent with policy.

The behaviour change that would supposedly decrease HIV spread seems relatively simple. Do not sleep around. Do not cheat on your partner. Use a condom. Unfortunately, data suggests that most people, even in good, responsible relationships, at one or another time in their lives stumble at each of these messages. In the approach to drug users or sex workers, public health implementers have long used a successful 'risk reduction' approach, where it is acknowledged that drug users may use drugs but that this can be made safer (clean needles, medication to prevent transmission, accessible services) or sex workers are at risk (provision of condoms, STD checks, legislative reform). This approach merits exploring in more conventional relationships, such as emphasising the ways to protect a partner after an affair, or assistance with disclosure, or what to do if a condom was not used.

Several researchers contend that the culture of 'multiple concurrent partnerships' is a driving factor behind the epidemic in southern Africa, and simply decreasing the number of sexual partners that each person has is not enough. Partners on the side are the problem. Efforts to introduce a well-researched and well-intentioned 'One love' monogamy programme were totally undermined by revelations regarding President Zuma's sex life. Repeated high-profile media revelations meant that he had to confess to multiple affairs, often with women decades younger than himself. A savage critique of the data to support the theory of 'multiple concurrent partnerships' was published in 2010 by the *Journal of the International AIDS Society*, challenging the conventional wisdom that this drives HIV transmission. However, it seems unlikely that this behaviour has no contribution to HIV-transmission dynamics, and making this part of an education programme may be beneficial.

It was believed in the recent past that HIV testing itself would lead to behaviour change; anecdotes of the temporary fear felt by those awaiting a test result favoured a world view of reflection and introspection that would hopefully lead to more 'responsible' sexual behaviours. Data supports this fairly strongly for those who test positive, where people who know they have the virus appear to be more likely to practise abstinence, use condoms and restrict their number of partners. This has not, however, been convincingly demonstrated when people test HIV negative. In fact, some studies indicate that 'risky behaviour' may even increase after testing negative. Efforts to improve post-test counselling in those who test negative, often regarded programmatically as the people who require the least effort, may need a strong reappraisal, especially as mass testing programmes may cause possible harm if there is sufficient post-testing risk-taking behaviour.

Legislative frameworks have been proposed to criminalise HIV transmission in other countries in Africa. Attempts to criminalise sex acts have universally caused behaviours to go underground, and this new proposed legislation would be negative in terms of public health, as well as human rights. One area, however, where legal reform would be most useful, is through the decriminalisation of sex work. Police harassment of sex workers has proved to be a consistent impediment to implementation of risk-reduction interventions in this group, and this would be a relatively easy win for the prevention movement.

Finally, we do not understand enough about African sex lives. Anecdotal reports of diverse local sexual cultures are countered by a stereotyped national view of a heterosexual, monogamous culture. In the US, it took the Kinsey Reports to finally uncover what actually went on in American sexual relationships. We know very little about what happens in African bedrooms, brothels, schoolyards and churches, in terms of sex. Kinsey Reports for African countries most affected by HIV, to help us understand a largely sexually transmitted epidemic, are long overdue.

Non-HIV infectious diseases

Infectious diseases extract a huge toll in Africa, even in countries where HIV prevalence is low. In developed countries, the decrease in the prevalence and severity of infectious diseases has accounted for some of the biggest gains in life expectancy. Many middle-income countries have made gains, such as Mexico and China; however, economically matched countries, such as South Africa and Botswana, still experience a large infectious disease burden.

TB is a major killer of Africans, and is the classic disease of poverty. It spreads easily through respiratory secretions, can be challenging to diagnose in its early stages and relies on prolonged therapy to be cured. The failure of conventional TB control measures recommended by the WHO during the 1990s and 2000s, yet poorly implemented by health departments, has come home to roost, with sub-Saharan Africa the only area on the globe with rising TB incidence. HIV makes people extremely susceptible to TB, and has further contributed to this failure of TB control, with areas of South Africa describing new incident infections higher than ever described in human history. An almost untreatable drug-resistant variant ('XDR') of TB in the mid-2000s was described in KwaZulu-Natal and sent warning messages across the world. A *Lancet* editorial described the rise of drug-resistant variants, first found in South Africa and subsequently documented in other countries in the region, as 'public health negligence'. An unappreciated area of this escalation in TB was the increasing rates of TB seen among health-care workers, due to high exposure to infected patients and poor infection control within clinics and hospitals.

The escalating public recognition of HIV has paradoxically revived efforts to address the moribund TB programmes, as TB became the number one cause of death among HIV patients in Africa and many other developing countries. 'TB activism' has emerged for the first time, asking awkward questions of poorly performing TB programmes. Demands for better diagnostics and treatment by HIV activists, as well as increasing criticism of ineffective public health programmes and recommendations by organisations like the WHO, has led to a wave of new research and focus in these areas. The first new anti-TB drugs in decades have proved to be effective in early study. A new diagnostic test allows for rapid detection of TB and drug-resistant variants. Lessons from HIV programmes in Africa, where adherence and outcomes are far better than for TB, have allowed for more ambitious and creative thinking when it comes to delivering TB services.

In many parts of Africa, malaria alone accounts for a huge health burden, and is one of the most potent hindrances to economic growth in many countries. Out of over 200 million infections annually, more than 90% of global malaria deaths occur in sub-Saharan Africa, mainly in children. Pregnant women who become infected are at risk of spontaneous abortion, as well as increased mortality. Despite the scale of the problem, until recently malaria has not had much creative energy paid to it. Even the understanding of shifting epidemiology and drug resistance was poorly understood, although now is being remedied through international monitoring collaborations. Fuelled by large amounts of new research and programmatic money, including from the Gates Foundation and Wellcome Trust, new and more effective anti-malarial treatments, vector control, prophylaxis and the aggressive marketing of insecticide impregnated bed nets have provided hope and safety for large numbers of Africans fortunate enough to be able to access this care. In particular, new drugs have allowed health-care workers to use effective treatment in environments where multi-drug resistant disease had rendered older treatments almost useless. In some areas, malaria has been largely eradicated through control programmes, suggesting that this may be possible in other areas of Africa, with sufficient public health will and resources. Control programmes may be hampered by poor inter-country collaboration and co-ordination, where malaria belts cross borders. Altering geographical malaria belts have been controversially blamed on climate change, altered irrigation and migration, although there is little agreement as to which of these drivers are the most important.

Beyond TB and malaria, a host of largely preventable or treatable infectious diseases continue to extract a toll on the continent. Other infectious agents have a field day in Africa, and span a bewildering and complex array of diseases, from typhoid to rabies to worms. Respiratory and diarrhoeal illnesses, a consequence of malnutrition, poor ventilation, poverty and unsafe water, account for the vast majority of preventable and treatable diseases. Hookworm infection accounts for large numbers of people with iron-deficiency anaemia, and river blindness is a catastrophic disability in poor communities. While improvement in treatment of these diseases may make some difference, the experience from developed and other developing countries suggests that the most rapid and effective way of addressing these diseases is through sustained improvement of social and economic systems, coupled with public health focused interventions.

Vaccines have made a profound impact on individuals' (especially children's) susceptibility to many common, severe infectious diseases, including polio, measles, rubella, diphtheria, pertussis and tetanus. While vaccine coverage as a whole has steadily improved across the continent, it still falls far short of the targets set by benchmarking organisations such as the WHO. The fact that the African region cannot make the necessary breakthroughs that would allow the region to eradicate polio, and that in 2010 there was a major regional outbreak of measles, indicates that vaccine services are failing in many African countries. Newer vaccines to protect against human papilloma virus, hepatitis B, pneumococcal and rotavirus disease could dramatically improve adult and child health. Unfortunately, successful vaccine programmes are too often hampered by poor health-delivery systems. Poor accessibility, inadequate storage, intermittent supply, lack of trust in health-care provision, poor education and expensive vaccines all play their part in preventing many African children from receiving adequate vaccination services. In addition, until relatively recently, there has been little political pressure to move life-saving vaccines into poor countries with any sense of urgency. Hepatitis B is an infection that causes significant mortality in the developing world but which has much less impact in the developed world. While the hepatitis B vaccine was successfully introduced into the developed world, it took twenty years to make the vaccine widely available in the poor countries that most needed it. The shameful public health lesson changed the global approach to vaccine access, and long delays in the introduction of new vaccines caused by high costs and political inertia, are no longer acceptable in the public health world.

Newer vaccines, such as the human papilloma virus vaccine, whose delivery focuses on young adults, will face huge challenges, as there is little experience of providing vaccines to anyone other than small children. Despite vaccine preventable diseases being relatively easy to control for public health interventions, funds to support vaccine initiatives are inadequate. The global effort to eliminate polio is a good example as despite its incremental successes, the programme has had to scramble for ongoing funding each year. Even more challenging is the introduction of vaccines for neglected diseases, such as rabies, into needy communities, as well as raising money for the new lifesaving vaccines such as rotavirus. The GAVI Alliance (Global Alliance for Vaccines and Immunisation), which aims to accelerate the distribution of new vaccines to the world's poorest countries, has to raise $3.7 billion to deliver on its targets up to 2015, and neglect to do this means that vaccine programmes in the poorest African countries could fail.

Finally, vaccine development is largely funded by pharmaceutical companies. The diseases that demand vaccines disproportionately affect poorer countries, which do not have adequate financial inducement to foster research. More recently, philanthropic organisations, such as the Gates Foundation, and occasionally governments, such as the South African government, have provided resources to address this, often partnering with pharmaceutical firms and providing speculative funding.

Vaccines are one of the most important health technologies that we have for the African region. The new global decade of vaccines, due to be adopted by the World Health Assembly in 2011, aims to galvanise international vaccine efforts but only time will tell if this renewed effort to support one of the world's best public-health interventions, will yield its intended results. In the interim, African leaders must step up to the plate and prioritise public health efforts on vaccines. If vaccine services fail, health ministers should be held accountable, as there are few excuses for the extraordinary death toll that vaccine preventable diseases reap on African children and populations every year.

Access to affordable and safe medicines and laboratories

The difference in disease profile between the developing and developed world, especially the burden of infectious diseases, has meant that pharmaceutical firms have not focused on research that would benefit Africans. Indeed, in the last twenty years, other than HIV drugs, only a handful of new infectious diseases drugs have been developed. The last drug developed for TB occurred decades ago, although new medications appear to be on the horizon. The profit in developing countries is very small compared to the huge markets found in the US, Japan and Europe, where making similar drugs carries far less risk and more predictable profit than trying to research, register and market a new drug class in Africa.

However, several things have changed this equation. Major philanthropy groups, such as the Gates Foundation, as well as pharmaceutical companies and even international agencies, have begun to support newer drug and vaccine development and look at ways to use existing drugs more economically. The rise of major generic companies, many of which are in developing countries, accompanied by community activism highlighting pricing and the cost in human life, has allowed for the manufacture of older drugs at a fraction of the cost. In the process, the price of HIV drugs has plummeted, new medicines are available for drug-resistant malaria, programmes to facilitate access to the treatment of river blindness and fungal meningitis have been implemented, support to pharmaceutical companies to develop new drugs has occurred, and more attention to efficient manufacturing processes may further diminish manufacturing costs.

However, safe medicines face several challenges not just related to cost. Systems of delivery frequently break down, meaning that drugs do not arrive, arrive in insufficient quantities, arrive expired or inadequately stored. Weak legislation means that drugs that should be controlled can be purchased over the counter, paving the way for the introduction of counterfeit drugs with resultant toxicity, lack of efficacy and drug resistance.

It is often under-appreciated what the cost of laboratory diagnosis and monitoring services contributes to cost and complexity in health systems. Effective treatment of malaria, HIV and TB, as well as many other illnesses, relies heavily on laboratories, and inadequate provision of services makes a considerable impact on programme effectiveness. Recently, the notion that centralised laboratories should provide services has been challenged, with an explosion in research on 'point of care' immediate results using robust machines that are often independent of electricity supply. In addition, new diagnostics may potentially transform the TB field, and alternatives to expensive HIV monitoring appear to be possible.

Pregnancy

In Victorian times, women in developing countries faced huge mortality during childbirth, with up to a third of them dying in the 1800s, dropping to 1/100 at the start of the century. This has plummeted to less than 5/100 000 is some countries, and dropped by a third globally in the last 30 years, largely due to the expansion of effective programmes in developing countries. Indeed, this may be modern medicine's most significant contribution to mortality reduction, and many countries have formal investigations into maternal deaths, largely regarded as almost always preventable. Maternal mortality and illness has been long recognised as a problem in developing countries, with over 90% of global maternal deaths occurring there, and largely related to bleeding, infections, unsafe abortions, eclampsia (a form of hypertension) and associated illnesses such as HIV. The WHO and others use maternal mortality ratios to judge how well a health system functions, again using it as an MDG, and the World Bank has estimated that good maternal care is one of the cheapest and most effective health investments developing countries can make. Addressing maternal health is also an effective way to decrease the impact of poverty, as the loss of a mother negatively affects the household economy and the survival and health of the remaining children. Despite this, maternal mortality is actually rising in several

African countries, including South Africa. Ensuring the availability of good quality post-natal care, and rapid referral systems for women needing emergency treatment, will make a significant difference in maternal health and to the survival of healthy infants.

Next to vaccines, contraception is one of the highest impact public health tools that we have. Frequent and/or unintended pregnancies increase the risk of maternal death and ill-health, including the risks associated with unsafe abortion. Child spacing of more than two years increases the chance of survival and good health in children. Yet contraceptive services have experienced a declining priority in recent years, with many services seeing a reduction in the types of methods on offer. Contraceptive services need to be put back on to the priority list of services and need to be given more attention and funding than is currently the case.

Violence

Interpersonal violence, especially gender violence and rape, is a feature across Africa. Studies in many different settings have shown that the low status of women and the cultural tolerance of gender-based violence have allowed this problem to escalate. Rape has become a feature of life in some countries affecting both women and children. Genocide and war continue to feature in Africa, with obvious overt health consequences. The aftermath of war can leave severe psychological scars, as in Sierra Leone and Rwanda, as well as ongoing physical danger, as seen in the landmines sown during the Mozambique civil war that continue to disable or kill civilians decades after the cessation of conflict. More locally, statistics in South Africa suggest that homicide is a common cause of death; men often kill or harm other men under the influence of alcohol. Similarly, women are often victims of an intimate partner, as are their children. In many African settings, guns are a vestige of war and enjoy long circulation in societies, even where legislation prohibits their use. Unlicensed firearms account for much of the devastation of crime, alcohol and gender-induced violence.

Solutions to violence obviously range widely, but recognition by governments that goes beyond 'days of activism' must be considered. This should include focused interventions, including gun and alcohol control, enforcement of legislation especially around gender-based violence, and in the case of civilian violence during conflicts, international responses that target perpetrators at all levels.

Cancers

As in the developed world, cancer is a major killer in Africa, although the types of cancers differ and are changing. All medical students know about Burkitt's lymphoma, a cancer identified in the 1950s in West Africa and known to be associated with the Epstein-Barr virus. Cervical cancer caused by the human papilloma virus, is the largest cancer killer amongst African women, and in areas where HIV is common the severity and the incidence of the disease is increasing. With rapid urbanisation and the Westernisation of diets and lifestyle, new cancer trends are emerging. From the limited evidence we have, cancer of the breast and cancer of the colon are becoming increasingly common. The high prevalence of HIV in many countries has contributed to a change in the patterns of cancers with Kaposi's sarcoma becoming one of the most common diagnoses made in HIV-infected individuals.

The weakness in health-service infrastructure predicts a poor outcome for many African cancer patients, so while the mortality from many cancers has decreased in developed countries the same cannot be said in the African region. Firstly, most countries have weak or non-existent cancer registries, which make it hard for policy-makers to track cancer trends and to develop appropriate interventions. From a clinical perspective, the early diagnosis and treatment available in the developed world has contributed to reductions in cancer deaths but this has not been the case in Africa. Sophisticated screening techniques, advanced surgical options and improved radiotherapy and chemotherapy simply do not exist.

Screening approaches, such as cervical cytology for cancer of the cervix, are inappropriate in countries where laboratory services are non-existent, transport is a problem and asking patients to come back for results creates insurmountable barriers to care. The impact of all this is that women are presenting with advanced disease to services that are ill-equipped to treat them. Apart from the over-arching need to strengthen health services, creating a better approach to cancer management in Africa will need to look to incorporate technologies that are appropriate for low-resource settings. An example of this can be found in cervical cancer screening where a simple on-site test that detects the human papilloma virus associated with cancer of the cervix has been shown to radically improve detection of early disease when cure is still possible. New technologies that remove cervical lesions that may develop into cancer if left untreated have been successfully introduced into low-resource outpatient settings, making treatment accessible and affordable to services and women alike. The introduction of a vaccine against human papilloma virus, widely available in rich countries but not yet available in the public sector anywhere in Africa, could change the whole landscape of cervical cancer in the region. To achieve this, the cost of these vaccines must be reduced, something that the pharmaceutical companies are now willing to consider. Political leadership informed by scientists and public health experts could in some cases transform the approach to cancer management in poor African countries.

Traffic accidents

Death rates from traffic accidents are high in Africa considering the lower number of cars per capita and competing with similar rates in much of Russia, the Middle East and Asia. Throughout the world, car injuries are playing a steadily increasing role in life expectancy and cause of disability, although the death rate per accident in Africa appears to be amongst the highest in the world, largely as pedestrian involvement is evident in over half of these incidents. A WHO study suggested that drivers had an almost 1/100 chance of having an accident each day in Africa, against a global average of 1/5 000. Yet again, children carry a disproportionate level of the mortality burden. Internationally, there has been a move to avoid the term 'accident', as it implies in many people's minds that the incident could not have been prevented, when this is not the case in the vast majority of traffic-related injuries. Traffic incidents consume huge economic resources, through subsequent medical care, traffic flow restoration, loss of economic activity and road repair, with an estimate in South Africa alone of US$5 billion annually. Data examining causation is lacking overall on the continent, but the root causes that have come from studies such as South Africa is unsurprising and mirrors that found in other countries with similar data – alcohol intoxication, unroadworthy and over-loaded vehicles, reckless driver behaviour and speeding, as well as poor roads.

Traditionally, enforcement has been the focus for reducing traffic accidents, including monitoring for alcohol limits, seatbelt use, car safety and speeding. More recently, advocacy has begun for better road construction after research has demonstrated that improved road and intersection design could significantly decrease driver error. Upgraded street lighting, cars driving with lights on and more pedestrian crossing options could contribute to addressing the high numbers of pedestrian casualties.

Cigarettes

Tobacco smoking is possibly the most important worldwide individually modifiable risk factor when it comes to disease prevention. In particular, commercially manufactured cigarettes, which are specifically designed to deliver the maximum dose of addictive product, have been linked to a long list of diseases including lung, bladder and mouth cancers that are rare in non-smokers. Smoking is a major risk factor for common diseases, such as cardiac disease and stroke, and an important contributor to emphysema, influenza, lung infection and TB acquisition. 'Secondary smoke' appears to be a major contributor to respiratory problems in children living with smokers, and pregnant women who smoke can harm their babies. It is estimated that the average smoker lives for a decade less than a lifelong non-smoker.

The burden of health care is substantial when it comes to smoking, both for the individual and for the health system. Many of the common serious illnesses associated with smoking are difficult to treat, even in a sophisticated health-care system. Other forms of tobacco use, especially chewing tobacco and snuff, also have adverse health impacts.

Africa traditionally has not been a major tobacco market, and not a single country figures in the 'top ten' of tobacco-consuming states. However, in an era of decreasing smoking tolerance and declining tobacco company revenues, Africa may represent a new and poorly regulated market. Lifelong smokers generally start smoking in early adulthood; African populations are generally younger than the rest of the world, with a disproportionate number of the population below the age of 20, representing a huge potential new customer base. The WHO has noted a steady increase in tobacco smoking across Africa, although country-specific data varies. Tobacco companies taking advantage of lax promotional laws, as well as cultural changes and perceptions of smoking as an aspirational activity, have meant that tobacco use on the continent is projected to double in just over a decade. In some countries, tobacco is an important crop, providing employment and taxes for states desperate for both, and allowing tobacco farmers and companies in particular to wield political power, challenging anti-smoking legislation in Kenya and Zambia. The city of Harare was constructed around the lucrative tobacco trade. While the majority of African smokers are male, an increase in women smokers has been noted.

While certain countries in Africa have installed legal restrictions on tobacco products with good effect, other countries could more rigorously implement the WHO's Framework Convention on Tobacco

Control, which proposes a series of interventions that would dramatically limit tobacco use, through outlawing smoking in public places, increasing taxation and restricting advertising. South Africa is a relative success story when it comes to tobacco control, where smoking kills three times more people than traffic accidents. The new democratic state instituted a series of restrictions on advertising and public space smoking while simultaneously increasing taxation on tobacco, leading to a drop of almost a third in active smoker numbers in the space of ten years. This followed a decade of increased smoking amongst South Africans, predominantly women, on the heels of aggressive tobacco advertising during the 1990s.

Alcohol and other substance use

Alcohol abuse patterns in Africa, as elsewhere, are tied to a broad array of health effects. Alcohol is implicated in traffic accidents, interpersonal violence and sexual risk taking and HIV acquisition, along with liver dysfunction, mental diseases, oral cancers and a host of other illnesses, as well as the personal, social and family effects of alcoholism. Some South African communities have the highest rates of foetal alcohol syndrome in the world. While there is clearly cultural diversity with regard to drinking, it is unclear whether patterns of abuse differ in Africa as compared to other areas. Alcohol controls could be improved through legislation, taxation and education and there are successes in Africa in this field.

There is also an increase in the abuse of other drugs ranging from heroin to local cheaper drug mixtures. International drug routes and the porous borders are contributing to this problem, although it appears to be nowhere near the levels experienced on many other continents. It is clear that proactive legislation should be implemented before this problem assumes the proportions it has reached in some developed countries.

How can we improve the health of Africans?

While acknowledging the dreadful toll of colonialism, the decimation of communities by the slave trade and systematic migration policies, the cynical manipulation of countries' political systems and their borders by protagonists during the cold war, African governments can do far better with their resources in securing their nations' health. Other developing country data suggests that equally poor and complex health problems can be quickly and adequately addressed with sufficient political and programmatic will. Botswana is able to treat over 80% of its HIV-infected population, while its giant, richer South African neighbour is barely able to treat half of those affected. Poverty-stricken Cameroon reaches 85% of childhood vaccine coverage, while neighbours Nigeria can get to just over 50% and Gabon 38%. Eighty per cent of Malawi's population has access to safe water, against less than 60% of Kenya's population. History is an important factor in understanding reasons for under-developed systems such as these, but many countries with limited resources have made rapid and major strides in addressing social issues, despite huge resource constraints. As with so many other public services, the solutions to improving health care lie largely with the improvement in systems, coupled with mechanisms to address poverty.

So what can African countries do? First, we should implement what we already know. We have the interventions, diagnostics and affordable drugs and vaccines to immediately tackle problems such as vaccine-preventable diseases, maternal ill-health, TB, malaria, river blindness, hookworm, and many other serious infectious diseases, even in the poorest of countries. New drugs and vaccines, legislation and approaches will be held as much hostage to the consistently poor health service delivery as older interventions.

Difficulties are compounded when over-stretched and under-resourced public health systems are given vastly different priorities, with messages from international agencies, the media, public opinion and vested pharmaceutical, diagnostic and researcher interests all jockeying for position and resources. These same service providers frequently have the least accurate local information to base decisions on, and the least resources to do anything with. Each country has a different disease demographic and competing resource priorities: Nigeria's health needs are very different from those in South Africa.

However, pleading country-level ignorance and poverty has masked an often inconvenient truth for African governments and that is that they routinely underfund or neglect the health budgets within their countries. Some governments still do not have line items in their national budgets for vaccines and depend entirely on outside donor agencies to fund this staple of child health services. Furthermore, as discussed above, in the fields of nutrition, water supply, environmental protection and legal enforcement of traffic and other legislation, all of which have profound implications for individual and public health, African governments have often made poor choices. Some poor countries have made major inroads in many seemingly intangible problems, despite having limited resources, so the excuse from leaders that implementing known public health measures is either too difficult or too expensive needs to be carefully evaluated and health ministers need to be called to account for failure.

Southern Africa's future with regard to HIV and TB is likely to be grim unless it prepares itself for a dogged, determined and long-term battle. In short, southern Africa finds itself with a hyperendemic illness that is effective but expensive to treat, and relies on frail health infrastructure. The virus is not going to disappear due to natural selection, a biological intervention or spontaneous changes in human behaviour in the near future. There is little foreseeable change in the numbers becoming infected, at least in the short term. The accrual of healthy patients on antiretrovirals will further strain the public health system, and the increasing cost of the programme will test political fiscal discipline and patience. Calm, dedicated and reflective heads are needed to lead interventions that focus on results, and that are not afraid to overturn conventional wisdom and public opinion when it is required.

The global activism that occurred around access to new drugs and vaccines in the developing world has changed the international consensus about what is ethical when it comes to making life-saving technologies rapidly available to poor countries. Pharmaceutical companies are willing to negotiate on parallel pricing structures for rich and poor countries, and international normative agencies such as the WHO now push for the rapid introduction of new technologies. But this approach cannot be taken for granted and activists will need to be continually vigilant if this new global norm is to be maintained.

Finally, Africa should pay attention to probable future health developments: traffic accidents, obesity, tobacco use, pollution and counterfeit medication can all be tackled with intelligent use of legislation, education and enforcement.

FRANCOIS VENTER is the Deputy Director of the Wits Reproductive Health and HIV Institute (WRHI), a research and training institute of the University of the Witwatersrand in Johannesburg, South Africa, and an Associate Professor in the Department of Medicine at the University of the Witwatersrand. He is the Head of Infectious Diseases at the Charlotte Maxeke Johannesburg Academic Hospital and is currently President of the Southern African HIV Clinicians' Society.

HELEN REES OBE is the Executive Director of the WRHI and ad hominem Professor in the Department of Obstetrics and Gynaecology at the University of the Witwatersrand. She is an Honorary Professor and the 2010 international Health Clarke Lecturer in the London School of Hygiene and Tropical Medicine. She holds numerous national and international positions and is currently the Chairperson of the World Health Organization's Strategic Advisory Group of Experts on Immunization, a member of South Africa's National Advisory Group on Immunisation, the co-Chairperson of the South African National AIDS Council's Programme Implementation Committee and Chairperson of the HIV Prevention Research Sub-Committee. She has won many awards for her work in South Africa and in global health.

References and suggested reading

Abdool Karim, S.S. and Abdool Karim, Q. (eds.) (2005) *HIV/AIDS in South Africa* (Cambridge University Press, Cape Town).

Beattie, A. (2010) *False Economy: A Surprising Economic History of the World* (Riverhead Books, New York).

Black, R.E., et al. (2010) 'Global, Regional, and National Causes of Child Mortality in 2008: A Systematic Analysis' in *The Lancet* Vol. 375, No. 9730, pp. 1969–87.

Kinsey, A.C. ([1948] 1998) *Sexual Behavior in the Human Male* (Indiana University Press, Bloomington, IN).

——— ([1953] 1998) *Sexual Behavior in the Human Female* (Indiana University Press, Bloomington, IN).

Lancet Editorial (2011) 'Natural Disasters: Taking a Longer Term View' in *The Lancet* Vol. 377, No. 9764, p. 439.

Sankaranarayanan, R. (2010) 'Cancer Survival in Africa, Asia, and Central America: A Population-based Study' in *Lancet Oncology* Vol. 11, No. 2, pp. 165–73.

Sawers, L. and Stillwaggon, E. (2010) 'Concurrent Sexual Partnerships do not Explain the HIV Epidemics in Africa: A Systematic Review of the Evidence' in *Journal of the International AIDS Society* Vol. 13, No. 34.

Sen, A. (1993) *Poverty and Famines: An Essay on Entitlements and Deprivation* (Oxford University Press, Oxford).

Usher, A.D. (2011) 'GAVI Takes Steps to Address Funding Woes' in *The Lancet* Vol. 377, No. 9764, p. 453.

WHO (2004) 'World Report on Road Traffic Injury Prevention', available at who.int/violence_injury_prevention/publications/road_traffic/world_report/en/index.html.

WHO (2005) 'The Global Immunization Vision and Strategy (GIVS) of the World Health Organization (WHO) and the United Nation's Children's Fund (UNICEF)', available at who.int/immunization/givs/en/index.html.

WHO (2010) 'The Abuja Declaration: Ten Years On', available at who.int/healthsystems/publications/Abuja10.pdf.

WHO (2010) 'Health Systems Financing: The Path to Universal Coverage', available at who.int/whr/2010/en/index.html.

WHO (2010) 'Trends in Maternal Mortality', available at whqlibdoc.who.int/publications/2010/9789241500265_eng.pdf.

WHO (2011) 'Global Status Report on Alcohol and Health 2011', available at who.int/substance_abuse/publications/global_alcohol_report/msbgruprofiles.pdf.

7

The Mauritius Success Story
Why is this Island Nation an African Political and Economic Success?

L. AMÉDÉE DARGA

From Alladin Ibrahim to Arvind Subramanian and Devesh Roy, some have called it the 'Mauritian miracle'. More recently, Jeffrey Frankel remarked: 'Whether through luck or skill, throughout its history, Mauritius has been able to adapt to changed circumstances.'

It is indeed a remarkable road that the Mauritians have travelled but it is no miracle. It is the doing of the Mauritian people. It is about the pragmatic management of the challenge of vulnerability. It is about how social forces resolve to interact for wealth creation and accumulation. It is about how the dynamics of social forces shape the type of leadership that emerges and about how leadership manages the interaction and contradictions between social forces to ensure continued progress.

Why is Mauritius considered a success? What are the policies and strategies that explain the country's achievement and how have Mauritians done it?

Mauritius has managed to prove two much-revered intellectuals wrong. In 1961 and 1972 respectively, James Meade and V.S. Naipaul, both Nobel Prize winners, made one damning verdict: post-independence Mauritius had little hope but to await a bleak future.

In 1972, Naipaul famously labelled Mauritius 'The Overcrowded Barracoon', saying its 'problems defy solution'. He considered that

Mauritius was then overpopulated with a starving people, idled by unemployment and plagued by despair.

The economist James Meade concluded that the outlook for peaceful development in Mauritius was poor and that population pressure must inevitably reduce real income per head below what it might otherwise be. That surely was bad enough in a community that was full of political conflict. In the absence of other remedies, it must lead either to unemployment (exacerbating the scramble for jobs between the Indians and Creoles) or to even greater inequalities (stocking up still more the envy felt by the Indian and Creole underdog for the Franco-Mauritian top dog).

Forty-two years after these two dire prognoses the Mauritian population has travelled from a per capita income of US$260 to US$11 400, placing it highest in Africa and 71st in world gross domestic product (GDP) per capita ranking, almost at the same level as Turkey. Accolades too numerous to list have been received by Mauritius, but they include being ranked 17th out of 183 economies in the World Bank's 'Doing Business Survey 2010', making it the star of the African region for the second consecutive year. It was listed 55th out of 139 nations in the Global Competitiveness Index 2010–11 of the World Economic Forum; 1st in 2009 and 2010 of the Mo Ibrahim Index of African Governance; and 26th out of 167 countries in the Democracy Index 2008 of the Economist Intelligence Unit. Port Louis ranked as the best quality of living among African cities in the Mercer Survey 2009 of Quality of Living Global City Rankings.

Indeed, Mauritius has achieved what almost no other sub-Saharan African countries have been able to attain since independence – sustained progress in economic conditions. Mauritius has travelled a long way in its 43 years of independence, from a mono-crop economy where sugar accounted for about a third of the GDP at factor cost, for most of the cultivated land, for a third of the total employment in the country and for nearly 92% of total export earnings, to one working on eight economic pillars: the cane industry, manufacturing with textiles and clothing as the locomotive, a seafood sector, the global business and financial sector, tourism, information technology (IT) and Business Process Outsourcing (BPO) and, more recently, a growing knowledge service export sector.

Between 1977 and 2008, Mauritius averaged a 4.6% GDP growth rate, compared with a 2.9% average in sub-Saharan Africa. More importantly, it has also accomplished what only a minority of fast-growing economies have achieved – reductions in inequality and real human development in almost all spheres of life.

Its performance on the Human Development Index (HDI), which draws on data for income, education and health to form a composite index, has been exceptional – not only by sub-Saharan African standards but also by international standards when compared with South Asia, the Arab states and East Asia and the Pacific, performing on a par with Latin America and the Caribbean.

Mauritius has successfully translated economic growth into concrete poverty reduction and improvements in human development. With a low taxation of 15%, both for corporates and individuals but on an expanding economic output, Mauritius manages to provide free primary and secondary schooling, free health care and free bus transport to students and elderly citizens. In addition, it spends 58% of its national budget on community and social services, of which 36% is paid as a non-contributory Basic Retirement Pension to any citizen above the age of 60. The citizens of Mauritius have on their part invested in acquiring their homes and the country boasts an 86% home ownership rate – one of the highest in the world. Inequality as measured by the Gini coefficient fell from 45.7 to 38.9 between 1980 and 2007. Its poverty rates remain low by international standards, with less than 1% of the population estimated as living on less than US$1 a day. Vector-borne diseases such as malaria have been successfully eradicated from the island, and life expectancy at birth has increased from 61 overall in 1965 to 69.3 for men and 76.1 for women in 2008. The net enrolment rate in primary education is 97% and 97.6% of learners reach Grade 6. The literacy rate of those between 15 and 24 years of age is 95.4%. All households are provided with safe drinking water and 99.9% have improved sanitary facilities. Access to free essential drugs is provided to 100% of the population. In fact, the Mauritian citizen has free medical treatment even of the highest technology, such as open heart surgery or eye laser treatment. At least one free antenatal medical care visit is provided to 93% of women, 83% have at least four visits, and 99.4% of births are attended by skilled health personnel.

So what did Mauritius do to achieve such successful economic and human development? As it was for the East Asian development experience in the 1970s, described in the World Bank Report of 1993, the Mauritian case is the subject of much research to find the 'model'.

For some time in the 1980s, the World Bank proudly claimed Mauritius to be a vivid example of the virtues of the magic potion of a structural adjustment programme (SAP), which it said it had applied to the Mauritian economy. In fact, Mauritius never underwent the World Bank SAP package so many African countries were subjected to. This is one example of how Mauritius did things differently (see further discussion in Bheenick's paper presented at the University of Mauritius in 1991). The first lesson was not to wait until you are completely broke to meet your banker; do so when you still have some room to manoeuvre. Mauritius recognised its predicaments in time and entered into talks with the International Monetary Fund (IMF) when it was not yet on its knees. Secondly, Mauritius agreed with the IMF on the end results but not on the prescription. It refused to eliminate subsidies on staple food and the cost recovery on education and health. Together with the private sector, the government worked on a number of other measures to reduce deficits.

Why Mauritians can

Notwithstanding a very strong political current of socialism advocated between 1969 and 1982 by the Mouvement Militant Mauricien (MMM), led by Paul R. Berenger who became prime minister in 2003 and whose programmes championed the need for nationalisation, all political leaders (including the MMM itself when it came to power in 1982 as well as the elite of Mauritius) have always taken a pragmatic approach to development. This has meant first deciding on the desired objectives, then determining the means to achieve such objectives. The objectives have consistently included the following: ensure employment for all; broaden and sustain a welfare state for the people; ensure sustainably growing national wealth; and ensure most equitable distribution of wealth.

Nobody owes us a living

When you have no valuable resource endowment except land and people, when you have a very small domestic market which cannot be a lead driver in growth, when you are very far away from developed markets and are a tiny speck in the ocean, when you are no longer an important geopolitical pawn, particularly after the opening of the Suez Canal, you can either despair or you can rise to the challenge of your vulnerability. This has been the psyche of the Mauritian people since independence. Political leaders still repeat the leitmotif 'nobody owes us a living'. Development has been a matter of survival strategy against all odds, the capacity to find solutions to challenges.

Managing diversity: We cannot sink the other one without sinking ourselves

Ethnicity is double edged. On the one hand, ethnic groups will tend to promote the forces of modernisation and advance the private capital accumulation of their members, and thus they can constitute a form of social capital as James S. Coleman defined it. On the other hand, ethnic groups will organise politically and if they cannot find the space to advance the self-interest of their members, they are likely to engage in violence, destroy wealth and destabilise the system in which they exist. Ethnic groups can thus both generate benefits and inflict costs on societies.

Mauritius became independent in the worst of political conditions. Whereas independence was unanimously welcomed by the people in all other African countries, 44% of Mauritians voted against Mauritius achieving independence. The campaign for and against independence was extremely bitter in rhetoric and pitched along ethnic division. In the months preceding and immediately after independence day, ethnic violence claimed a number of lives.

However, the contending forces, on the one hand the new ruling political elite and on the other hand the landed bourgeoisie, quickly determined that such conflict would only mean a lose-lose situation for each other and that a strategy of accommodation would be a better outcome for future options. Other components of the elite, intellectuals, media and the church argued using the same perspective. In this way, key groups managed to engineer the consociational accommodation that has characterised the country's political land-scape for the last 42 years. The power sharing and elite collaboration that characterise consociationalism ensured governmental stability, the survival of democracy and the avoidance of ethnic violence. Since independence, Mauritius has held nine general elections. They have all been fought between two coalitions of parties, except in 1976 when it was a three-way contest. Fracture lines between ethnic groups remain and it has happened, as it did in February 1999, that under-lying frustrations surge and express themselves violently. But there are always more firefighters than there are pyromaniacs and there is a quick pull back from the brink.

Invest in human capital development

Most natural resource commodities are finite; by contrast, human resources are infinite and renewable. Probably because it has no natural resources, Mauritius decided right from independence that its most precious asset was its human capital.

There are two ways to invest in human capital. The first is by the state investing in the infrastructure and the resources to provide services to that effect, namely health and education. The second is through investment by the families themselves. Mauritius actioned both options.

First, primary school was free and then in 1976 secondary schooling was also made free. Since the 2000s tertiary education provided by the University of Mauritius has been free. Free education accounts for 18% of government expenditure.

Similarly, health services have been maintained free through the 42 years of independence with 9% of government expenditure devoted to the provision of health services.

Families equally invested in the education of their children as a way to achieve social mobility. Given the limited capacity of the University of Mauritius, families have often saved over long periods to send their children for tertiary education overseas. Government provided further support by allowing part of the expenditure on this item to be exempt from income tax.

Welfare transfers account for 60% of government expenditure; besides education and health this includes non-contributory old-age pension, as well as social aid to widows, orphans and the handicapped.

Never kill the goose that lays the golden eggs

At independence, political power shifted from the colonial master to a new bourgeoisie while economic power was in the hands of a landed bourgeoisie in the sugar industry. This landed bourgeoisie also controlled the milling capacity for sugar while a relatively large mass of small planters and plantation workers were the constituency of the new ruling elite. The small planters were in an exploitative relationship with the landed bourgeoisie for milling their sugar cane. Those in political power made the decision not to kill the goose that laid the golden eggs but rather to drive a three-prong strategy. It left the landed bourgeoisie to continue the process of wealth creation and accumulation; in fact, it provided support to it through

diplomatic negotiations with European partners to ensure the maintenance of preferential market access at highly remunerative prices.
The ruling elite rather extracted from this support better deals for
the workers and the planters by imposing the state as a mediator of
the economic relationship. Furthermore, it also extracted revenues
for the state through an export levy on all sugar exported. The levy
was at its highest at 22% of sugar earnings, that is, the total export
value of the sugar export proceeds. Grudgingly, the sugar barons
paid but it benefited their capital accumulation. The goose was
kept happy, more golden eggs were laid and more and more were
captured by the state for the benefit of other stakeholders. The large-
scale commercial sugar plantation has been a key base for fuelling
investment in the further development of the country.

The same approach has been maintained to date. In the 1990s,
when the sugar sector was losing competitiveness, the then government supported the centralisation of milling capacity, removed the
levy and agreed to a downsizing of its labour force, but extracted
through the negotiated competitiveness enhancement programme a
number of concessions for small planters, for workers who were
retiring and, more importantly, a restructuring of shareholding of
the sugar companies by creating the Sugar Investment Trust where
all planters and workers of the industry were made shareholders.
The Sugar Investment Trust now owns 35% shares in all sugar
companies.

In the face of the recent loss of preferential market access, quotas
and the reduction of sugar prices, the state has supported the
sector to reform and adjust by further downsizing its labour force,
modernising qualitatively through the development of green power
production capacity which the state-owned power distribution body,
the Central Electricity Board, buys under power purchase agreements,
and use of the least productive part of the land for high-value real
estate development.

Build a petite bourgeoisie and even a middle class from small-scale planters

Small-scale sugar planters are largely owners of small plots from one to three acres. They till and plant using family labour and in previous times mobilised forces of neighbours and friends who were remunerated at friendly rates for cane cutting. The process of capital accumulation here, albeit tiny, was supported on the one hand by the state mediation for a fairer deal for those planters from the millers and on the other hand by additional transfers by the state itself. Such transfers included those in the form of subsidised access to capital for land preparation and plantation. The major part of the capital accumulated by these planters was used in the first two decades after independence for investing in the tertiary education of their children mainly abroad and/or in other small business activities. Thus, within one generation after independence, the small planter class had become an engine contributing to economic development either through increased consumption, savings or through investment in human capital development.

Build an entrepreneurial class to drive job creation and national wealth creation

The political leaders of Mauritius made and have maintained the choice right from the beginning: private entrepreneurship drives wealth and job creation, not the state. The state steers the direction for doing the same, lays down the terms for doing business and facilitates as it deems necessary to ensure the outcome.

As the ruling elite accommodated the goose that lays the golden eggs, it needed to devise the appropriate strategies to:

- offer a profitable avenue for the capital accumulated to be invested in the country rather than seek the opportunity elsewhere;
- be sensitive to the need to manage diversity and offer avenues for others to create wealth and accumulate; and
- ensure more and more job creation.

Once again there was no dogmatic approach, no textbook prescription, but a search for concrete solutions to achieve concrete objectives through dialogue with stakeholders, which, in this case, were the landed bourgeoisie on the one hand, and the petite bourgeoisie of the other ethnic groups on the other hand, composed mainly of traders and emerging professionals.

Two new avenues were created: tourism and industrialisation. Capital from the sugar sector was invested in tourism while the emerging entrepreneurs engaged in industries, essentially at first to tap up domestic market needs. Special made-to-measure schemes were set up to support each of the two sectors with fiscal and other incentives. Tourism benefited from prime beachfront state land that was allocated on cheap long-term lease. To support the weaker emerging class of entrepreneurs, the government set up the Development Bank of Mauritius to provide access to cheaper capital and low-priced, rented industrial buildings.

The new industrialists benefited from a relatively protectionist trade policy, even for an African country. Average tariffs were high. The argument made by Arvind Subramanian and Devesh Roy that it is the openness of Mauritius to trade that explains the 'Mauritian Miracle' is an over-simplification. However, pragmatism did prevail when it was decided to create the institutional structure of an export processing zone (EPZ) for the development of an export-orientated industrial sector. Mauritius offset the burden on its EPZ operators with tariff-free access for productive inputs, tax incentive subsidies and relaxed labour market regulations.

Consistently, Mauritius has opened new avenues for investment and wealth creation while adding more pillars to its economy, thus reducing the inherent risk of dependence on only one or a few sectors, while supporting growing competitiveness of the previously existing ones. This can be seen in the following sectors: tourism and domestic-orientated industries in the late 1960s; export-orientated industrialisation from the early 1970s; freeport trading business in the early 1990s; offshore business and the financial sector in the mid-

1990s; IT and BPO in the late 1990s; the seafood sector in early 2000; international high-value real estate development; and, more recently, health and tertiary education services export.

The most important lesson rarely highlighted about the 'Mauritian success' is the critical role its indigenous entrepreneur class has played since independence in the development of its economy.

The following conditions have gradually built and reinforced an entrepreneurial class: space for capital accumulation created by the state; facilitating business operating conditions; and support through access to finance. This entrepreneurial class, comforted by policy stability and relative predictability of macro parameters for wealth creation, has accumulated in the country and sought further opportunities for snowballing through investment in the newly created sectors. In fact, the creation of new sectors and pillars of the economy has been the result of prompting and dialogue between the entrepreneurial class and the state: the first in the quest for new avenues for wealth creation; the second for developmental purposes. Foreign direct investment has never been barred from any of the sectors; on the contrary, it has been actively sought. Still, the entre-preneurial class has managed to develop enough to be able to cut itself a good share of any new area of opportunity that is opened, not by way of legal enforcement but through its own capability.

Industrialising: The brick and mortar economy is crucial

In the heat of the international crisis, British analysts were seriously questioning the wisdom of the United Kingdom having neglected its industrial sector. Countries such as Singapore and even Switzer-land still have a manufacturing sector that accounts for 25 to 30% of their GDP.

Mauritius has a manufacturing sector that accounts for 20% of its GDP. From cheap labour-intensive industries, it has graduated to higher value-added production, capturing more value chains. Four lessons emerge from the Mauritian industrial experience. The first is that raw materials are less important, value addition is more so.

Mauritians have never seen a cotton plant, and yet the country has been one of the biggest exporters of textiles and garments of sub-Saharan Africa for the past 40 years. Not one carat of rough diamond has ever been mined in Mauritius, but Mauritians export cut diamonds competitively.

The second lesson is that competitiveness is not about pricing, it is about a range of factors. Mauritius managed to compete with China on garments not on the basis of pricing but on its flexibility in production and its capacity to service its customers on time with zero-defect products.

The third lesson is about markets. Both domestic and export markets count. Diplomacy is about national interest and national interest is about finding favourable market access for your products.

The fourth lesson is that while foreign direct investment is important, nowhere is indigenous entrepreneurship, including crucially small and medium enterprises (SMEs), more important than in manufacturing.

Strong and participatory institutions

The fact that since independence Mauritius has maintained and sustained a democratic system and strong participatory institutions has undoubtedly contributed to its developmental achievements.

In addition, the need to conciliate the various ethnic groups led to the development of participatory political institutions, which 'have ensured free and fair elections, the rule of law, a vibrant and independent press, and respect for property rights, all of which have made Mauritius an attractive investment location' (Subramanian, p. 21).

In Mauritius, national and local elections are held regularly, based on rules prescribed by law. The legitimacy of these elections has never been in question. Elected governments have the effective power to govern, and the opposition sticks to parliamentary rules. Both government and parliament accept their respective roles as part of the political system. Thus, political institutions have proven to perform effectively and to be stable, capable of surviving government crises when they occur. Change in political leadership has, however, never meant a fundamental change in development strategy; it has always been 'change within stability'.

Rule of law prevails. The judiciary is a truly independent third power.

Mauritius is not the only African country to have inherited a democratic political system with some good institutional capacity at independence but it is one of the rare ones to have maintained, developed and domesticated it to serve its developmental imperatives. This has been possible only on the basis of realisation of the need for accommodation, of managing diversity away from its destructive potential. This can only be achieved by having rules of engagement that all agree serve or safeguard their interest. The competitive democratic system with clear rule of law is for want of any better system still the best for the purpose. One of the mechanisms for such accommodation is the special electoral provision for eight 'best losers' seats over the 62 elected members to parliament to ensure adequate representation of minorities in the National Assembly by reserving eight seats for candidates who, although having lost by majority rule, nevertheless win a sufficiently high percentage of the vote to qualify under this clause.

The permanent concern for accommodation has given rise to, at the political level, a practice of consociationalism, which in its essence involves negotiated compromise. This culture of the political elite has imbibed the practice of leadership in Mauritius. Decision-making is often the outcome of consultative processes and negotiations between the state and various formal or informal divergent forces including the private sector, trade unions, civil society, ethnic lobbies and contending interest groups of the entrepreneurial class and are aimed at mitigating conflicts and maintaining social cohesion.

Those who are regulars at regional or international economic negotiations have noted that the Mauritian delegation always includes representatives of the private sector. They might at times be in conflictual relations at the national level, but they are partners for national interest in the international arena.

Desired outcomes should determine policies

It is evident that the right policies count. There is no one-size-fits-all policy and the same policy does not always facilitate the same outcome. This has often been the mistake of World Bank and IMF economists, who believe that economics is a mechanistic science and do not take into account that economics is systemic and involves human behaviour. As stated earlier, Mauritius never adopted a dogmatic approach to policy determination. The leaders were focused on outcome. Desired outcome was determined; then policies were crafted to achieve the outcome. In the 1980s, when Mauritius had to borrow from the IMF, it refused the structural adjustment pre-scriptions for removal of subsidies on staple food, withdrawal of free education and health services and other measures; it only agreed on the outcome, which was to reduce its deficit. Mauritius found its own ways to reduce the deficit. This lesson of the Mauritian encounter with SAPs has rarely been projected by the Bretton Woods institu-tions. When Mauritian leaders needed more revenue for the state, it facilitated the creation of additional jobs by incentivising investment in enterprise creation by the locals themselves. It exempted dividends from income tax. As more people earned revenues from jobs or business, they consumed more. Taxing consumption brought more revenue for the state. As Mauritius wanted people to invest in their own housing, government exempted mortgage payment from income tax for a considerable period of time. Today, 86% of Mauritians own homes. What the state lost from such exemptions, it captured through the consumption tax from the inputs for construction. Multiple examples can thus be given but they all point to the same principle: determine what you want as outcome for your people, then define the policies to achieve the outcomes.

Conclusion

Mauritian economic and social development is no miracle. It is the result of how people and leaders managed their realities for the creation of wealth and how they managed the wealth created to ensure their well-being – and here well-being also means absence of conflict.

Like Mr Jourdain in the *Bourgeois Gentleman*, the people and leaders of Mauritius have built for themselves a developmental state without knowing it. The Mauritian post-independence leaders determined to establish a state that builds its legitimacy on the basis of its objective to promote sustained economic and social development and increasingly higher rates of economic growth. To do so, the state chose not to kill the goose that lays the golden eggs but strike a balance where more wealth creation could be achieved while enough eggs could be picked for the benefit of sustaining the state itself and for the benefit of others. The state strengthened itself by building and sustaining its institutional, technical, administrative and political capacity.

The state did not itself participate as an actor but as a facilitator for wealth creation. It steered the way, determined the policies and avenues that opened new space for wealth creation and accumulation in a way that both strengthened the older bourgeoisie and allowed a growing entrepreneurial class to emerge and empower itself. While actively opening and pursuing the attraction for foreign investment, Mauritius followed the wisdom expressed by the words of Paul Kennedy: 'In the final analysis, only powerful and capable local interests – public as well as private – possess a degree of permanent, all-profound commitment to national need sufficient to generate the momentum required for a successful onslaught against the condition of dependent, distorted and restricted development' (p. 191).

In order to ensure that the state could achieve and maintain its relative autonomy, the political leaders sought social anchoring through the use of the democratic system, which enabled it to gain adhesion of the majority of the polity and key social actors. In fact, there could have been no other viable alternative. In societies that are ethnically divided, development can only be possible when co-operation is promoted between competing groups to achieve a viable proposition and a functioning reality with common goals. And the state must be perceived as an honest broker for ensuring balanced distribution of benefits.

L. AMÉDÉE DARGA is a social science researcher and former member of parliament and minister of Mauritius. He is a trustee of the Southern and Eastern African Trade and Information Network (SEATINI) and a Member of the Bureau of the Committee on Human Development and Civil Society of the United Nations Economic Commission for Africa.

References and further reading

Auty, R. (2009) 'Elites, Rent Cycling, and Development: Adjustment to Land Scarcity in Mauritius, Kenya and Côte d'Ivoire'. UNU-WIDER Conference on Elites in Economic Development, Helsinki, June.

Bheenick, A. (1991) 'Beyond Structural Adjustment'. Paper presented to seminar studies on Deficit Financing and Economic Management, University of Mauritius, Reduit, Mauritius.

Bowman, L.W. (1991) *Mauritius: Democracy and Development in the Indian Ocean* (Westview Press, London).

Bräutigam, D. (1997) 'Institutions, Economic Reform, and Democratic Consolidation in Mauritius' in *Comparative Politics* Vol. 30, No. 1, pp. 45–62.

Coleman, J.S. (1988) 'Social Capital in the Creation of Human Capital' in *American Journal of Sociology* Vol. 94, pp. S95.

Dukhira, C. (2002) *History of Mauritius: Experiments in Democracy* (Brijbasi Art Press, New Delhi).

Frankel, J.A. (2010) 'Mauritius: African Success Story'. HKS Faculty Research Working Paper Series RWP10–036, September.

Ibrahim, M.A. (1993) *Economic Miracle in the Indian Ocean: Can Mauritius Show the Way?* (Editions de l'Ocean Indien, Port Louis).

Kennedy, P. (1988) *African Capitalism: The Struggle for Ascendancy* (Cambridge University Press, Cambridge).

Mannick, A.R. (1989) *Mauritius: The Politics of Change* (Dodo Books, Mayfield, East Sussex).

Meade, J.E. et al. (1961) *The Economics and Social Structure of Mauritius: Report to the Government of Mauritius* (Methuen, London).

Naipaul, V.S. (1972) *The Overcrowded Barracoon* (Random House, New York).

Nath, S. and Madhoo, Y.N. (2008) 'A Shared Growth Story of Economic Success: The Case of Mauritius' in Ndulu, B.J., O'Connell, S.A. and Azam, J-P. (eds.) *The Political Economy of Economic Growth in Africa*, Vol. 2 (Cambridge University Press, Cambridge).

Seldon, S. (2005) *A Comprehensive History of Mauritius: From the Beginning to 2001.* 2nd edition (Mauritius Printing Specialists, Port Louis).

Subramanian, A. (2007) 'The Mauritian Success Story and its Lessons'. UNO-WIDER Research Paper No. 2009/36, June.

Subramanian, A. and Roy, D. (2002) 'Who Can Explain the Mauritian Miracle: Meade, Romer, Sachs or Rodrik' in Rodrik, D. (ed.) *In Search of Prosperity: Analytic Narratives on Economic Growth* (Princeton University Press, Princeton).

Taylor, T. (2008) 'Challenging and Resilient, 1968–2008: Genèse d'un Miracle'. L'Express Édition Spéciale: 40 Ans d'independence, 10 March, p. 40.

Wellisz, S. and Saw, P.L.S. (1993) 'Mauritius' in Findlay, R. and Welliz, S. (eds.) *The Political Economy of Poverty, Equity, and Growth* (Oxford University Press, New York).

World Bank (1993) *The East Asian Miracle: Economic Growth and Public Policy* (World Bank, Washington, D.C.).

8

Fraudulent Elections Lead to Pseudo-Democracy

How Can the Crisis of Democracy in Africa be Overcome?

GILBERT M. KHADIAGALA

> Transitions from authoritarian rule are inevitably fraught with
> uncertainty and danger. It is not democracy or elections that
> are so dangerous, but rather the chaos and mayhem that sitting
> regimes are capable of fomenting in their efforts to squeeze
> the most out of eroding power monopolies.
>
> — Frank Holmquist and Michael Ford

Introduction

Almost two decades since the inauguration of democratic experiments
in Africa, there has been widespread disillusionment about the role
of elections in the process of building democracy. Recent discussions
of democratic transitions in Africa have been less celebratory and
sanguine than the previous cheerleadership and triumphalism that
marked the so-called 'second liberation' struggles of the early 1990s.
Moreover, as more African countries have witnessed violent and
contested elections, critics have questioned whether Africa can evolve
systems that overcome the fragmentation and polarisation that still
scar most of these societies. Lofty intellectual analyses have focused

on the formidable obstacles of creating democracies on the basis of ethnic and sectarian divisions; the absence of a genuine middle class to underwrite participation and cosmopolitanism; and the limited number of enlightened and autonomous elites to propel broad-based agendas devoid of the narrow and selfish domain of elitism, ethnicity and sectarianism.

Rather than rehashing all these arguments, this chapter picks up on a few ideas that, while sympathetic to the structural impediments to democracy, are anchored more in the conventional and modest explanations that scholarly accounts often obscure. I proceed from the assumptions that elections and electoral dynamics that undergird the project of building democracy in Africa have not emanated from endogenous and demand-driven processes. After a very brief spell when African societies rose up in anger and protest against misrule and authoritarianism, the democratisation agenda all over Africa has settled in the comfortable inertia of complacency, largely attributable to the proliferation of a donor-driven industry around election financing, monitoring, observation and civil society building. The outcomes of donor-driven processes have invariably yielded the phenomenon of pseudo-democracy or democratisation on the cheap that reproduces Africa's fragile participation and governance systems. Democratisation on the cheap furnishes the illusion of political change, reinforces the patterns of weak democratisation and postpones the creation of solid institutions for democracy. After a short analysis of the structural explanation for Africa's weak democracies, the chapter reviews the experience of elections and democratisation over the last twenty years through specific themes and examples. It concludes with what needs to be done to return to the business of building local systems of accountability, participation and governance that draw inspiration from the universal norms and ethos of democratisation.

Africa's democratic travails: The structural arguments

Irrespective of one's disdain for academic theorising, it is difficult to escape the structural assumptions of the lackadaisical nature of democracies in Africa. Democracy, according to these perspectives, is underpinned by competition in ideas, vistas and voices at the social, economic and political levels, permitting regular changes in leadership, meaningful choices in the marketplace and freedoms that enshrine a whole array of individual and social rights. In 1966, Barrington Moore, an American sociologist, pithily summarised the dilemma of accomplishing these objectives: 'No bourgeois, No democracy'. Beneath this simplistic characterisation was Moore's profound message that democracies were, in fact, built on middle classes embedded in systems of property ownership (bourgeois) that dominate the social and economic spaces and influence political decisions in most industrialised economies. In subsequent rendering of this argument, scholars pessimistically spoke of the impossibility of building participatory and competitive democracies on the backs of large peasantries who were often isolated from each other through limited infrastructure, cultural differences and regional differentiations. Africa fitted the profile of peasant economies, which had years to go before attaining the 'democratic requisites', as scholars called them. In addition, African countries seemed to confirm the argument of being unprepared for democracy by virtue of the existence of narrowly based elites who often mobilised their ethnic constituencies against ethnic challengers within the same territorial boundaries.

Proponents of the structural explanations prevailed throughout the post-independence period as the admixture of weak economies and authoritarian leadership coincided agreeably with mass apathy and ethnic conflagrations to lay the brittle foundations for democracy in Africa. Moreover, Africa's degeneration into militarism and single-party regimes reinforced the narrow bases of middle classes that could not develop or organise outside state sponsorship and guardianship; instead of an autonomous bourgeoisie that would tactically shape the course of politics, the overriding picture in Africa was of parasitic economic classes beholden to what were, for the most part, ethnic state machines. Predictably, the contestation over state sinecures also bred the source of further fragmentation that brought African economies and polities to their knees before the end of the cold war in the 1990s and marked a departure from the way of organising politics.

Transition or interregnum? Toward the 'second liberation'

The combination of external pressures from donors, who were increasingly disillusioned with the course of politics in Africa, and internal protests that stemmed from economic impoverishment, opened a window of opportunity in reshaping the debates about Africa's democracy. The puzzle, however, was whether these pressures would produce significant momentum to constitute a transition from the old authoritarianism order to a new one of participation, accountability and transparency or whether the new phase would be a mere pause in an unchanging progression of events. Amidst grinding poverty and despondency, would proponents of structural arguments be shamed as African countries transited into prosperity through democracy? Or would the forces of the old order seize the opportunities occasioned by external and internal pressures to reorganise their authoritarian hold on society, confirming again the views of the structural theorists? Twenty years since the momentous events of the 1990s, the picture is emerging of an interregnum rather than a democratic transition.

At the heart of the resurgent order was the role of elections. Single-party and military regimes had given elections a bad name, holding them occasionally to legitimise their authoritarian rule and ward off prying opponents. With the inauguration of the new era, elections at first seemed to regain some meaning, particularly with the legalisation of opposition parties to lend a participatory flavour to the new order. A few African states saw attempts to rewrite the rules of political competition through national conventions at the onset of multiparty democracy. National conventions functioned as the transitional mechanism in nine Francophone countries – Benin, Gabon, Congo, Mali, Madagascar, Togo, Niger, Zaire and Chad – five of which experienced a successful change of government after the first elections. The bulk of the elections in the early to mid-1990s, however, were conducted against the backdrop of previous constitutional arrangements. As a result, regimes and parties that seemed under siege from multiple pressures recovered very quickly once they conceded to hold elections in the absence of significant alterations in the rules of competition. Overall, while a few incumbents lost power to political opponents after the 'second liberation', the majority of ruling parties used the elections to regenerate and regroup domestically and shore up their sagging international legitimacy.

Why did international legitimacy remain a critical calculus among African regimes? Fundamentally, there had been no appreciable changes in the economic circumstances that had prevailed since the 1980s; changes that had consigned African countries to a whole array of economic reforms to promote accountability and the new donor mantra of 'good governance'. For all intents and purposes, in the early 1990s, the era of donor budget support, social sector investment, the empowerment of women, debt relief and poverty alleviation was just beginning. Thus, as elections became a central component in the new legitimation regime of good governance, it was important for governments to seek to meet the minimal requirements of this bargain to keep the foreign aid taps open. Equally important, despite the invocation of democracy and good governance, donors had decidedly short attention spans to meet the weightier mandates of institution-building and cultural change that genuine democratic transitions entailed. Thus, by default, donors latched on to the cheaper versions of democratisation in Africa: electoral support, primarily through periodic election monitoring and observation, and 'building civil society'.

Election monitoring was popularised by the Ronald Reagan administration in the mid-1980s to guarantee that leftist regimes in

Central America, particularly the Sandinistas in Nicaragua, would not cheat in elections they were supposed to lose to their right-wing opponents. Election monitoring and observation stemmed from the assumptions that target states were either too internally divided or lacked the capacity to conduct fair and free elections. This explained the importance of an externally imposed surveillance mechanism that would guarantee outcomes that donors could live with. Moreover, the participation of the United Nations and non-governmental organisations (NGOs), such as the Carter Centre, in the initial monitoring processes furnished these elections with a global stamp of legitimacy as these countries gradually built the capacity to graduate out of international electoral surveillance. Subsequently, the international election monitoring and observation became a global industry linked both to the United Nations system, governments and NGOs. Thus, what were supposed to be transitional systems to help weak democracies and countries in conflict to overcome the momentary transitional pains of building participatory institutions transmogrified into permanent institutions.

Also vital in the inauguration of weak electoral and democratic processes was the externally driven push for civil society building. The enterprise of nurturing civil society as an adjunct of democratisation drew inspiration from the post-communist transitions in Eastern Europe where NGOs played significant roles in producing democratic breakthroughs. Civil society building in Africa started in earnest in the 1980s as an external project to sidestep the weak and seemingly incompetent state, particularly as donors sought alternative avenues of engagement to foster economic development and service delivery. In the mid-1990s, however, there were more frontal efforts to unleash the power of civil society to jumpstart democratisation. Proponents of this trend suggested that while a politically active civil society plays a central role in deepening democracy, in most emerging African democracies civic organisations had little knowledge of democratic principles and practices, hence the priority of promoting competent and active civil society. Subsequently, the discovery of civil society became a policy industry whereby NGOs, community-based organisations (CBOs) and other bodies sought donor financing to ostensibly contribute to Africa's democratic maturation.

The global civil society building regime was misguided from the outset in the assumption that NGOs could be steady vehicles for regenerating democracy in Africa. Almost twenty years since the bid to galvanise African civil society, there is very little to show in terms of its contribution to democratisation; instead what has emerged is the proliferation of multiple and competitive institutions whose *raison d'être* is the search for donor funds apparently for the cause of building participatory structures. NGOs have become a vast industry concerned more with perpetuating themselves in the donor funding supply chains than in the business of promoting accountable or participatory governance. More savvy politicians in some African countries such as Tanzania have also joined the bandwagon, forming NGOs to leverage donor resources that underwrite narrow patronage-based networks. No wonder the quality of these legislatures has suffered immensely. More pertinent, intellectual energies that should have been devoted to building participatory institutions, such as strong political parties with clear mandates to mobilise wider citizenries for national reconstruction and agenda-building, have been frittered and diverted into unproductive civil society activities that only succeed in lining the dollar pockets of international NGOs and their local 'partners'. Rather than promoting learning that benefits society in the long run, African universities are perennial prey to hungry NGOs that poach valuable expertise. In turn, this expertise does not produce innovative knowledge, but recycled policy briefs that regurgitate the gospel of building civil society.

The experiences of African democratisation
Democracies that germinated in the inhospitable climate of external superintendence via election monitoring and civil society construction had few chances of 'consolidation', despite repeated elections. Instead, the foremost pattern since the mid-1990s has been the coalescence of

non-democratic forces and actors around the agenda of democratisation and the profound reversal of the gains produced by preliminary
impetus of external pressure and internal protests. Elections that
were held in the first phase of the 'transition' in the 1990s produced
few remarkable changes in rules, regimes and leadership. Throughout
most of Africa, one-party regimes perennially invoked the language
of good governance and 'free and fair' elections to retool themselves
and legitimate their power. As rewards for conducting elections and
overcoming the early hurdles of democratisation, international donors
resumed aid and assistance to regimes even though these elections
were hardly free and fair. Capturing what became the pet phrase of
international monitoring missions in African elections was the evasive
phraseology used by the Commonwealth Observer Mission after the
Kenyan elections in 1991: 'In many instances, the results directly
reflect, however imperfectly, the will of the Kenyan people.'

Once regimes that had no real commitment to democratic practices mended fences with donors, there emerged complex cat-and-
mouse games between African and external actors around elections.
For the most part, African countries without any stakes in democracy
shifted the burden of election organisation and financing to donors.
The logic for this shift was simple: since donors want elections, they
should fund them. As most countries increasingly regarded elections
as ritualistic exercises to ward off the prying eyes of donors, they
made only perfunctory attempts to invest in endogenous mechanisms
of electoral financing or administration. That is why, at the turn of
every election, countries made frantic appeals for donor funding of
elections and, in some instances, if donor funding was not available
countries postponed elections. Thus devoid of local content and
meaning, elections inevitably made limited contributions to political
change. For their part, donors continued to invest in flawed elections
on the assumptions that they would, over time, create the circumstances for the learning of democratic practices. Some donors justified
the flawed elections on the basis of cultural and structural factors.
Consequently, most countries were held to minimal electoral stand-

ards that they were not even expected to meet, reinforcing the half-hearted electoral endorsements by international observation missions.

Apart from electoral financing, there was an alliance of sorts between donors and authoritarian and semi-democratic African governments around questions of building the institutions for competitive elections. Despite widespread consensus that political parties were the essential ingredients of democratisation, throughout the early phase of African democratisation, authoritarian regimes were at the forefront of disorganising and dismembering opposition parties. Although opposition parties faced teething problems of building constituencies beyond their narrow regional and ethnic bases, the most formidable challenges stemmed from their inability to organise. Donors, on the other hand, refrained from engagement in political party development, afraid of government accusations of political interference. Yet, African governments showed little reluctance when the same donors provided funding to NGOs in the name of building civil society. As a result, numerous NGOs proliferated without any organic links to the goals of strengthening participation. Besides, authoritarian regimes increasingly tolerated the funding of NGOs because they allowed governments to abdicate their social and economic responsibilities.

From the late 1990s, some African governments tried to underwrite the weak democratic dispensations with institutional rules that would foster pluralism and enhance political competition. Borrowing from the experiences of the national constitutional conventions, these efforts culminated in constitutional amendments and reforms, particularly the creation of impartial and independent election monitoring bodies, more freedom for opposition groups and expansion of media freedoms. Like before, however, the breadth and depth of constitutional reforms hinged on whether ruling parties and alliances could countenance constitutional changes that could potentially undercut their power. In some cases, mass violence and agitation forced constitutional reforms on reluctant elites who then caved in only to regain ground after the pressure had dissipated. More critical, there are few successful models of constitutional changes in Africa that have reversed the fortunes of authoritarian leaders; most countries are still at a very elementary stage of launching reforms that would undo the stranglehold of dominant parties on the political and economic spheres. In Nigeria, for instance, there have been persistent calls since the first multiparty elections in 1999 for constitutional reforms through a national consultative process, but none of the democratically elected governments have entertained such reforms. Instead, after the 2007 elections, which observers termed the worst elections in Nigeria's history, the government contemplated some changes in the electoral rules, oblivious to the fact that electoral reforms need to be anchored in broader constitutional reforms.

Tentative steps toward constitutional reforms have been the exception rather than the rule. For the majority of African countries, the reform process has been accurately characterised by one step forward and two steps backwards. Constitutional changes that have weakened parliaments, increased presidential tenures and clamped down on opposition parties are the norm in countries from Algeria to Uganda. In the latter, Yoweri Museveni, who has been in power since 1986, has constantly intimidated and cajoled parliament to amend the constitution to prolong his power indefinitely. Since donors weighed on him to permit multiple parties in 2005, he has consistently used elections to legitimise what essentially remains a military regime. In Burkina Faso, Blaise Compaoré, who has been in power since 1987, is fond of changing the constitution to prolong his tenure. In 1991, Burkina Faso changed the constitution to restrict the presidency to a seven-year term. In 2000, however, the constitution was amended to reduce the presidential term to five years, permitting President Compaoré's re-election in 2005. In early 2010, Compaoré announced that he would run again for re-election in November 2010; more poignantly, his party has pledged that after he wins again, it is prepared to change the constitution so that Compaoré can run in the presidential elections in 2015. In Angola, long-awaited presidential elections were expected to be held in 2009, but faced countless delays, and in January 2010, parliament approved a new constitution abolishing direct elections for the president. This meant that President José Eduardo dos Santos, who has been in power since 1979, will be in office until 2012, when the current parliamentary mandate runs out. In addition, the constitutional amendment strengthened the power of the presidency, prompting opposition parties to accuse the government of destroying democracy.

In countries such as Gabon, Togo, and potentially, Egypt, Libya, Senegal and Uganda, where there were expectations that democratic change would emanate from the demise of dominant leaders, the outcomes are forms of dynastic rule that have further undermined democratisation. Although Faure Gnassingbé (Togo), Ali Ben Bongo (Gabon), Karim Wade (Senegal), Gamal Mubarak (Egypt) and Muhoozi Museveni (Uganda) purport to represent generational leadership changes, in reality they denote the institutional inertia and culture of authoritarianism and militarism that their fathers visited on these countries. Militarism has also recently resurfaced on the African political landscape through the overthrow of civilian regimes in Madagascar, Mauritania, Niger and Guinea. Attempts to ostracise these regimes through the African Union's (AU) principle that condemns unconstitutional changes in government have failed miserably as African countries have been unable to marshal consensus against militarism. In Niger, a military coup took place in February 2010 when renegade soldiers stormed the presidential palace and deposed President Mamadou Tandja, who had been accused by opposition forces of anti-democratic practices. Where the military has intervened to prevent the return to a semblance of democratic order, as in the case of Guinea in December 2008, the intervention compounds the political paralysis. After the first round of presidential elections in Guinea in June 2010 produced a stalemate, the leading presidential candidates faced off in a second round in November 2010, in a process that was marred by violence and recriminations. The political stand-off in Madagascar since the military propelled Andry Rajoelina to power in March 2009 also demonstrates the political stalemate that ensues in the face of power imbalances between civilian and military institutions.

Most countries that have held elections to mark a departure from civil conflicts have not fared any better in terms of political renewal. In countries such as Burundi, Côte d'Ivoire, Democratic Republic of the Congo (DRC), Sierra Leone, Liberia and Rwanda, the international community understandably committed considerable resources in electoral processes to jump-start post-conflict reconstruction. But most of them can barely run credible elections once the United Nations and other actors have moved on. Burundi is instructive here. After almost twelve years of civil war, Burundi held parliamentary and presidential elections in 2005 where a Hutu president, Pierre Nkurunziza, was elected. In the subsequent elections in June 2010, opposition parties boycotted the elections claiming massive fraud by Nkurunziza's party. In effect, given the intolerance that undergirds Burundi's politics, it is premature to characterise it as a post-conflict country. In neighbouring DRC, following the landmark presidential and parliamentary elections in 2006 that were funded by donors, expectations that these elections would lead to a legitimate democratic dispensation were frustrated by President Joseph Kabila's draconian rule. There are increasing doubts as to whether Kabila will be able to conduct transparent and free elections in 2011, particularly since the United Nations will have wound down its mission. Similarly, Rwanda held its second elections in August 2010 since the genocide in 1994 against the backdrop of increasing intolerance of criticism by President Paul Kagame and the blatant intimidation and imprisonment of opposition leaders. With no real opposition, Rwandan elections allowed Kagame to legitimate his excessive centralisation of power.

Before the recent incidences of electoral violence in Kenya and Zimbabwe jolted African and international efforts to seek solutions, many countries, including Kenya itself, had a history of severe violence before and after elections. Rather than representing a new phenomenon, electoral violence and contested elections are part of the unresolved dynamic of weak democracies that have struggled to build participation on the basis of fragile social consensus. Disputed polls held in 2000 in Côte d'Ivoire led to widespread violence that laid the groundwork for the division of the country between the rebel-held north and the government-held south. After repeated delays, Côte d'Ivoire held presidential elections at the end of October 2010 in which none of the candidates could garner a majority. The run-off presidential elections in November 2010 led to renewed strife between the north and south after President Laurent Gbagbo refused to vacate office. In 2005, Ethiopia held elections in which nearly 200 opposition supporters were killed and a comprehensive crackdown on the opposition followed, with the detention of opposition leaders. Furthermore, after the 2005 elections, the government systematically marginalised opposition regions, denying them foreign aid, which it receives in large numbers because of President Meles Zenawi's professed 'development' record. Predictably in the May 2010 elections, only one opposition member of parliament was elected in Ethiopia's 536-seat parliament.

The solutions to electoral violence are sturdy institutional rules that inure these societies from electoral uncertainties and stabilise competition, but the distinctive outcomes in Kenya and Zimbabwe also reveal that leadership and elite consensus matter. Both countries (and more recently political parties in Zanzibar) opted for a transitional government of national unity (GNU) to manage the fragmentation that stemmed from the electoral violence. The GNUs were, in principle, transitional vehicles to construct new rules of competition to stem future violence. In the Kenya case, a functional working relationship among the key leaders plus growing fear about descent into state failure helped galvanise the move toward a new constitution that may, if implemented, restore a semblance of stability to the Kenyan electoral process. Zimbabwe, however, has witnessed a profound leadership stalemate from the outset; both during and after the negotiations for the Global Political Agreement, President

Mugabe and Morgan Tsvangirai were incapable of forging a relationship that would resolve the deep-seated problems that bedevil
Zimbabwe. In addition, the absence of elite consensus was compounded by the inordinate reliance by the two leaders on regional
mediators in circumstances where they should have, like their Kenyan
counterparts, sought local solutions. With the constitution-making
process so far behind and the looming end of the two-year GNU,
Zimbabwe stands on the precipice of another electoral calamity and
potential return to civil war.

What is to be done and where do we go from here?

Fraudulent elections and the resultant cheap democracies in Africa
are the logical outcomes of the global trends that have privileged
easy and quick democratic fixes at the expense of local ownership
of the difficult challenges of institution-building and behavioural
change. Democratisation on the cheap has engendered weak participatory systems that have fortified local power imbalances, particularly
by emboldening regimes that have only feeble stakes in participation
and accountable systems of power. Approaches out of this quagmire
require the return to a healthy balance between international and
local responsibilities. Weak democracies thrive on an international
regime of irresponsibility where resources and responsibilities for
democratisation fall disproportionately on external actors. The era
of externally driven democratisation is over: Germany and Japan are
the post-world war exceptions that required enormous military and
economic investments by the United States. Post-cold war attempts
to replicate the previous imperial ventures in Afghanistan and Iraq
are only reinforcing the limits of exogenous democratisation and
stabilisation processes. International actors such as the United Nations
have also confronted obstacles in engineering democratic outcomes
in war-torn states.

Despite the disappointment with pseudo-democracies, opinion
polls in most African countries reveal that citizens remain optimistic
about the possibility of building democracies even against the back-

ground of prevailing limits to create more representative and participatory democracies. Although Africa does not reflect the prerequisites often associated with democracy (economic development, a sizeable working class and a developed market economy), the optimism for a transition rather than an interregnum inheres in the progress made over the last two decades and the growth of role models in democratisation. Furthermore, the optimism is driven partly by the African resilience of overcoming obstacles. But questions about whether Africa can transcend the era of strongmen and pseudo-democracy and move into an era of constitutionalism and competition hinge not just on hopefulness, but on practical steps that African societies need to embark upon, as I illustrate below.

Firstly, the global system of election financing, observation and monitoring is broken and needs a quick fix out of existence. Africa should get out of the pattern of irresponsibility fostered by the regime of election financing and monitoring. Democracy on the cheap underwritten by donors is at the heart of the faltering participation processes. Once donors engineered elections from above rather than local actors demanding them for their own benefit, the temptation was for regimes to hold them grudgingly to appease the donors. Since the 1990s, this dependence has not changed a bit and most African countries are reluctant to wean themselves from it because the system reproduces itself through complex international and national actors and infrastructures around elections. If elections are important, they should be budgeted from local resources; neither the United Nations Development Programme (UNDP) nor the European Union (EU) should be in the business of African elections that they constantly deride and tolerate. The tolerance for, and increasing acceptance of flawed elections, has contributed to strengthening the prevailing solidification of authoritarian and semi-democratic regimes. This invariably emboldens authoritarian regimes in their use of electoral violence and other malpractices to stay in power. When elections are not regarded as national priorities, governments have no incentives to invest in them. Elections need to be intrinsically linked to notions of sovereignty with dignity and responsibility, where countries mobilise national resources to guarantee the routine but monumental tasks of power rotation, the socialisation of new leadership and the creation of responsive and reciprocal institutions between the governors and citizens.

Secondly, there should be recognition of the trade-offs between creating functional political parties for sustainable democracy and the inordinate focus on building NGOs. The disproportionate investment in NGO activities has sapped energy and resources from political parties, the fundamental institutions for participation and accountability. This is not an argument for clamping down on NGOs (as authoritarian governments are wont to do), but it speaks to the priorities that should inform future institution-building. A case could be made for promoting NGOs that deliver social and economic services rather than the amorphous and multi-purpose 'activist' ones that seem to litter the African political landscape. Leaders of such NGOs should devote more time building political parties than engaging in elusive 'civic education'. Political parties have always been the weakest links in democratisation in Africa, beset by problems of unsatisfactory leadership, poor organisation, limited constituencies, few resources and harassment from incumbent parties. If half of the donor funds committed to civil society building were devoted to party development, there would be a significant improvement in the quality of competitive institutions. Ultimately, local financing of credible opposition parties is the most realistic approach to building parties that are based in local dynamics of accountability and responsibility. Local financing of parties may also deepen transparency around electoral financing, particularly by reducing the abuse of national resources by incumbent parties. Solid parties with coherent leadership, ideas and programmes may also transform the sorry state of African legislatures which still struggle with the legacies of pseudo-democracies: lack of consequential input in national deliberations, co-optation into authoritarian executive structures and parliamentary absenteeism. Again, if many countries invested in educated and enlightened legislatures rather than legalising briefcase NGOs, the quality of representative institutions would improve markedly.

Thirdly, as we debate Africa's democratic future, it is futile to run away from the structural analyses that posit the preconditions of democracy on firm structures of property rights, a thriving middle class and the expansion of the private sector. While these perspectives are often lost in the intellectual debates about the tensions between markets and states, they need to be at the centre of vigorous policy discourses about creating meaningful democratisation within a broad-based local socio-economic base. Conventional thinking about governments as providers of macroeconomic and political stability, public goods and friends of private enterprise are now part of routine wisdom about state-market relations in Africa. But this wisdom is rarely incorporated in the debates on elections and democratisation: how do expanding private-sector activities contribute to the building of genuine middle classes who then have stakes in participation and good governance? What are the consequences of parasitic middle classes on political participation and the expansion of electoral options? How can Africa's vast natural resources be harnessed for economic growth, poverty reduction and social equity – the preconditions for stable democracy?

Finally, there is currently a false trade-off between democracy and development that has arisen from two major trends. Firstly, it has been popularised by external actors caught in the so-called donor's dilemma: whether donors should support authoritarian regimes, such as Ethiopia and Rwanda, who supposedly have a stellar development record. The donor's dilemma is compounded by the reluctance to withhold economic assistance despite the egregious democratic and human rights violations. Realistically, the donor's dilemma obscures the double standards that are at the core of engagement with Africa: countries with democratic traditions continually invoke the impossibility of attaining these values abroad. This is the mentality that also contributes to the generous support for flawed elections and the reproduction of semi-democratic regimes in Africa.

Development cannot be disengaged from the dynamics of losers and gainers, issues that are mediated by power relations. There are few developmental states in Africa because the use of power has always been tilted to achieve development outcomes that benefit only narrow and sectarian interests. Without genuine democratisation of power and the establishment of institutions that tie the hands of errant elites, development will remain an elusive goal. Thus, donors need to be reminded that the donor's dilemma is not an African problem but one of their own creation. For instance, the practice of donor budget support for authoritarian governments in Africa has, over the years, undermined not just the democratic project but state capacity to collect local taxes for endogenous development. Countries that do not receive budget support have innovated in mobilising local revenues and resources in more useful developmental directions.

Secondly, there is currently a detrimental distraction in the development discourse about emulating the 'developmental states' in Asia, particularly the Chinese model. Some African elites have opportunistically conjured up the Chinese development model in their attempts to deny democracy at home. Often these arguments conflate China as a trading partner with China as a development model. As stated above, authoritarian regimes in Africa have not produced the developmental outcomes of China in the past; neither are they going to do so in future.

In Africa's quest to build development with participation, China should be a trading partner, not a model. Despite its developmental outcomes, which are due to a myriad set of conditions, China is an authoritarian political system that would be dangerous for Africa to emulate. Moreover, as a culturally homogenous state, China can have the luxury of not being a democracy while in Africa, managing ethnic diversities makes democracy an imperative. For this reason, the populist campaign by repressive regimes for the 'Chinese way' of development is disingenuous, framed largely to distract attention from the crisis of pseudo-democracies.

GILBERT M. KHADIAGALA is the Jan Smuts Professor of International Relations and Acting Head of the School of Social Sciences at the University of the Witwatersrand in Johannesburg.

References and further reading

Holmquist, F. and Ford, M. (1992) 'Kenya: Slouching Toward Democracy' in *Africa Today* Vol. 39, No. 3, p. 23.

International Peace Institute (2010) 'Election-Related Disputes and Political Violence: Strengthening the Role of the African Union in Preventing, Managing, and Resolving Conflict'. Report of the AU Panel of the Wise, The African Union Series, July.

Lindberg, S.I. (2006) *Democracy and Elections in Africa* (Johns Hopkins University Press, Baltimore).

——— (2009) *Democratization by Elections: A New Mode of Transition?* (Johns Hopkins University Press, Baltimore).

Lipset, S.M. (1959) 'Some Social Requisites for Democracy: Economic Development and Poltical Legitimacy' in *American Political Science Review* Vol. 53, No. 1, pp. 69–105.

Matlosa, K., Khadiagala, G.M. and Shale, V. (eds.) (2010) *When Elephants Fight: Preventing and Managing Election-Related Conflicts in Africa* (Electoral Institute for the Sustainability of Democracy in Africa, Johannesburg).

Moore, B. (1966) *Social Origins of Dictatorships and Democracies: Lord and Peasant in the Making of the Modern World* (Beacon Press, Boston).

Wallis, W. (2010) 'Perfidious Donors Betray Africa's Democracy' in *Financial Times*, 10 August.

9

Traditional Agriculture
How Can Productivity be Improved?

MANDIVAMBA RUKUNI

Introduction

One of the most serious post-independence errors of judgement by African nations is the lack of political wisdom to give priority to agriculture and rural development. The needed long-term public sector investments into this key sector are still lacking. This chapter is premised on a perceived need to deal with issues of agricultural development in a broad context. Moreover, issues of smallholder agricultural development can no longer be divorced from issues of democracy, politics and governance on the continent. Global trends now have significant impact on the potential for recovery and growth of African agriculture. In particular are the negative impacts of climate change, the energy crisis and food aid policies which dampen long-term growth prospects. In addition, and central to this chapter, is the need to intensify the search for workable solutions to increasing the productivity and competitiveness of African agriculture.

In 1956, when the wave of political independence started in Africa, the continent was food secure, self-sufficient and, in general, Africa was a net food exporter. Today, Africa is mostly hungry and it is the most food insecure continent in the world, causing a slow-down in productivity and growth. Ironically, governments in rich industrial countries, where farmers are few in number and already productive, tend to support investments in farming more than governments in poor agricultural countries where hunger persists and productivity is lagging. Sub-Saharan Africa, where 50% of the food insecure are farm households, has not only had slow progress in accelerating agricultural growth but is typically vulnerable to shocks such as conflicts, climate change, high and volatile food prices and financial crises. Agro ecosystems in sub-Saharan Africa are severely constrained by factors such as droughts, poor infrastructure, undeveloped input and output markets, as well as weak governance and institutions.

The importance of developing agriculture in Africa is central because nearly 75% of the population is rural. The social and economic progress of these people is largely dependent on increasing the productivity of agriculture and natural resources. Agriculture is the backbone of the African economy and will continue to be so for the foreseeable future. Even in economies where agriculture contributes a single-digit percentage to the gross domestic product (GDP), the performance of the agricultural sector still determines the economic fate of most people and all other sectors continue to depend significantly on the performance of agriculture. Unfortunately, agriculture in most countries on the continent is substantially underperforming relative to its potential. Water control and irrigation management, particularly small-scale water harvesting, irrigation and drainage systems, are critical for averting famines and developing a more productive and competitive agriculture. But in Africa, only 7% of arable land is irrigated, compared to 14% in Latin America and the Caribbean, 38% in East and Southeast Asia, and 42% in South Asia. Fertiliser use in Africa currently amounts to about 9 kg/ha of arable land per year, compared to 120 kg/ha in South Asia. Meanwhile, Africa utilises only 1.6% of its water resources, compared to 14% in Asia. The challenge posed by the HIV/AIDS epidemic is now felt in the rural areas posing a heavy burden on millions of people who are infected and their families, both in terms of their capacity to produce and to buy their food.

Public and private sector investments in the prime movers of agriculture are the primary solution to achieving sustainable improvement in agricultural productivity. The prime movers that require substantial investment to achieve sustainable agricultural development are as follows:

- Investments in land development and improved land tenure systems for land users;
- New technology produced by public and private investments in agricultural research or imported from the global research system and adapted to local conditions;
- Human capital in the form of professional, managerial and technical skills produced by investments in schools, agricultural colleges, faculties of agriculture and on-the-job training and experience;
- Sustained growth of biological capital (genetic and husbandry improvements of crops, livestock and forests) and physical capital investments in dams, wells, irrigation, storage facilities, roads, and so on;
- Improvements in the performance of farmer service and support institutions such as marketing, credit, research and extension, and settlement; and
- Favourable economic policy environment and political support for agriculture in the long term.

Significance of agriculture in overall economic development

The agricultural sector in Africa contributes an estimated 35% of the region's gross national product (GNP), employs up to 80% of the total labour force and accounts for up to 40% of the total foreign exchange earnings. The future of Africa is closely intertwined with the development of its agricultural sector. In countries that are not dominated by mining, agriculture is the largest contributor to total foreign exchange earnings. According to an article by C. Peter Timmer in the journal *International Agricultural Development*, general economic growth has to be preceded or at least accompanied by solid agricultural growth. Agriculture has historically played this central role since the English Agricultural Revolution, which paved the way for the Industrial Revolution. This transformation process still applies today. Africa will not be an exception, neither is it likely that Africa will be able to jump this vital stage of development. The traditional roles of agriculture are essential in overall economic growth and these include:

- Providing adequate and affordable food for increasing populations. The process of industrialisation and urbanisation is more efficient when food is cheaper for the growing industrial labour force;
- Supplying raw materials to grow and diversify domestic industrial sectors;
- Releasing labour for the growing industrial sector;
- Enlarging the size of the effective market for the products of the domestic industrial sector;
- Providing employment and livelihood as well as alleviating poverty for a large percentage of the rural population;
- Earning and saving foreign exchange through exports; and
- Accumulating domestic savings for investment and capital formation.

Timmer (1998) provides a conceptual framework for agricultural and economic transformation which shows four stages of development as follows:

- **Stage one**: Where agriculture has been adequately nurtured and starts growing and creating new wealth at a rate that allows direct and indirect taxation and this feeds into other major public assets and infrastructure.
- **Stage two**: Where agricultural growth becomes a direct contributor to overall economic growth through greater links with industry, improving efficiency of product and factor markets, and continued mobilisation of rural resources.

- **Stage three**: Where agriculture is fully integrated in the market economy. Prices of food and the share of food in urban budgets continue to decline.
- **Stage four**: Where agriculture is part of an industrial economy. Productivity and efficiency of agriculture is a major issue, and environmental and other concerns assume greater significance.

Africa in general, it would appear, is only entering the first stage of the transformation. Some countries in Asia and Latin America, on the other hand, seem to have entered this first stage with some in the second and third stages. In the 1950s, it could be argued that there was little difference in the level of development among the three regions. As agriculture goes through these stages, its share in the national accounts figures diminishes, and increasingly the population becomes more urbanised. African politicians have unfortunately misinterpreted this as a decline in the importance of agriculture. In reality, agriculture is politically alive in industrial economies; even where farmers and rural people represent only 2–3% of the population, they still command the attention of governments.

One unfortunate situation in Africa today is the premature movement of large numbers of rural people into urban areas. This rural to urban migration is unfortunate and premature because most of these people do not have jobs or homes in the urban-industrial sector. Most do not possess the life and economic skills to be gainfully employed in the urban areas. As a result, urban decay is on the increase in Africa as the over-stretched infrastructure breeds ill-health, crime and social breakdown of family structures. Moreover, the movement is largely by young adults. This drains the rural areas of the young and energetic force that is desperately needed for agricultural development in these areas.

Why the focus on productivity?

High and sustained rates of agricultural growth, largely driven by productivity growth, will be necessary if African countries are to accelerate economic growth. This is because agricultural growth has powerful leverage effects on the rest of the economy, especially in the early stages of development and economic transformation, when agriculture accounts for large shares of national income, employment and foreign trade. The food, agriculture and national resources sector in Africa is strategic to the long-term growth and development of the economies. And since the majority of the estimated half billion African population lives in rural areas, and their livelihood is tied to agriculture directly and/or indirectly, it follows therefore that this sector will continue to be the backbone of the African economies for a few more decades. Agricultural productivity in Africa has hardly increased during the last four decades. Since then, Asia and Latin America have seen yields of staple crops more than double (to about 3 tons/ha in Asia, and about 2.6 in Latin America). In Africa, the yield increases of staple crops have been modest at about 1 ton/ha. In fact, in many rural areas, where 70% of the poorest 1.2 billion in the world live and work, agricultural productivity is declining sharply. Much of this is due to land degradation, decline in soil fertility and climate change.

In many cases, declining agricultural productivity forces people to encroach on forests, grasslands and wetlands, creating a downward spiral of further environmental degradation and poverty. Improving agricultural productivity is thus essential to the sustainable development goal of reducing both poverty and stress on the environment. Problems posed by climate change, droughts and floods contribute to the unsustainable and unproductive use of land resources and, consequently, poverty.

African agriculture has undergone major market reforms and external liberalisation during the past three decades. All in all, however, these reforms have failed to generate sufficient supply responses to enable agriculture to play a central role as a main driver of growth and poverty reduction. Instead, food availability per capita has declined by 3% in sub-Saharan Africa since 1990, in sharp contrast with increases of more than 30% in Asia and 20% in Latin America.

Also, Africa currently imports 25% of its food grains. The poor performance of African agriculture implies that the continent has been lagging behind in adapting to the structural transformation of the international agro-food market which has opened up new business opportunities for developing-country producers, while at the same time increasing competitive pressures. In 2006, the African average cereal yield was only 40% of the Southeast Asian average.

This alone explains the significant difference in overall economic growth, particularly between Asia and Africa. In the fight against poverty, hunger, malnutrition and unemployment, Africa has to get its agriculture moving and focus squarely on productivity and competitiveness. African countries participate in the expansion of world agricultural trade but their contribution is relatively small. Looking at the evolution since the mid-1980s, the share of African products in world agricultural imports has actually declined from 5.4% in 1985 to 3.2% in 2006. Moreover, agricultural exports are highly concentrated in a small number of countries. Africa's share in global trade dropped from 6% in 1980 to about 3% in 2007. Eight of the ten lowest ranked countries on the Global Competitiveness Index are sub-Saharan African.

Around the world, the ratio of arable land to population is steadily declining. Between 1960 and 2000, it declined by about 40%, but in developing nations the decline has been most rapid. In Africa, the ratio of arable land to population declined by 55% in the same period. Over the last three decades, and as discussed later in more detail, productivity increases in agriculture have largely been through increases in area cultivated as opposed to yield. Productivity increases are therefore needed in terms of increases in yield per unit area, as well as per unit of labour. In addition, the costs of production have to decline for a unit of produce. Competitiveness is partly a function of productivity since volume and lower production costs allow for more effective penetration of local and export markets. Competitiveness in terms of efficient and effective supply of local and export markets, however, requires additional capacities and competencies.

213

The quality of produce at the production end is central for enhancing the product quality, particularly for niche markets. The ability to penetrate and maintain market share requires timely access to knowledge and information on market trends and traits, as well as technology to allow cost-effective production, processing and packaging. Africa has to meet the twin target of getting its agriculture moving, and at the same time integrating the rural with the industrial economy in order to accelerate overall economic growth, incomes, employment and food security.

Recent trends in African agricultural performance

Productivity levels of smallholder agriculture in Africa, in terms of both land and labour productivity, still lag far behind other developing regions. Within Africa, the situation is especially marked in southern and eastern Africa. Low growth rates in cereal yields and production in Africa have translated over the years into falling per capita food production and increased imports, contributing to high levels of food insecurity at both national and household levels (20% of African cereal consumption depends on imports, including food aid). Much of the growth of output in Africa has been due to expanded use of land, labour and livestock, until the 1990s, when recent estimates imply that productivity growth has played an increasingly larger role. Total factor productivity (TFP) grew at an annual rate of 1.3% on average during the 1990s, accounting for approximately 40% of the 3.1% annual growth in agricultural output.

Growth in the traditional inputs of land, labour and livestock accounted for the other 60% of agricultural output growth. To achieve the desired agricultural growth rate of 6% or more will require TFP growth rates of 4.4% per year. This is because the growth in land and labour inputs are unlikely to continue to grow at the same rate as in the past, and productivity must increase at a faster rate for output to grow. The expansion of the labour force is tied to the demographics of the region and changes in the recent past show a reduction in the growth of labour. While the economically active population in sub-Saharan Africa increased at an average growth rate of 2.1% during 1981–90, this growth was reduced to 1.9% per year in the 1990s and projected to be even less in the post-2000 era. Current world food price increases, propelled by a mixture of structural and temporary factors, are allied with diminishing food stocks and difficulties in accessing food by some communities, particularly in sub-Saharan Africa. During this same period, the value of food imports into Africa has increased from US$4.2 billion to US$7 billion.

The uniqueness of African agriculture: Issues and challenges for agricultural productivity in Africa

Africa has some unique features that differ from Asia, where the green revolution had a positive impact on productivity. Recognising these is an essential prerequisite to the formulation of strategies and priorities in raising productivity, particularly as far as science and technology are concerned. This is because these features not only present as unique features but are the actual factors affecting the performance of African agriculture. These delineate the options available to science and technology to influence productivity and imply that African agriculture is more likely to experience numerous 'rainbow evolutions' that differ in nature and extent among the many systems, rather than one green revolution as in Asia, where irrigated rice-wheat systems predominated. Because of these features, more investment in agricultural research and development (R&D) per unit of productivity gain will likely be required in Africa as compared to other continents. The unique features of African agricultural systems are as follows:

Diversity of cropping systems

If one drives around in most parts of rural Africa, one notices the many combinations and permutations of various crops. There is also a great diversity of staple crops: maize, sorghum, cassava, plantain, cooking banana, rice, yam, and so on. This means that increasing productivity requires investment in a lot of different crops. Most staple crops are grown under rain-fed conditions. This differs from Asia where the whole green revolution was based on a few crops, namely rice and wheat, grown mainly under irrigation.

Thin rural infrastructure

Poor infrastructure, especially rural and trunk roads, constitute another significant challenge to agriculture in Africa. While one half of the rural population of South Asia lives within a one-hour journey of a market, nearly 50% of African farmers still live five hours or more from a market. Not only are there few rural roads, but transport costs in Africa are among the highest in the world, reaching as much as 77% of the value of exports. Poor infrastructure and information leave farmers effectively isolated from regional or international markets.

Undeveloped markets

The commodity market structure is generally characterised by a lack of market linkages. There is a lack of functioning competitive markets as a result of low purchasing power in domestic markets and poor access to global markets due to trade distortions such as agricultural subsidies in rich countries. This means limited opportunities for adding value by post-harvest processing and high post-harvest losses, which are estimated at 30% for grains and 50% for other more rapidly perishable products. Where opportunities exist, farmers can rarely take advantage of them because they are not empowered or sufficiently informed.

Minimal mechanisation

Smallholder farmers in Africa still rely on manual labour. The productivity of agriculture will therefore benefit from access by these small farmers to appropriate machinery that reduces the drudgery of labour and that can be manufactured locally and made available at reasonable prices.

Limited seasonal financing

Rural financial markets are under-developed in Africa and this reduces the capacity to finance their seasonal expenses.

Competition with food aid

Often food aid over time increases the dependency of rural households; in addition food aid can dampen local markets leading to poor prices and reduced local incentives to produce.

Dominance of weathered and inherently infertile soils

Environmental degradation affects soil nutrient depletion, soil erosion and the destruction of water catchment areas and salination. The soils of the continent's vast land surface are typically old and leached; 16% of the surface land is classified as very low in nutrients as opposed to just 4% in Asia. An estimated 65% of sub-Saharan Africa's agricultural land is degraded as a result of water and soil erosion and chemical degradation. African soils are estimated to be losing nutrients worth US$4 billion per annum. Yet farmers use fertiliser at a rate of only about 8 kg/ha and less in smallholder farming, compared to a target of 50 kg/ha. This may not be surprising, given the cost that sub-Saharan African farmers must pay for fertiliser, which is up to three times that paid by their counterparts in Brazil, India or Thailand.

Weak agricultural support systems

There is an under-investment in R&D and infrastructure which leads to a lack of conducive economic and political enabling environments, inadequate manpower and poor skills for planning, policy formulation and analysis. In addition, poor budgetary outlays for programme implementation and monitoring and evaluation all contribute to this situation. Limited government capacity, especially where centralised government dominates, leads to unclear or inadequate sector policies and strategies with respect to identifying proper sequencing of development priorities.

Poor agricultural policies

There are trade-offs between present-day political gains versus long-term development policies in Africa.

Solutions for African agriculture's productivity challenge: An elaboration to the prime movers

Favourable policy environment and political will

The single most important step in getting agriculture moving in Africa is generating greater political commitment to this sector by politicians, parliamentarians, policy-makers and ministries of planning and ministries of finance. Greater fiscal commitment to agriculture will provide a more conducive policy environment. This will create the appropriate environment for long-term and sustainable investments, particularly from the private sector. Macroeconomic stability and favourable pricing and marketing policies are crucial for providing the necessary incentives for generating a supply response.

Of particular importance and practical significance in the creation of a favourable policy environment for agriculture is the strengthening of governance and institutions. In a 2009 report, the Food and Agriculture Organization (FAO) notes that in the 1960s and 1970s, support to small farmers through the provision of inputs, the purchase of their output, credit and extension services were provided by public institutions and national marketing boards. In the 1980s, in line with market liberalisation policy and as part of the structural adjustment programmes, these institutions were weakened and in some cases even dismantled. Yet, no effective and consistent policies or continuous operational programmes were adopted and implemented to ensure their replacement with adequate private or semi-private institutions to continue to provide the same services to small farmers. It has become clear today that small farmers need public policy and institutional support to enable them to organise themselves to collect information, improve their production and benefit from economies of scale in input access and product marketing.

Realigning of institutions serving farmers and agriculture

Realigning of Africa's farmer-support systems that include extension/ training, research, credit and private-sector supply of inputs for smallholders is critical for raising agricultural productivity in Africa. Donor-initiated economic policy reforms have failed to achieve the desired increase in aggregate agricultural output in many countries in Africa. There is now ample evidence that these reforms must be complemented by indigenous efforts to revitalise farmer-support institutions. There is also a growing awareness that an array of public and private institutional models is needed, particularly because of the uniqueness and peculiarities associated with the African situation outlined in preceding sections.

There is a need for financial intermediation through bridging savings and credit. Public sector credit programmes have collapsed in Africa and the commercial banks have not really moved into rural areas to service that market. The debate on farm credit in Africa therefore joins the traditional debate around micro-finance for rural small and medium enterprises. Too little capital is flowing into the rural areas and micro-enterprises, and micro-finance initiatives cannot fill the gap. In addition, micro-finance is largely subsidised by other institutions and unsustainable. Micro-finance efforts are disconnected from the mainstream money markets. Mainstream money markets are conservative and reluctant to learn new rules and values in working with poor people and communities. Africa needs functional rural financial markets capable of both savings and investment financing. The focus has to shift toward holistic 'financial intermediation'. This implies a shift from subsidised programmes to self-financing programmes.

Resolving security of land tenure and property-rights issues

Land-tenure rights of people is an issue that is assuming greater significance in every African country, and will increase in the twenty-first century. African governments have to appreciate that transforming agrarian systems into urban-industrial economies invariably requires fundamental changes in many institutions, including those of land tenure. The distribution of land ownership is a major factor that influences this transition from one form of social and political order to another. Barrington Moore in *Social Origins of Dictatorship and Democracy* sums up the experience of all industrialising countries in the separation of a substantial segment of the ruling classes from direct ties to the land. There is growing evidence that agricultural growth and efficient management of natural resources are dependent on the political, legal and administrative capabilities of rural communities to determine their own future and to protect their land and land-based natural resources and other economic interests. The lack of this power (or lack of democracy) is translated into insecure tenure rights, abuse of common property and resources, disenfranchisement of rural people, particularly women, and the breakdown or weakening of rural economic institutions. The management of the environment and the effectiveness of community-based natural resource management are all dependent on clearly defined land rights and support systems for rural communities.

Natural resources managed as common property now face severe degradation in most African countries. When local institutions are unable to resolve conflicts over the use of common resources, governments often make the mistake of assuming direct control and administration of these resources. In some instances, the government is simply interested in exploiting the resources to the exclusion of local communities, as is sometimes the case with wildlife and national parks. The deprived communities often lose interest in protecting the natural resources and may actually contribute to unauthorised exploitation and poaching. For resources under common usage, governments should shift towards a policy that employs a transparent decision-making process to control access to natural resources. Meaningful community governance is possible mainly where political power and fiscal responsibility are decentralised to institutions that represent local stakeholders. In practice, however, two widespread policies inadvertently undermine indigenous tenure systems.

- **Unregistered land is state land**: Most prevalent is the practice that all land with no registered title is state land. According to the book *Searching for Land Tenure Security in Africa*, the reality, however, is that the majority of Africans continue to believe in and hold their land under indigenous customary tenure systems, irrespective of the formal legal position under national law. Organs of central government are generally inappropriate for local administration and management of land tenure, and invariably undermine the local and traditional institutions. Moreover, this leads to corrupt practices by influential politicians and bureaucrats. Although governments acknowledge this de facto prevalence of customary tenure, they continue to maintain the *de jure* state ownership. In this situation, land conflicts escalate, and traditional conflict resolution mechanisms are rendered ineffective.
- **Common land is private land**: The second practice is the attempt to replace customary land tenure with state-imposed individual property rights to land and resources. This change is assumed to be more compatible with the protection and sustainable exploitation of natural resources, as well as the intensification and commercialisation of agriculture. There is mounting evidence, however, that land titling and registration programmes have not yielded positive benefits. Moreover, formal title has not necessarily increased tenure security, according to the authors in an article in the leading *American Journal of Agricultural Economics*.

The weakness of government institutions in Africa leave these state-imposed individualised tenurial systems in a vulnerable position. State-imposed tenure systems are often based on European or North American legal and administrative codes. A host of institutions is required for this tenurial system – and soon. These types of institutions, including surveyors, courts of law, legal practitioners, police and banks, are generally absent in rural Africa. African customary laws and values that guide tenure policies also differ or even conflict with the alien ones. Where the state imposes alien tenure systems, conflicts often arise in the interpretation of these at customary level. Examples include differences in values surrounding group versus individual rights and inheritance and succession.

Mandivamba Rukuni, chairman of the Commission of Inquiry into Appropriate Agricultural Land Tenure Systems, claims that these practices are so debilitating that in Zimbabwe, for example, highly centralised systems of government were judged as the most serious threat to tenure security for land users under all types of tenure. This problem is most acute for communally held land and state land occupied by communities under customary rights. Communities occupying such land have limited exclusive rights because bureaucrats and politicians also claim institutional authority over the land. In the worst case, these state functionaries may be the de facto landlords.

Tenure security

Traditional African land tenure systems have all the key ingredients of secure tenure. Land tenure security can generally be defined as the certainty of continuous use, and is associated with four sets of rights:

- **Use rights**: Rights to grow crops, trees, make permanent improvement, harvest trees and fruits, and so on;
- **Transfer rights**: Rights to sell, give, mortgage, lease, rent or bequeath;
- **Exclusion rights**: Rights to exclude others from using or transferring; and
- **Enforcement rights**: Refer to the legal, institutional and administrative provisions to guarantee use, transfer and exclusion rights.

Who enforces rights?

According to Gershon Feder and David Feeny, in an article in the *World Bank Economic Review*, these four property rights define the legitimate uses and users of land in a given period. Rights may be subdivided almost infinitely. In parts of Africa and South Asia (as was the case in medieval England), rights to the crop are private whereas rights to the stubble after harvesting are communal. Similarly, in some parts of Africa, land and tree tenure are not held by individuals. Rather, they are defined at community level. Economist John Taylor claims that rights may be enforced by formal institutions or informal customs, beliefs and attitudes. Enforcement often requires a buttress of instruments such as courts, police, banks, lawyers, surveys and valuation and record-keeping systems.

Who enjoys rights?

All tenure systems fall into four broad categories of ownership: open access, communal, private and state (see Table 9.1). In most countries, few areas are truly open access; some land may appear open, but usually it is state or communal land over which the state or community lacks adequate enforcement capacity, or such capacity comes under pressure. The result is insecurity of tenure, manifested in land-use patterns that mimic open-access systems.

Exclusivity defines the degree of tenure security. Under communal tenure, exclusive-use rights are assigned to a group. Individual- or family-use rights are also assigned under most traditional tenure systems.

Table 9.1 Categories of land tenure systems.

Category	Ownership of Exclusive Rights
Open access	None
Communal	Defined group
Private	Individual legal entity
State	Public sector

Private property rights are the most prevalent form of tenure in industrialised Western countries. Many Africans view these rights as a creation of the state, not as God-given or sacred rights. The experience in Africa has therefore been that where private property rights are not viewed as legitimate, or not generally viewed as working in the public interest, or where they are simply not enforced adequately, they become quite insecure. In extreme cases, *de jure* private property can deteriorate into de facto open access. In the *World Bank Economic Review*, Shem Migot-Adholla and fellow authors have argued that communal tenure in indigenous African land rights systems do not necessarily conflict with Western property rights systems. Holding exclusive-use rights in traditional tenure systems can be as secure as private property rights in Western industrialised countries.

There is no tenure system that is good or bad, right or wrong. Most important is a tenure system that is secure, appropriate and able to facilitate the needs of a community or society. At issue is who confers the rights. Where freehold rights are assigned to a family or an individual by the community under the traditional tenure system, these rights can be very secure.

Contrary to popular belief by Western scholars and observers, traditional systems of tenure are quite secure, and do not necessarily constrain productivity and conservation. A growing body of research on tenure demonstrates that the most important characteristic of tenure security under indigenous systems is the ability to bequeath land. Authors Frank Place, Mark Roth and Peter Hazell examined existing studies by the World Bank and the Land Tenure Centre, and also researched a number of African countries, to produce a comparative analysis of Burkina Faso, Ghana, Kenya, Rwanda, Senegal, Somalia and Uganda. This analysis confirmed that indigenous systems do not hinder productivity or investment. In addition, land registration has not necessarily led to tenure security. Recent research also demonstrates that the high productivity increases enjoyed by smallholders in Kenya and Zimbabwe had, and still have,

less to do with individual tenure, than with the removal of pro-
hibitions and other bottlenecks for smallholders that were more
important than land tenure changes. Government intervention makes
sense, therefore, only after the causes of tenure insecurity and the
bottlenecks to rural development have been identified.

Research has also exposed two other economic fallacies associated
with state-imposed individual tenure reforms. First is the fallacy of
economies of scale in agricultural production. Worldwide evidence
shows no real scale economies, and, if anything, small farms can be
even more efficient than large farms. The second fallacy is the view
by governments that the practice by African farmers of holding
multiple parcels of land in separate locations is not efficient. Once
again, evidence is showing great wisdom in the holding of multiple
parcels of varying suitability for the wide spectrum of crops grown.
These two fallacies lead governments into pursuing policies of consolidating holdings rather than subdividing land.

Investment in social capital and physical infrastructure

Compared to other regions of the developing world, much of rural
Africa is characterised by a dispersed rural population and low
population densities, according to researchers Sudhir Wanmali and
Yassir Islam. The centre-periphery model described by John Friedman
in *Regional Development Policy* is characterised as a colonial relationship in which the principal factors of production, including raw
materials and agricultural goods, are drawn from the periphery 'rural'
to the centre 'urban' where they are used to produce higher valued
manufactured goods. Over time, infrastructure is concentrated in
urban areas and availability declines in rural areas. Researchers
Dunstan Spencer and Ousmane Badiane claim that rural roads in
Africa today are less developed than they were in India at the
beginning of the green revolution. A puzzling question, for instance,
is why Africa, in spite of recurring droughts, has not developed
innovative and locally appropriate means of small-scale irrigation

that supports rain-fed agriculture. The irrigation infrastructure in Africa is thin and its role in a future agricultural revolution, albeit small in area, can be significant in terms of productivity increases, diversifying crops into higher value ones and supplying lucrative markets at their time of shortage. As explained in earlier sections, improvements in infrastructure represent one single area where huge benefits in African agricultural productivity could be reaped.

Improvements in technology to transform traditional agriculture
Most National Agricultural Research Systems (NARSs) in sub-Saharan Africa are having difficulty in producing a steady stream of new technologies for small-scale farms and in generating adequate financial support from their governments. The experiences to date have shown that there is no blueprint for reforming NARSs in Africa. Donors can assist the reform process by supporting local initiatives to craft smallholder-driven research systems that are staffed with accountable scientists who are adequately financed from local sources. According to a 1998 article in *World Development*, since independence in most African countries, agricultural institutions have been in transition. Since independence, African research managers have been forced to grapple simultaneously with five complex transitions which ultimately will influence the productivity and competitiveness of African agriculture:
- Managerial transition from colonial to local administrators;
- Scientific transition from expatriate to indigenous scientists;
- Financial transition from dependence on financial support from colonial governments and large-scale farms to mobilising support from governments and donors;
- Political transition from commercial farms to smallholders in dual agrarian societies; and
- Transition from public to private institutional forms and new forms of public/private/NGO partnerships.

African R&D systems have performed better with 'disembodied' technology in terms of improved management and husbandry recommendations for cropping livestock. Successes with 'embodied' technology are rare because of the limited capacity to manufacture. R&D and industrial capacity is needed for the manufacture of 'embodied' technology such as machinery, seeds, fertilisers, chemicals and materials. Disembodied technology, by contrast, refers to knowledge, techniques and management practices that increase productivity and are largely transmitted through extension and advisory services. Energy and power for smallholder farmers is a major drawback to productivity. The continued decline in draught animals, coupled with a lack of appropriate small machinery, means that farmers' yields are held back. Since most of the increase in production is from new areas opened up, as opposed to technological breakthroughs, this means greater pressure on the environment.

Promotion of traditional principles of agriculture
Traditional principles of agriculture, such as preservation of the gene pool, practising holistic resource management, inter-cropping, use of organic fertilisers, integrated pest control, conservation agriculture and agro-forestry, which ancestors understood without science or formal education, need to be promoted. Africa is a de facto organic continent and African farmers need to exploit the growing international markets for organic products, including vegetables, flowers and herbs.

The principles of agricultural renaissance also provide a useful guide on how African governments should intervene in their agricultural sectors. These principles include:
1) Promotion of small family farms.
2) Regarding farming as a:
   - Tradition: Knowledge and skills passed on to next generations;
   - Business: To create rural wealth; and
   - Way of life: Custodian of culture and the environment.
3) Promoting integrated crop and livestock management.

Commercialisation of smallholder agriculture through value-chain development

Value-chain development should be based on the small family farms in line with the principles of agricultural renaissance explained above.. Family farming units can be intensively trained in the technical aspects of production, value addition, entrepreneurship, wealth creation and basic value chain management. The process of wealth creation at community level does not necessarily depend on formal education but involves:

1) Building physical and biological assets:
   - Improved quality of trees, herbs, animals, etc.; and
   - Roads, wells, grain bins, improved houses.
2) Circulating local products and services:
   - Family businesses;
   - Using extended family as business model; and
   - Localising exchange of goods and services.
3) Promoting the value of self-employment:
   - Starting own business and projects; and
   - Refusing to work for someone else after a certain age.
4) Bequeathing life and survival skills to the youth:
   - Food production and preservation;
   - Home improvement; and
   - Project management.
5) Transmuting problems and challenges into business opportunities:
   - Cultural industries and cottage industries as lucrative businesses in future.

This requires building the spirit of entrepreneurship and does not hinge on formal education but involves being equipped with skills in:
- Seeing opportunities where others do not;
- Having the courage to act;
- Having the courage to do things that have never been done before; and
- Having courage to be innovative and creative.

Make trade open, transparent and fair for African smallholder farmers

National governments should eliminate existing harmful trade restrictions and refrain from newly imposed ones in order to reduce food price volatility and enhance the efficiency of agricultural markets. In addition, transparent, fair and open global trade should be ensured. In 2009 the FAO reiterated that a rules-based international agricultural trading system that is open, non-distorted, non-discriminatory, equitable and fair can promote agricultural and rural development and contribute to world food security.

Agriculture accounts for 11% of the value of all world exports. According to the FAO in 2002, the measures and strategies that would ensure that the poorest and most vulnerable countries and population groups receive an equitable share of the benefits of trade liberalisation should be aimed at:

- Eliminating direct and indirect export subsidies;
- Rationalising and simplifying access to the Organization for Economic Cooperation and Development (OECD) markets. Specifically, rationalise and simplify trade preferences, assist countries whose preferences have been eroded through multilateral liberalisation and deepen existing preferences for very poor countries;
- Reducing OECD tariffs and consumer taxes on processed agricultural products, with special preferences for products from developing countries;
- Eliminating tariff escalation for tropical commodities in the developing as well as the developed countries. Tariffs are rising even faster in the former than in the latter group. The purchasing power of China's or India's rapidly growing middle class could turn these countries into major importers of some tropical agricultural products over the next 30 years; and
- Creating or expanding safety nets and food distribution schemes to ensure that low-income consumers are not penalised by rises in the price of food imports.

Integrate climate change into strategies at all levels

Climate change affects agriculture directly through changes in agro-ecological conditions and indirectly by affecting growth and distribution of incomes, and thus demand for agricultural produce. Changes in temperature and precipitation associated with continued emissions of greenhouse gases will bring changes in land suitability and crop yields. To reduce the vulnerability of poor people to climate change and moderate the impact of climate change, a combination of adaptation and mitigation strategies is needed at the global, regional, national, basin and local level. Options for climate change adaptation in agriculture include improved land management, adjustment of planting dates and introduction of new crop varieties, while the mitigation options include improved energy efficiency and crop yields, and land management techniques to increase carbon storage. In particular, community-based adaptation strategies that strengthen the community's capacity to cope with disasters, enhance land-management skills and diversify livelihoods should be supported.

Conclusion

The necessary long-term public sector investments into this key sector are still lacking and there is a need for a major improvement in the political and fiscal commitment of governments to agriculture. The importance of developing agriculture in Africa is central because the majority of Africans are rural. The social and economic progress of these people is largely dependent on increasing the productivity of agriculture and natural resources. Agriculture is the backbone of the African economy and will continue to be so for the foreseeable future. Africa's agriculture is unique in terms of the diversity of cropping systems; thin rural infrastructure; undeveloped markets; minimal mechanisation; limited seasonal financing; competition with food aid; dominance of weathered and inherently infertile soils; weak agricultural support systems and poor agricultural policies. The prime movers that require substantial investment to achieve sustainable agricultural development include: investments into land development and improved land tenure systems; new technology produced by public and private investments in agricultural research; professional, managerial and technical skills produced by investments in the right educational systems; sustained growth of biological capital and physical capital investments; improvements in the performance of farmer service and support institutions; and, more importantly, a favourable economic policy environment and political support for agriculture over the long term.

MANDIVAMBA RUKUNI is founder and Director of the Wisdom Africa Leadership Academy, based in Harare, Zimbabwe.

References and further reading

Bruce, J.W. and Migot-Adholla, S.E. (eds.) (1993) *Searching for Land Tenure Security in Africa* (Kendall/Hung Publishing Company, Dubugue, IA).

Bruce, J.W., Migot-Adholla, S.E. and Atherton, J. (1993) 'The Findings and their Policy Implications: Institutional Adaptation on Replacement' in Bruce, J.W. and Migot-Adholla, S.E. (eds.) *Searching for Land Tenure Security in Africa* (Kendall/Hung Publishing Company, Dubugue, IA).

FAO (2002) 'World Agriculture: Towards 2015/2030', FAO Corporate Document Repository.

—— (2009) 'Agricultural Investment Production Capacity and Productivity', FAO Corporate Document Repository.

Feder, G. and Feeny, D. (1991) 'Land Tenure and Property Rights: Theory and Applications for Development Policy' in *World Bank Economic Review* Vol. 5, No. 1, pp. 135–54.

Friedman, J. (1966) *Regional Development Policy: A Case Study of Venezuela* (MIT Press, Cambridge, MA).

Migot-Adholla, S.E., Hazell, P. and Place, F. (1991) 'Indigenous Land Rights in Sub-Saharan Africa: A Constraint on Productivity' in *World Bank Economic Review* Vol. 5, No. 1, pp. 155–75.

Moore, B. (1966) *Social Origins of Dictatorship and Democracy* (Beacon Press, Boston).

Place, F., Roth, M. and Hazell, P. (1993) 'Land Tenure Security and Agricultural Performance in Africa: Overview of Research Methodology' in Bruce, J.W. and Migot-Adholla, S.E. (eds.) *Searching for Land Tenure Security in Africa* (Kendall/ Hung Publishing Company, Dubugue, IA).

Roth, M., Barrows, R., Carter, M. and Kanel, D. (1989) 'Land Ownership Security and Farm Investment: Comment' in *American Journal of Agricultural Economics* Vol. 71, pp. 211–14.

Rukuni, M. (Chairman) (1994) *Report of the Commission of Inquiry into Appropriate Agricultural Land Tenure Systems* (Government Printers, Harare).

Rukuni, M., Blackie, M.J. and Eicher, C.K. (1998) 'Crafting Smallholder-Driven Agricultural Research Systems in Southern Africa' in *World Development* Vol. 26, No. 6, pp. 1073–87.

Spencer, D. and Badiane, O. (1995) 'Agriculture and Economic Recovery in African Countries' in Peters, G.H. and Hedley, D.D. (eds.) *Agricultural Competitiveness: Market Forces and Policy Choice* (Ashgate, Farnham).

Taylor, J. (1988) 'The Ethical Foundations of the Market' in Ostron, V., Feeny, D. and Picht, H. (eds.) *Rethinking Institutional Analysis and Development: Issues, Alternatives and Choices* (Institute for Contemporary Studies Press, San Francisco).

Timmer, C.P. (1998) 'The Role of Agriculture in Indonesia's Development' in Eicher, C.K. and Staatz, J.M. (eds.) *International Agricultural Development*. 3rd edition (Johns Hopkins University Press, Baltimore and London).

Wanmali, S. and Islam, Y. (1997) 'Rural Infrastructure and Regional Development' in Haddad L. (ed.) *Achieving Food Security in Southern Africa: New Challenges, New Opportunities* (International Food Policy Research Institute, Washington, D.C.).

10

Rethinking Africa's Re-industrialisation and Regional Co-operation

What is the Best Way Forward?

THANDIKA MKANDAWIRE

Africa is the least industrialised continent today, whether this is measured by the share of industry in gross domestic product (GDP) or by industrial value added per capita. Consequently, any scheme of regional co-operation must place the industrialisation of Africa at the core of its agenda. This chapter discusses Africa's short-lived attempt at industrialisation and the need to rethink regional co-operation in light of this experience.

Post-colonial experience

At independence, around the modal year of 1960, Africa was the quintessential 'late industrialiser', having missed out on two occasions during which many developing countries embarked upon industrialisation. The first occasion was the Great Depression in the 1930s and, later, the Second World War as many countries were forced to manufacture hitherto imported industrial products. This industrialisation was carried out spontaneously in response to the rupture in international trade. After the Second World War, new international arrangements allowed considerable space to nation states, thus facilitating reconstruction and development of various welfare regimes in developed countries and developmental regimes in developing countries. During this period, the import substitution by default of the 1930s and 1940s was formalised into an industrial policy of import substitution industrialisation (ISI), which involved protection of infant industries through tariffs, preferential treatment in allocation of credit and provision of all kinds of subsidies. The purpose of import substitution was not autarky as has been often suggested, but the diversification of export products through the structural transformation of the economies. This new strategy was systematically pursued by countries such as India and Brazil. Such a strategy of industrialisation was premised on the existence of an independent nation and autonomous state able to pursue such a policy. This basically ruled out much of Africa until the 1960s. It was, after all, imperial policy to treat colonies either as protected markets for its export industries or as monopolised sources of raw materials. The achievement of either goal was not likely to encourage any far-reaching industrialisation in the colonies. Colonial powers thus discouraged local industrial production for the domestic market of the colony and the export of manufactured goods from the periphery. Only the relatively more autonomous 'settler' economies of Kenya, Southern Rhodesia and South Africa managed to set up some industry during this period.

Thus, for most of Africa, it was only with independence that the 'right to industrialise' was attained. The ISI strategy dovetailed neatly with the nationalists' quests for industrialisation and was sanctioned and facilitated by prevailing trade arrangements, which, as noted above, gave considerable space to national governments while promoting global trade. Furthermore, it was conventional wisdom that import substitution was the way to go and, according to Professor Lynn Mytelka, every World Bank mission to African countries argued in this vein. In addition, the strategy had strong historical and theoretical grounds based on theories of market failure and problems of market co-ordination, the experience of 'late industrialisers' and the spectacular industrialisation of the Soviet Union. Pursuing a light version of this strategy, African countries enjoyed for a while rates of industrialisation during the first decade or so of independence that, if sustained, would have significantly transformed the African economic landscape (see Table 10.1).

Table 10.1   Manufacturing production (average annual growth rate, percentage).

Region/country	1961–79	1980–94	1995–2010
Brazil		2.2	1.4
India	6.8	5.5	6.9
Indonesia	8.3	12.6	3.9
Korea, Rep.	18.2	9.9	6.5
Latin America and Caribbean	4.6	1.5	2.3
Middle East and North Africa	10.5	5.5	6.5
South Asia	5.4	5.8	6.7
Sub-Saharan Africa	5.6	1.7	3.1

(Source: Calculated from World Bank Live)

The era of de-industrialisation

By the mid-1970s and even before the oil crisis, it became clear that the import substitution strategy pursued by individual African economies was showing signs of premature exhaustion. This, in many cases, was magnified by shortages of foreign exchange and collapsing domestic markets following the economic crisis of the latter half of the 1970s.

In official circles, there were two major divergent diagnoses of Africa's poor performance in terms of industrialisation. The first one was the position of African regional organisations (the Organisation of African Unity or OAU together with the United Nations Economic Commission for Africa or UNECA, both based in Addis Ababa) that produced the Lagos Plan of Action. The second position was espoused by the World Bank, which produced a document in 1981, *Accelerated Development in Africa: An Agenda for Action*, more popularly known as the 'Berg Report'.

Table 10.2   Selected indicators of economic size in 2005 (in constant 2000 US dollars).

Country name	GDP	Manufacturing	Industry
Sub-Saharan Africa (all income levels)	430 324 114 211	47 898 734 409	129 565 257 578
Belgium	251 239 846 692		57 349 290 982
New Zealand	62 290 519 519		14 395 630 728
Nigeria	61 902 502 732		
Norway	187 788 450 771	17 689 188 523	65 205 340 529
Sweden	282 364 681 299	60 611 294 118	76 512 693 163
South Africa	160 367 192 374	26 678 154 581	44 487 613 332

(Source: World Bank Online Datasets)

The Lagos Plan of Action was premised on a number of critical observations about Africa's industrialisation experience. The first of these noted the inadequacy of domestic markets as a basis for far-reaching industrialisation under import substitution. African economies are small. The entire GDP and industrial production of sub-Saharan Africa are each only twice that of Belgium or less than that of Norway and Sweden combined (see Table 10.2). And yet both Sweden and Belgium have felt it necessary to enter some larger economic entity. It is not surprisingly that problems of excess capacity arose in many countries.

The second observation was technological dependence. This in itself is not a problem as an initial condition. The problem arose when this dependence undermined or precluded 'learning by doing'. Furthermore, many governments failed to bargain with foreign investors on matters of transfer of technology. This was partly because of the weak bargaining position of small African economies and the weak management capacity, which compelled them to provide incentives that tended to favour the importation of capital goods. It was also the result of the small size of the markets that did not allow for a 'deepening' of the import substitution process to include capital goods that are crucial in reducing technological dependence.

The third problem was that of the financing of imported producers' goods (capital goods and intermediate goods). Many countries in Africa believed they could finance the importation of these goods with earnings from their primary goods; and with buoyant prices for raw materials in the 1970s this seemed a rational strategy for resource-rich countries. But it also ensured that the strategy would ultimately run into the 'Prebisch constraint' of secular decline in terms of trade as the demand for imported capital and other producers' goods outpaced the earnings from exports of raw materials. Furthermore, while the exports of the continent may be fairly diversified, individual countries continued to be monocultural economies, often along the lines mapped out for them by their erstwhile colonial masters.

The fourth problem was the weakness of the domestic industrial class, both in terms of financial and managerial capacity and political clout so that effectively the industries that enjoyed state protection were largely foreign-owned or parastatals.

Finally, in a world where the global trade order was premised on bargaining, the attempts by individual African countries to assert themselves proved futile. It was necessary that African countries act collectively to strength their positions through regional integration.

The Berg Report had an entirely different diagnosis which, over the years, was to completely dominate policy-making in Africa. Thandika Mkandawire and Charles Soludo note in *Our Continent, Our Future* that it drowned the voices from the UNECA and OAU in Addis Ababa and this had far-reaching consequences for African economies. The dominant neoliberal analysis which the Berg Report peddled attributed the crisis to state interventionism in general and industrial policy in particular. It argued that African countries had remained in the import substitution phase too long and had only managed to produce *enfants terribles* that had failed to grow behind the protective walls. The argument that was initially aimed at countries in Latin America or India was now extended to Africa. While, by the 1970s and definitely by the 1980s, this argument may have held for

237

Latin American countries, its transposition to the African case was definitely misguided since by the time of the 1973 crisis most African industries were barely a decade old. The literature on Asia clearly suggests the need for persistence through various 'learning' stages of import substitution in order to allow for adaptation and in-novations that make the industry competitive, not only on the basis of cheap labour or favourable exchange rates but on the basis of productivity. Both time and intensity of policy clearly suggest that ISI was not pursued sufficiently long enough or vigorously and systematically enough in much of Africa, again with the exception of perhaps Rhodesia and South Africa. Indeed, Roger Ridell has rightly argued that import substitution did not fail in Africa; rather it was never tried.

The new diagnosis did not only confine itself to economic analysis, it was immediately partnered by a political analysis that identified the culprits behind the failed policies. If earlier criticism of import substitution was levelled at dependence and the weakness of the national capitalist class, the new analysis was informed by public choice theories that attributed industrial policies to rent-seeking activities of beneficiaries of such studies, as suggested by authors such as Robert Bates. It was later joined by a more culturalist's institutional turn, which attributed bad polices to the 'logic of neo-patrimonialism' that led to the allocation of resources and licences on purely clientalist grounds. Both these views suggested that the political logic would trump economic logic and both views counselled against 'industrial policy' since it would be 'captured' by the wrong interest groups. Even those policies that worked elsewhere in the developing countries were deemed too complicated for African governments. Or as the World Bank put it in 1994:

> In promoting exports governments should not try to pick 'winners'. Because most African countries are small, the market segments they succeed in will be narrow. That makes it unlikely

> that government (or international agencies) can identify those segments in advance: governments can best help entrepreneurs discover and develop competitive exports by getting out of the way (p. 192).

One consequence of this political economy was that while the policies it advocated or implied were 'pro-market', they were fundamentally 'anti-business' and left the state with neither sticks nor carrots with which to drive private initiative in a collectively desirable direction.

Under the structural adjustment regime, policy towards industry was anchored on trade liberalisation, privatisation and exchange rate manipulation. The assumption now was that trade liberalisation would lead to efficiency through the mechanisms of competition, which would weed out inefficient industries and assist the economy in identifying its true comparative advantage. Getting rid of foreign exchange distortions (through devaluation) would make industries more competitive. Financial liberalisation would increase the supply of investable funds, which would be made available to the many profitable projects that had hitherto been 'crowded out' by the state or starved of funds due to credit rationing. Efficiency would be further enhanced by privatisation. By the end of the 1980s, virtually every African country was pursuing some structural strategy pro-gramme under the tutelage of Washington financial institutions. The consequences of these programmes were dire as the deflationary and procyclical nature of the policies made things worse. For industry, this meant the dismantling of industrial policies and the protective trade policies and financial arrangements that they had spawned. This produced de-industrialisation in many African countries. But, most significantly, the new conditionalities that went with this policy regime forbade use of the instrument of protection that had been used by many other countries in the past. Ever since it was formally articulated by Alexander Hamilton, the notion of 'learning by doing' and the need to provide such a facility for 'infant industry' through some protective measures has been a crucial aspect of all late industrialisers, according to Henry Bruton in the *Journal of Economic Literature*. Africa was thus expected to engage in the unprecedented act of industrialisation without 'industrial policy'.

Regional integration: Some lessons

The list of problems identified by the African regional organisations were widely recognised in Africa's political circles. After all, Kwame Nkrumah had forcefully stated the case for regional integration. In light of these weaknesses, the Lagos Plan of Action argued for deepening the process of import substitution through regional integration, collective efforts for technological acquisitions, mobilisation of Africa's rich natural resources, improving the pan-African infrastructure and collectively negotiating Africa's position in the global order. The political leadership recognised these issues in the Lagos Plan of Action and a range of regional arrangements was embarked upon. And yet, by the end of the twentieth century, regional integration was far from being a feature of African political economies. It is important to recall some of the problems with past experiments of regional integration if we are not to repeat the errors.

'Lack of political will'

One feature of the debates on regional integration in Africa has been the complete lack of domestic political anchoring of the regional integration project. This is often referred to as 'lack of political will', which in fact refers to the absence of political constituencies in the business, mass movements and the technocratic intelligentsia that would push for regional integration. There have been few well-articulated or well-organised national economic interests seeking large markets, which are collectively protected against extra-regional competition. At the national level, it is often some pan-Africa sentiment that has provided a modicum of ideological support to regional co-operation but this has been undermined by narrow nationalism that was unprepared to make the kinds of commitments that a pan-African project demanded.

Authoritarianism and regional integration

A major political stumbling block was authoritarian rule. Regional integration among authoritarian regimes in Africa failed partly because such rule could not countenance any higher authority than that exercised at the national level. Furthermore, it meant that any commitments made on a continental level were at the whims of individual personalities who met at some gathering and were not subject to national debate or scrutiny. In this, the New Partnership for Africa's Development (NEPAD) was unique in that it did provoke some debate at various African levels and among civil society organisations, although it eventually failed to sustain the public interest.

Regional technocracies and regionalism

In a number of cases, international agencies, such as the UNECA, have taken the initiative, while in other cases it was foreign donors that provided the impetus for regional co-operation. Pan-African bureaucracies, however, were under no political obligation to answer questions of what costs or benefits would be borne by any individual nation. Instead, they were content with stating convincingly the case for regional integration. And yet, if regional integration was to have political anchoring at the national level, it had to be embraced by key political actors at that level. It thus had to address explicitly the national costs and benefits of integration.

False premise of 'planned' national industrialisation

Endeavours at regional integration took place in the era of 'development planning'. Naturally, regional integration had to be of a 'planning' type – an approach celebrated and incorporated in the Lagos Plan of Action. Significantly, it was the ministers of planning of the respective member states that played a key role in the drawing up of the Lagos Plan in 1980. And ironically this was the year that also marked the beginning of the demise of the roles of the ministries of planning in African policy-making as the World Bank's Berg

Report produced at the behest of African ministers of finance was to set the tone of the policy discourse for the next quarter of a century.

The view that one was dealing with planned economies was a fatal misunderstanding of the nature of the economies of constituent members and had serious repercussions on the thinking about and functioning of the whole. Such an approach automatically led to emphasis on complementarities and on planned and concerted allocation of economic activity and ignored problems of competition and its regulation within a protected market. As a result, regional integration in Africa has been of the 'plan mode' type whereby efforts at regional integration have focused on deciding how to allocate what was conceived as essentially complementary activities in order to exploit economies of scale rather than in creating an internally competitive market that was 'governed' in such a way as to encourage regional industrialisation while preparing local industry for eventual competition in the global market.

Such an approach proved difficult to sustain partly because it was not easy to pick the winners and decide exactly where they would be allocated and partly because every country sought to produce all the products it could. Consequently, this approach opened up a Pandora's box. First, the efficiency of the particular allocation of industry in terms of the entity's and components' development was questioned. Second, given the uncertainty about outcomes of any investment, satisfaction or dissatisfaction with a particular allocation was based largely on subjective reasons. Third, there was an absence of enforcement mechanisms for decisions taken by regional entities, worsened by the lack of respect for the administrative allocation of economic activities by member states. Finally, member states did not enjoy full control of investment decisions in their respective countries. Where the logic of the administrative allocation of industrial activities collided with the global investment strategies of transnational corporations, most states complied with the exigencies of the latter, facilitated by the fact that the transnational corporations brought money while the regional entities charged with allocation of economic activities had unfunded ideas and mandates. This was made worse by the fact that they had no way of imposing their administrative allocation because they simply had no enforcement mechanisms.

The challenge of industrialisation in the era of NEPAD

NEPAD has emerged during an era characterised by three features: (a) the crisis of 'de-industrialisation' of member states under the grip of structural adjustment; (b) the problem of reconciling regional integration among countries pursuing structural adjustment; and (c) the exigencies of globalisation and structural adjustment premised on liberalisation of domestic markets and international trade. All these have implications for how Africa must proceed.

As noted above, one consequence of structural adjustment has been de-industrialisation and the failure to induce export diversification that included industrial products other than mining. The premature end of import substitution had resulted in the absence of capacity and productivity enhancing measures in industry. In turn, this has meant that gains from exchange rate manipulation have tended, like much else in orthodox adjustment, to have a one-off character. In most cases, the gains in exports were not due to new export-oriented manufacturing capacity but in the redirection of existing manufacturing production from domestic to export markets in response to altered price structures and depressed domestic markets. In addition, the collapse of infrastructure as public investment was reduced and the fact that promised private investment in infrastructure was not forthcoming, meant that the new price regimes did not have their intended effects. Nor would the simple freeing of markets lead to greater regional trade when transport and communications had collapsed.

The second problem was that of reconciling preferential treatment and co-ordination in any programme of regional integration implicit in NEPAD and the structural adjustment programmes (SAPs) through which member states were being 'globalised'. SAPs had no interest in regionalism that assumed some form of protectionism and preferential treatment. Indeed, neoliberalism and regionalism are fundamentally in contradiction. The SAP reform agenda was opposed to regional integration and simply advised each country to open its markets to the 'world economy'. The main reason was that in general regional integration leads to the collective adoption of import substitution industrialisation, a strategy of economic development that these institutions strongly condemned and have sought to reverse with SAPs. In addition, these institutions believe that the economies should be 'open' to the entire world – buying from the cheapest supplier and selling to the best buyer, neither of which need to be immediate neighbours with whom one sought to integrate. This undermined preferential treatment of member states of a particular regional arrangement over non-members, which is an inherent part of regional co-operation. We should also recall that one major thrust of the policy of the International Financial Institutions (IFIs) was the dismantling of the developmental state and its replacement by regulatory states. Not surprisingly, donors have tended to focus on the regulatory and normative functions of NEPAD (good governance and 'peer review') and not on its strategic developmental potential. It has also meant depriving regional institutions of truly developmental mandates and instruments.

Critics have pointed out that NEPAD started off with the assumption and hope that its member states were market economies in the mode of the Washington Consensus, each pursuing export-oriented strategies and desperately seeking foreign investment. If earlier arguments for regional integration were premised on the quite reasonable assumption that further import substitution would be facilitated by widening this market, the NEPAD argument was premised on the implausible assumption that failed neoliberalism will be sustained by regionalism.

A third feature of the new environment was globalisation. The agenda of regional co-operation has always involved providing a collective shield against forms of globalisation that were inimical to

African interests, more specifically imperialism and neo-colonialism. Regional integration is still about strengthening one's bargaining position in a highly regulated world market. It implies the preferential treatment of member states (or, as in the European case, 'community preference') while the rhetoric of globalisation insists on 'level playing fields' and 'non-discriminatory' behaviour towards all countries party to the new global order. This recourse to regionalism in the face of globalisation that was weakening individual states was, of course, not peculiar to Africa. One common response to globalisation has been the intensification of regional efforts. Indeed, there is ample evidence suggesting that in the more successful countries increase in trade within regional blocs has played a much more important role than globalisation. 'Globalisers', such as African and Latin American countries, have performed less well than 'regionalisers' such as European and Asian economies.

Developmental regionalism

One major argument for regional integration is extending the size of the market to overcome the limits individually faced by constituent member states. Underlying arguments for regional integration was a strategy for 'deepening' import substitution whose 'easy' phase of production of consumption foods had been brought to a grinding halt by the limitations of the Lilliputian markets of African economies. However, it is important to stress that the case is often stated in such a manner as to suggest that size alone will do the trick. This is not as obviously true as it seems. Even such things as monetary unions do not guarantee better performance if they are not accompanied by proactive policies to achieve development. The CFA franc countries have not performed better than non-CFA ones and have thus far failed to exploit the benefits of such monetary co-operation. Economies of scale must be deliberately exploited and harnessed if size is to matter. And that immediately calls for a regional development strategy that spells out areas of co-operation and rules of competition. It also calls for a specific set of institutions to 'think' regionally and to 'govern' regional markets. More specifically for Africa, this will entail a regional industrial policy and the necessary institutions for planning, financing and implementing such a policy.

We noted that earlier regional integration schemes had partly failed because they were based on the false assumption about the 'planned' nature of constituent economies. What would be the implications of a contrary assumption of regional integration among market economies? The first would be the realisation that one is talking about regulating or 'governing markets', to use Robert Wade's felicitous phrase and not about co-ordination of 'plans'. In such a situation, a major task of the central authorities of integration schemes will be regulating markets to stimulate the dynamism of competition, to correct market failures and to attenuate the unequal spirals that markets can spawn – all this explicitly to give regional integration a developmental thrust. The second implication would mean that in addition to the focus on co-operation and complementarity one would also have to emphasise stimulation and regulation of competition within the region and co-ordinated exports into world markets. Regional integration involves, in one form or another, a preferential treatment of constituent members. It means that individual producers within these states would enjoy the advantages of a protected market. However, the regional market should not serve as the *chasse gardé* of monopolies but a training ground to give regional industries the opportunity to acquire a competitive edge in the global market. In other words, regional integration should not be merely import substitution oriented but should provide the platform for a competitive export-oriented industrialisation. Having gained the competitive edge and cost advantage in certain products, the new firms can be expected to seek additional markets for their fast growing output.

This immediately raises the question about the new configuration of the global order and how Africa should proactively engage this order. More specifically, the rise of China and India provide Africa with both challenges and opportunities. On the challenge side,

China's exports of a number of goods that were part of the infant industry of these countries is a contributing factor to de-industrialisation and places an additional constraint on the export-orientation of most African economies. On the opportunities side, both India and China can serve as possible sources of finance and as outlets for Africa's natural resources. Already, the significant improvement in terms of trade can be partially attributed to the demand from these two countries. China has also become a major source of investment while India seems to be playing an increasing role in various forms of technical assistance, including the management of infrastructure. However, left at this level, such opportunities can easily reproduce troubled Africa's relationship with her erstwhile colonial masters. It is important that Africans see these opportunities as part of the strategies of industrialisation and seek a regional framework to engage these new powers in a strategic manner.

Finally, there are growing inequalities among African countries that are being exacerbated by the uneven development among those countries. Such uneven development will have to be squarely faced by the regional authorities. It will also require various forms of solidarity in which better endowed countries assist the less fortunate ones. One version of the regional development of Asia was the 'flying geese' model in which first Japan, then Taiwan and South Korea and then other Asia-Pacific countries embarked on development. Similarly, in European integration France and Germany played leading roles in the process of integration. Which countries can play the lead role in Africa's development and how?

Conclusion: Some research issues

As things stand, there is little connection between the trade preoccupations of most regional groups in Africa and the developmental agenda of individual countries. There is no industrial policy under NEPAD. And the policies that might constitute the base for a 'developmental regionalism' have yet to be spelt out and the mechanism for their implementation identified. Obviously, most of what is required will ultimately depend on political leadership. However, as the case of Europe suggests, Africa's own 'Afrocrats' can play an important role by providing the knowledge base for political decisions. I have suggested that concerted industrialisation efforts must be the corner-stone of revamped efforts at regional integration. This will require strengthening the developmental capacity of constituent states and regional authorities to formulate and implement development strategies in a co-ordinated fashion.

Finally, we must bear in mind the political character of regional integration and avoid the technocratic design of regionalism in Africa that has hitherto dominated discourse on regional integration. New efforts at regional integration must be built on democratic arrangements within and among member states.

THANDIKA MKANDAWIRE is the former Director of the Geneva-based United Nations Research Institute for Social Development and is currently Professor and Chair of Africa Development at the London School of Economics and Olof Palme Professor at the Institute for Futures Studies (Stockholm).

References and suggested reading

Bates, R. (1981) *Markets and States in Tropical Africa* (University of California Press, Berkeley and Los Angeles).

Bennell, P. (1998) 'Fighting for Survival: Manufacturing Industry and Adjustment in Sub-Saharan Africa' in *Journal of International Development* Vol. 10, pp. 621–37.

Bruton, H. (1998) 'A Reconsideration of Import Substitution' in *Journal of Economic Literature* Vol. XXXVI, pp. 903–36.

Mkandawire, T. (1988) 'The Road to Crisis, Adjustment and De-industrialisation: The African Case' in *Africa Development* Vol. 13.

———— (2011) 'Rethinking Pan Africanism: Nationalism and the New Regionalism' in Moyo, S. and Yeros, P. (eds.) *Reclaiming the Nation: The Return of the National Question in Africa, Asia and Latin America* (Pluto Press, London).

Mkandawire, T. and Soludo, C. (1999) *Our Continent, Our Future: African Perspectives on Structural Adjustment* (IDRC, CODESRIA and Africa World Press, Dakar and Trenton, NJ).

Mytelka, L. (1989) 'The Unfulfilled Promise of African Industrialisation' in *African Studies Review* Vol. 32, pp. 77–8.

Ridell, R. (1990) 'Manufacturing Africa: Reflections on the Case Studies' in Ridell, R. (ed.) *Manufacturing Africa: Performance, and Prospects of Seven Countries in Sub-Saharan Africa* (James Currey, London), pp. 33–67.

Van de Walle, N. (2001) *African Economies and the Politics of Permanent Crisis, 1979–1999* (Cambridge University Press, New York).

Wade, R. (1991) *Governing Markets: Economic Theory and the Role of Government in East Asian Industrialisation* (Macmillan, London).

World Bank (1979) *World Development Report, 1979* (World Bank, Washington, D.C.).

———— (1981) *Accelerated Development in Sub-Saharan Africa: An Agenda for Action* (World Bank, Washington, D.C.).

———— (1994) *Adjustment in Africa: Reforms, Results and the Road Ahead* (World Bank, Washington, D.C.).

11

Regional Integration in Africa
What are the Challenges and Opportunities?

SINDISO NDEMA NGWENYA

Historical perspectives: Legitimation of regional integration in Africa

The need for regional co-operation and integration in Africa has its origins in the struggle for decolonisation and was initially articulated in a concrete way during the first Pan-African Congress that was held in 1958. When the Organisation of African Unity (OAU) was established in 1963, the OAU Charter provided for decolonisation of African countries and advocated regional integration as a bulwark against the former imperial/colonial power. It is worth noting that the name OAU denotes a loose association of sovereign countries that were bound together by a shared vision of liberating the continent from colonial rule. Whereas the founding fathers of the OAU espoused the integration of their economies and societies, they unanimously agreed to maintain the colonial boundaries and non-interference in the affairs of one another. This was an antithesis for integrating countries that were artificially created and partitioned amongst the colonial powers at the Berlin Conference in 1884. Consequently, the seeds for weak co-operation and integration, even, in the extreme, disintegration, were inadvertently sown.

This was in deep contrast to the benevolent regional integration that was to mark, for instance, Western and later the larger Europe, which espoused the assimilation that covered economic, social, political and cultural aspects, and climaxed with the setting up of administrative and legislative institutions.

The integration of African countries was not and is still not based on the common history of colonialism, which not only destroyed the common identity of Africans but their culture and institutions. The inherent philosophy and structure of regional integration in Africa tended to maintain and enhance this colonial foundation, which saw African economies as basic commodity and service (including labour) suppliers. This meant that the dynamics of the African economy and later regional integration were driven by the axis of colonisation rather than inherent internal dynamics and demands. Regional integration based on these principles of the OAU meant that the integration of African economies and its people were sub-ordinated to servicing the interests of the former colonial powers. Thus, the identity, culture and institutions were outwardly rather than inwardly propelled and driven. The internal dynamics were, therefore, left to the peril of regional integration and the perceived development paths were not designed or articulated internally for Africa but externally. Thus, regional integration was to undermine and dismantle the remaining African civilisation. Pan-Africanism became a copycat and re-enforcer of retrogressive colonisation.

The OAU was in essence an amalgam of countries that had strong economic and political relations with former colonial powers. History provides evidence that sustainable and mutually beneficial co-operation and integration is anchored on shared common history, values and vision. Indeed, the common history of enslavement and colonialism should have been the basis for regional integration. Alas, that was not the case. A comparison of other regional integration initiatives reveals that they were informed by the history of the countries that came together on the basis of common history and concrete programmes, rather than ideology.

Lessons from elsewhere: Europe and Asia

In the European example, the European Coal and Steel Community was formally established in 1951 by the Treaty of Paris and was first proposed by the French foreign minister, Robert Schuman, in 1950. 'The solidarity in production thus established will make it plain that any war between France and Germany becomes not merely unthinkable, but materially impossible' through the creation of a supra-national authority that would pool and control coal and iron ore which provided materials for making armaments of war. In 1967, the European Coal and Steel Community merged with the European Economic Community (EEC) – now the European Union (EU). The Schuman Declaration that created the European Coal and Steel Community had the following distinct aims:

- It would mark the rebirth of Europe;
- It would make war impossible between member states;
- It would encourage world peace;
- It would transform Europe by a 'step-by-step' process (building through sectoral supra-national communities) leading to the unification of Europe democratically, including both East and West Europe separated by the Iron Curtain;
- It would create the world first supra-national institution;
- It would create the world's first international anti-cartel agency;
- It would create a single market across the community;
- It would, starting with the coal and steel sector, revitalise the whole European economy by similar community processes; and
- It would improve the world economy and the developing countries, such as Africa (Schuman Declaration, pp. 1–2).

In the second example, the Association of South East Asian Nations (ASEAN) was created through the ASEAN Declaration of 1967 in Bangkok, Thailand, with the principal objective of promoting and enhancing security in the region. The security considerations were informed by the tragic experiences of the Second World War and previous colonisation of countries that founded ASEAN.

An interesting feature of both the European and ASEAN experience is that it was not informed by deterministic economic ideologies, but rather by pragmatism based on a developmental trajectory that did not serve the fetish worship of the markets, which is the case with African integration arrangements through the 'liberal market economy approach'. The East Asian development model is based on the functional concept of the 'social market economy approach', which Professor Ryokichi Hirono, chairperson of the Initiative for Development in East Asia (IDEA), described as characterised by the following:

- Importance of complementarity and balanced relations required between effective competition under market forces and effective co-operation among all actors at household, corporate, community and national levels among those institutions;
- Centrality of human centred development and growth with equity, prioritising investment in human capital for growth and social equity for income distribution, resulting in higher values for human development indicators such as literacy, enrolment ratios, lifespan and income distribution and lower values for under-five mortality rates, and population below the poverty line; and
- Overwhelming importance attached to pragmatism, as against ideology at all levels of decision-making in the formulation and implementation of economic, social and governance policies.

An overview of regional integration in Africa

African economic integration has been informed by economic determinism as evidenced by the Lagos Plan of Action and the Final Act of Lagos of 1980, and the Abuja Treaty and Constitutive Act of the African Union of 2002. These treaties envisaged the integration of African economies along neo-classical lines of linear progression or development from preferential trade areas, free trade areas, customs unions, common markets and ultimately the African Economic Community.

In recent years, particularly in the 1990s and the early years of the twenty-first century, there has been a tendency among academics, policy-makers and commentators to attribute the rise of regionalism in Africa to the phenomenon of globalisation. This rationalisation in the form of pseudo-science ignores the fact that Africa has since the time of colonisation been vertically integrated into the global economy on the basis of raw material supplier. In fact, the challenge facing Africa has been and still is to integrate into the global economy on the basis of modernisation and structural transformation.

There is evidence that some of the founding fathers of the OAU were keenly aware that without modernisation and surrender of sovereignty by independent African states the realisation of economic 'liberation' would remain a mirage. Kwame Nkrumah articulated the *raison d'être* of political and regional integration in Africa in the following statement:

> Never before have a people had within their grasp so great an opportunity for developing a continent endowed with so much wealth. Individually, the independent states of Africa, some of them potentially rich, others poor, can do little for their people. Together by mutual help, they can achieve much. But economic development of the continent must be planned and pursued as a whole. A loose confederation designed only for economic co-operation would not provide the necessary unit of purpose. Only a strong political union can bring about full and effective development of our natural resources for the benefit of our people (pp. xi–xiv).

Unfortunately, for Africa the vision of Kwame Nkrumah was not only diluted, but eviscerated by those leaders who belonged to the gradualist school of integration who sought to break up Africa into subregions on the basis of colonial history and common language.

The major weakness, if not a failing, of regional integration in Africa is that it is not informed by a vision, which was enunciated by Kwame Nkrumah. On the contrary, the integration programmes are informed by neoliberal ideology, which has a blind faith in the power of the market. The advocates of untrammelled power of the market appear to suffer from selective amnesia in that even in the developed market economies governments have historically planned and provided guidance to the market in the form of micro, meso and macro policies. The recent global economic crisis has amply demonstrated the limitations of the market when it is not regulated by governments. Indeed, the economies in Asia and China have fared better from the global economic crisis and its recession as a result of stronger regulation of the markets, which has provided stability and certainty to the private sector.

It is ironic that during the Asian financial crises in the late 1990s commentators and soothsayers were predicting the doom of these economies due to what they perceived as 'crony capitalism'. That the apocalypse of these economies has not come to pass is due to a development paradigm that is anchored on the 'social market economy'. With regard to regional integration, political security considerations have underpinned the programmes of the ASEAN.

Regional integration in Africa is ill-fated because it has no historical, cultural and ideological underpinnings based on subjective and objective conditions. It is no accident that trade integration that has been religiously espoused by all regional integration organisations has not produced the desired results because it is not based on social and economic modernisation of pre-colonial structures. On the contrary, the model of economic integration applied by African countries has deepened the dependence and predatory economic relations with the rest of the world. Hence, in the absence of structural transformation and modernisation, the post-colonial independent states have remained suppliers of raw materials and services, a role that was consciously assigned to them during the colonial era.

The critique and proposed solutions that follow in this chapter are a radical departure from conventional orthodoxy, which has reviewed African regional integration on the basis of flawed assumptions and deterministic economic models. The following aspects are addressed:

- Institutional and legal underpinnings of regional integration arrangements;
- Why the deterministic economic model is unsuitable for Africa;
- Funding of regional integration by member states;
- Open regional integration on the basis of a new global economy; and
- Proposed solutions for effective and mutually beneficial regional integration.

Institutional and legal underpinnings of regional integration arrangements

> The difficulty lies not in new ideas, but escaping from the old ones, which ramify, for those brought up as most of us have been, into every corner of our minds
>
> — John Maynard Keynes

The assumption of independence by the new leaders in Africa heralded a new dawn with a 'change of guard' from colonial governors/administrators to indigenous African leaders who inherited, lock, stock and barrel, the colonial institutions and laws. There is ample evidence to show that no sooner had the new elite stepped into the shoes of the departing colonial powers did they rigorously enforce the same oppressive laws that they had fought against. That this was the case is not surprising because most of the new rulers were educated by the same colonial powers and even imitated the culture and lifestyles of departing colonial administrators whom they held in awe and esteem. This is the difficulty that Keynes captured in the quotation above. Hence, the changes were invariably in the form of appearances rather than substance. Professor Adebayo Adedeji eloquently captures this malaise in an article in *Africa Report*:

'Unfortunately, the leadership that took over from the departing colonial authorities did not go back to our past and revive and revitalise our democratic roots. They took the least line of resistance and convenience and continued with despotism, autocracy and authoritarism. But the basic democratic culture is still there' (p. 58).

The institutions and legal underpinnings of regional integration should have as their basis the establishment of national institutions and legal reforms that expressly provide for regional integration. A review of the treaties of regional organisations reveals that their aims and objectives are to promote collective self-reliance at the regional level without accompanying measures at the national level. The concept of self-reliance implied autarky and interdependence among the participating countries and disengagement from the rest of the world. Paradoxically, there were no programmes at the national level to realise this laudable objective of self-reliance as each post-colonial state continued to implement policies and programmes of the previous colonial order.

The policies of import substitution have been mistaken for an attempt to disengage from the world economy. This is not the case because these policies were intended to create an elite business class that owed its allegiance to the ruling elite, and the economic rents of the parastatal companies were appropriated by both the political elite and the 'comprador bourgeoisie' who were appointed to run the companies. Import substitution policies were no different in terms of class interest to incipient industries that were established during colonial rule in that such industries were licensed on condition that they did not compete with industries in the metropolis.

The striking feature of regional integration is that the leadership is not accountable to the people because the decisions taken at the regional level are rarely subjected to popular debate in each country. In fact, post-colonial governments have not used the same skills and zeal that were used in mobilising the populace for liberation for nation building and regional integration in the post-independence era. This explains why regional programmes are not mainstreamed into national budgets and national development programmes as regional programmes are considered as residual to national development. The lack of accountability means that regional integration has remained elitist and bureaucratic. Whereas African countries have established regional secretariats, there have been no parallel programmes to establish institutions at national level to oversee the implementation of regional programmes. Even where ministries responsible for regional integration have been established, they have either not been adequately funded or they lack authority to ensure that regional integration programmes are implemented by other government ministries.

It is, therefore, not accidental that regional integration in Africa has not been accompanied by the establishment of capable institutions at both the national and regional level. At the regional level, countries have been openly hostile to the creation of supra-national institutions which are not only independent but have the power to enforce decisions. This explains why even the African Union (AU) Commission has no executive powers. In fact, an examination of the Constitutive Act reveals that the AU Commission is devoid of supra-national powers.

The exercise of sovereignty by each country has meant that decisions taken at the regional level are rarely implemented. This has given rise to a situation where the countries at the regional level have the capacity to make decisions but no capacity to implement the decisions. The lack of implementation has been interpreted by some analysts as reflecting lack of political will; yet this is simply due to the political and bureaucratic elite protecting their privileged positions. They cannot countenance sharing power with supra-national institutions. This position is equally true at the national level where the populace does not participate in policy formulation and review; this is the prerogative of the government in power.

Although some of the treaties require that decisions taken at the regional level are legislated at the national level, this is rarely done for most of the decisions, with the exception of those decisions requiring tariff reductions and harmonised legislation. It is common knowledge that most national parliaments do not schedule the adoption of legislation of regional decisions. The exceptions to this are the regional organisations that have regional parliaments that enact laws, such as the East African Legislative Assembly and the Economic Community of West African States (ECOWAS) Legislative Assembly. The issue of power relations between the executive and legislature is confirmed by the fact that there are regional and continental parliaments that have no power to legislate. The African Union Parliamentary Assembly is a case in point. Notwithstanding the existence of these legislative assemblies, they do not have the capacity to enforce decisions thus making them ineffective and redundant at worst.

The inability of African countries to build and nurture public institutions to support and facilitate national development and, by extension, regional integration has been the Achilles heel of post-independence development. This is in contrast to the Asian tigers and newly industrialising economies, which have accorded priority to ensuring that a capable state plays a decisive role in facilitating national economic development and regional integration, including integration into the world economy. This partly explains why China, which is ruled by a Communist Party, has been able to achieve unprecedented growth and poverty reduction since 1979. This is due to Deng Xiaoping, the father of the Chinese 'Four Modernisations' programme, the pillars of which were agriculture, industry, science and technology, and the military. There are lessons to be learnt from these emerging economies that have become key drivers and locomotives for the global economy. This tectonic shift in economic power is ably articulated by Singaporean intellectual and author, Kishore Mahbubani, in his book *The New Asian Hemisphere: The Irresistible Shift of Global Power to the East.*

Why the deterministic neo-classical economic model of regional integration is unsuitable for Africa

In the introduction it was demonstrated that the intellectual and philosophical inspirations to regional integration in the EU and the ASEAN were pragmatic and not ideological. This is in contrast to Africa where regional economic integration is informed by the ideology of neo-classical economic theory, major assumptions of which are not applicable to African economies where structures have hardly changed from the time of colonisation. The following statement by President John Kufuor of Ghana is instructive:

> Ghana was the first sub-Saharan nation to win its independence from a colonial power in 1957, yet the average per capita income of my people is lower than it was in the 1960s, four decades after independence. Some of the blame for this we Ghanaians must accept. My country must acknowledge that corruption is a cancer on our public and economic life and must be contained.
>
> One hundred years ago, our trading was limited to the supply of raw materials, mainly gold, timber and cocoa. One hundred years later, our trading consists of raw materials, mainly gold, timber and cocoa. I must admit that Ghana's path towards self-reliance has not been smooth. I am painfully aware that it has been characterised by one step forward and two steps backward (p. 5).

Admittedly, most economies in Africa fit into the description by President Kufuor. The fact is that Africa has not modernised its social and economic structures as evidenced by the continued dependence on the export of primary commodities. There is ample evidence that the adoption of the Vinerian model of economic integration has not focused the attention of policy-makers to address the policy measures that are required to bring about the structural transformation and modernisation of economies.

261

Without exception, most regional integration organisations in Africa use trade as a key driver for regional economic co-operation and integration. Given the fact that these economies are producers of primary commodities and have no industries to process the primary commodities, it is a leap of blind faith to expect that regional integration on the basis of trade liberalisation will result in increased intra-regional trade. This is simply because there is nothing to trade in due to the absence of product complementarities among countries. This explains why intra-regional trade remained on average at less than 10% of global trade. Due to incorrect diagnosis, orthodox analysts come to the wrong conclusion that intra-trade is low, inter alia because of poor infrastructure on tariff barriers and unsound regulatory policies. Similarly, there is a preoccupation with whether regional integration arrangements bring about welfare gains. Hence, economists spend their time analysing the so-called trade creation and trade diversion effects of regional integration. Regional integration is considered to be beneficial if there is trade creation, which means that trade liberalisation enables domestic/regional producers to supply goods at a lower price than foreign suppliers because they are competitive. Conversely, regional integration that produces trade diversion is considered not beneficial to consumers because through tariff preferences it replaces competitive foreign suppliers with high-cost regional suppliers. As is the case in economics with the 'all other things being equal' assumption, trade diversion and trade creation models do not take into account that there may be institutional support and policy measures that render the outcomes from the analysis meaningless. Lastly, primary commodity producers have to deal with issues related to inelastic demand and price fluctuations for their products.

Empirical evidence shows that regional integration that is based on neo-classical economic theory is inappropriate for social and economic modernisation. It is my contention that Africa would by now have made significant strides in both national development and regional integration if a production model of integration were

Primary commodity prices

Primary commodity dependence among African countries has meant a dependence on the uncertainty of price fluctuations over time. Despite recent upward pushes in prices of certain commodities, such as metals and food, commodity prices remain a challenge for developing countries in Africa because relative to prices of manufactures and services, they have declined over time. The consequence of this is that the incomes derived from exports of primary commodities have not kept abreast of the import costs of mainly manufactured products from mainly developed country partners (see Figure 11.1).

The last few years provide a clear picture of the effect of primary commodity prices. In the last four years, we have witnessed a major contraction in global trade induced by the global credit crunch. One of the key transmission channels of impacts of the global credit crunch in developing countries was commodity prices (Te Velde, 2009). Within the same period, the world has also witnessed rising food prices as a result of tighter global supply and demand balances, amongst other reasons.

Figure 11.1   Price indices of selected products, 1970=100.

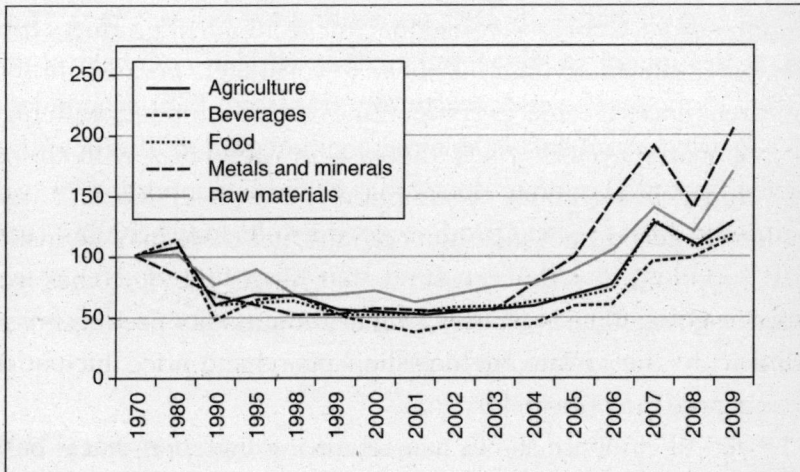

(Source: World Bank)

used. This is because without a dynamic production base that is driven by the private sector there are no goods and services to trade among the countries. Production integration entails government facilitation of the private sector, both domestic and foreign; development of infrastructure; and scientific and technological institutions that support technology transfer, innovation and industrial policies. The Asian tigers, including Japan, did not develop by accident but through conscious policies and result-oriented programmes or projects. The same applies to India, China and Brazil.

A case in point is the transformation of Shenzhen, which was a sleepy Chinese fishing village when Deng Xiaoping launched his economic reforms in 1979. Shenzhen was designated the first Chinese Special Economic Zone in 1980. According to a study by a Hong Kong-based consulting firm Enright, Scott & Associates, Shenzhen's population grew from 30 000 to 11 million between 1980 and 2005. Its economy increased at an average rate of 28% from 1980 to 2004. In real terms, the economy grew from US$32.5 million in 1980 to US$41 billion in 2004. During the same period, exports from Shenzhen reached US$105 billion in 2005, accounting for 13% of China's total. This is the model of development that African countries should emulate to modernise and structurally transform their economies in order to bring about sustainable regional integration. It is envisaged that the Special Economic Zones that China is supporting in some countries in Africa should produce good results in the coming years.

It is evident that the structural transformation of African economies is going to be elusive as long as these economies continue to be linked to the former metropolitan powers. Among others, the following are the principal reasons.

Firstly, the investments in manufacturing that were made in the colonies were those that did not compete with industries in the metropolitan countries. For example, the trade policy of the EU and successive conventions, starting with the Lomé Convention's preferences, ensured that African, Caribbean and Pacific (ACP) countries exported unprocessed primary commodities, which were then processed in Europe. The deterrent was that duties on processed commodities escalated according to the degree of processing. Hence, European companies could not invest in manufacturing plants in the ACP countries.

Secondly, the existence of enclave economies meant that the majority of the population that survived on subsistence farming with no disposable incomes were not attractive to potential manufacturers due to the small size of the market.

Funding of regional integration programmes/projects

With the exception of ECOWAS, which has an operational regional fund, most of the funding for regional integration projects is from multilateral financial institutions and from development partners. There appears to be confusion by both analysts and countries that are members of regional integration organisations in that funding invariably refers to the contributions they make to regional organisations and not to funding regional programmes and projects. It is instructive to note that the funding of regional secretariats is minuscule when compared to regional programmes and projects, which can often run into hundreds of millions of dollars. This has given rise to regional organisations being seen as off-budget vehicles for mobilising external resources for funding the financing gap. There is nothing wrong with this except that these resources are not subject to national governance oversight. Frequently, national parliaments and other stakeholders are not aware of this funding and its impact, if any, on the national economy.

It is unfortunate that countries would opt to co-operate and implement transnational projects that they do not contribute to in funding. This has implications for ownership and governance of regional institutions. Apart from the budget contributions to regional secretariats and related institutions, which are provided for in annual national budgets, there are no budget provisions for the implementation of regional programmes. This has resulted in a situation where cross-border infrastructure projects that are funded by development partners do not have counterpart funding because the expectation is that the development partners would provide all the funding.

Although the treaties establishing various regional organisations envisage the pooling of both financial and human resources, this has not happened in practice. In the few cases where technical assistance has taken place, this has been done on the basis of bilateral co-operation rather than regional co-operation.

Development partners have over the years provided Official Development Assistance (ODA) to governments and to regional organisations in the form of grants. The impact of the ODA flows has been minimal due to the fact that they have been exclusively to governments. Most donors have policies that will not allow the funds to directly benefit the private sector. Invariably, donor-funded projects have benefited the private sector from the donor countries because domestic companies in the recipient countries do not have the capacity to undertake the projects. This is because of failure on the part of African governments to put in place policies that support the development of the domestic private sector. This explains why aid has not been a dynamic for national development and regional integration. Lessons can be drawn from the Marshall Plan in post-war Europe whereby the plan was not a programme of charity aid or of government infrastructure but of support to local business. According to authors R. Glenn Hubbard and William Duggan, the key elements of the Marshall Plan were as follows:

> First, it made large loans from the United States to European governments. Second, each government spent the repaid funds on restoring public infrastructure to further boost production. Third, each government made pro-business policy reforms along the lines of the ten elements of *Doing Business*. Fourth, a European coordinating body reported to an American ad-ministrative body back in the United States (pp. 90–91).

Open regional integration on the basis of the new global economy

The past decade has witnessed seismic shifts with respect to political and economic governance in Africa, with the majority of African countries experiencing changes in government through multi-party elections. In addition, the rule of law and respect for property rights has become embedded in the social and political fabric of the majority of AU countries. The AU itself has adopted an interventionist policy in member countries by explicitly outlawing changes of government through non-constitutional means. Regional Economic Communities (RECs) have also become actively involved in ensuring that conflicts are resolved and that member states within each REC effect changes in governments through democratic means. This means that citizens are increasingly influencing and determining government policies, which was not the case in the majority of African countries in the post-independence era.

These political changes have been made possible by the ending of the cold war and the process of globalisation; particularly the information and communication technology (ICT) revolution. The latter has empowered individuals through, among others, the Internet and broadcast media to follow global events in real time. Recently, media such as Facebook and Twitter have been instrumental in producing political changes in some countries. There are cases where political leaders have used Facebook to announce not only their intentions to contest presidential elections but also to disseminate their political manifestos. The ICT era has the potential, unlike any other technology, to foster social and economic interaction and integration.

Effective and transparent institutions are key to national development and regional integration. This is because without effective institutions (that is, governments, independent judiciaries, etc.) at local, national and regional levels, good policies do not work. Institutional capacity building should be a continuous activity. For regional integration programmes to be owned and implemented by different stakeholders in society there is need for regional fora for consultations in programme design and ultimately implementation that includes governments, business, labour and civil society. It is this quartet that should set the agenda and dictate the pace of regional integration. The effectiveness of this mechanism requires constitutional reforms that will allow the different parties to engage as equal partners.

Taking into account that by and large the African economy structurally comprises the following triad, the formal economy, informal economy and subsistence economy, appropriate macro, micro and institutional strategies and policies should be designed at national and regional levels to bring about structural integration of the different sub-economies. The case in point is agricultural subsistence economy, which is the largest employer, yet it has remained outside the formal economy with the result that the labour of the peasant farmer is not priced when setting the price of agricultural commodities. This has effectively subsidised the urban population and locked the peasant farmer in the poverty trap due to incorrect government policies that set prices for agricultural staple foods that are produced by subsistence farmers.

Whereas big companies are important for employment, skills acquisition and technology transfer they need to be complemented by small and medium enterprises (SMEs). The latter can provide competitive services to big firms, as is the case in developed and emerging developing economies, which have coherent policies that facilitate market integration of SMEs. In most countries in Africa, there are no coherent policies that facilitate the growth of SMEs through linkages with big firms. Dynamic regional integration, therefore, entails the development of national and regional strategies and policies that facilitate market-driven complementarities and synergies between big firms and SMEs.

On the economic front, Africa has witnessed far-reaching economic reforms that have resulted in improved economic governance through sound macroeconomic policies. This partly explains why the recent global financial and economic crises have not had the same impact on African economies as in developed economies. Investment regimes have been liberalised and economies opened up to both cross-border and foreign direct investments. The process of globalisation, coupled with the shift in economic power from the industrialised economies to the newly industrialising economies, has produced healthy competition that African countries are taking advantage of.

The strategies for regional integration have been based on trade liberalisation through the removal of tariffs as a means of realising larger markets from which economies of scale can be derived by economic operators. Until recently, this strategy did not produce the expected result because it was not accompanied by commensurate investment. This situation was compounded by the fact that whereas there are explicit trade policies for regional integration there have been no corresponding regional industrial strategies and policies. Hence, the expected structural changes have not taken place. For instance, in the case of Africa, crude oil and copper were top export products in both 1970 and 2009, accounting for a significant proportion of the export profile. However, for ASEAN, manufactured products such as office machinery have come to dominate the export portfolio in 2009 when compared to the 1970 export scenario. Petroleum, though a major export of ASEAN, now contributes less to total exports than it did in 1970. In the case of the EU, its differentiated manufacturing export profile has remained consistent over the period under review. An additional key insight into the issue of realisation of larger markets is the fact that the export and import profiles of Africa have implied a comparatively lower level of the ratio of intra-regional trade compared to extra-regional trade (see Figures 11.2 and 11.3).

There is evidence that the economic structures are beginning to change due to increasing cross-border and foreign direct investments in manufacturing and the services sectors. These investments are mainly from Asia and China. Recently, South Korean and Japanese

Figure 11.2 Comparative analysis of African, ASEAN and EU shares of intra-regional export trade to total regional exports, 1970–2009.

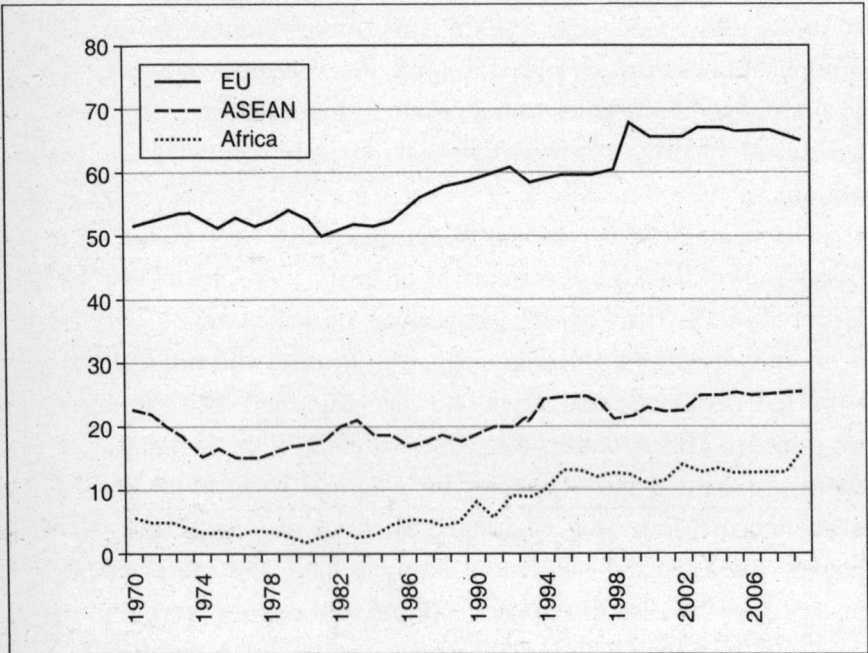

(Source: United Nations COMTRADE database)

companies have or are in the process of investing in various African countries. These market-driven investments will over time lead to intra-industry regional trade, which at present is marginal when compared to the ASEAN region and the Asia Pacific region, which is about 25% of intra-trade. For the EU it is even higher at 35%. Tables 11.1, 11.2 and 11.3 provide insight into the composition of export products that are traded in these regional blocs and which are mainly value-added products. In the case of Africa, it can be seen from the tables that there are limited opportunities for intra-industry trade. It is intra-industry trade that promotes technological co-operation and innovation, including a more integrated market and more competitive industries.

Figure 11.3 Comparative analysis of African, ASEAN and EU shares of intra-regional import trade to total regional imports, 1970–2009.

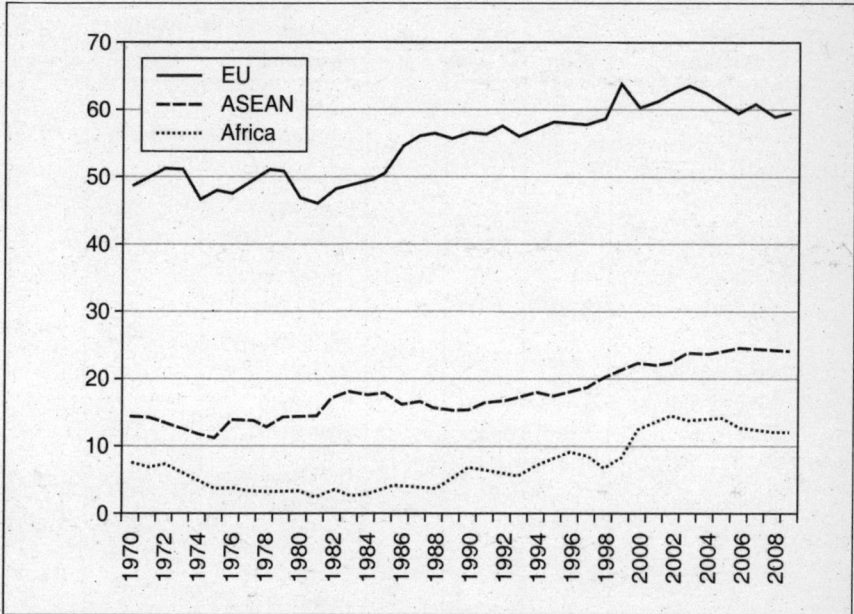

(Source: United Nations COMTRADE database)

To sustain these investments, there is need for RECs to come up with regional industrial policies that will promote regional value chains that are part of the global value chains. Effective regional value chains will require at the national level institutional support, extension of easy credit and formulation of coherent policies that allow entrepreneurs to thrive and excel.

Regarding agriculture, the sector by and large is characterised by a subsistence economy with the majority of the population mired in poverty. This is a sector that requires policies at the national level for modernisation and at the regional level for the implementation of policies that allow free trade in agricultural commodities, including regional value chains. Taking into account that governments do not have unlimited resources, both financial and human, this is a sector

Table 11.1 Africa's comparative product export profiles, 1970 and 2009.

Africa's top global export products, 1970				Africa's top global export products, 2009			
SITC*	Product description	Value, US$m	As a % of total	SITC	Product description	Value, US$ m	As a % of total
33101	Crude petroleum	3 155	57.1	33101	Crude petroleum	73 395	57.1
68212	Refined copper, including remelted	1 302	23.5	68121	Platinum, etc., unwrought or partly wrought	6 767	5.3
11212	Wine or fresh grapes	162	2.9	68212	Refined copper, including remelted	2 342	1.8
24231	Sawlogs and veneer logs, in the rough	161	2.9	84112	Women's, girls' and infants' outer garments	2 294	1.8
68226	Tube and pipe fittings of copper	142	2.6	84111	Men's and boys' outer garments, not knitted	2 209	1.7
65141	Cotton yarn and thread, bleached, etc.	56	1.0	51335	Phosphorous pentoxide and phosphoric acid	1 741	1.4
7232	Cocoa butter (fat or oil)	49	0.9	71923	Centrifuges and filtering machinery	1 692	1.3
65229	Other cotton fabrics, woven, bleached	39	0.7	84144	Outer garments knitted, not elastic	1 433	1.1
3201	Prepared or preserved fish	37	0.7	84143	Under garments knitted, not elastic	1 209	0.9
24331	Lumber, sawn lengthwise, etc. non-conifer	22	0.4	3201	Prepared or preserved fish including caviar	1 063	0.8
	Other products	406	7.3		Other products	34 423	26.8
	Total	5 529	100.0		Total	128 568	100.0

* *Standard International Trade Classification*
(Source: United Nations COMTRADE Database)

Table 11.2   ASEAN region comparative product export profiles, 1970 and 2009.

ASEAN's top global export products, 1970				ASEAN's top global export products, 2009			
SITC	Product description	Value, US$ m	As a % of total	SITC	Product description	Value US$ m	As a % of total
33101	Crude petroleum	453	27.2	71492	Parts of office machinery	24 107	8.8
24231	Sawlogs and veneer logs, in the rough	225	13.5	33101	Crude petroleum	16 370	6.0
28311	Ores and concentrates of copper	191	11.5	72499	Other tele-communications equipment	9 413	3.4
24331	Lumber, sawn lengthwise, etc. non-conifer	106	6.4	73289	Other parts for motor vehicles	7 921	2.9
63121	Plywood, etc. and veneered panels	63	3.8	71842	Excavating, levelling, boring, etc.	7 128	2.6
5481	Roots and tubers, fresh or dried, sago	49	2.9	73492	Parts of aircraft, airships, etc.	6 198	2.3
33251	Lubricating prep. cont. >70% by weight	26	1.6	89711	Jewellery of precious metal	5 593	2.0
73289	Other parts for motor vehicles	24	1.5	89111	Gramophones, tape recorders, etc.	5 285	1.9
71842	Excavating, levelling, boring, etc.	21	1.2	28311	Ores and concentrates of copper	5 258	1.9
72998	Electrical parts of machinery and appliances	20	1.2	71829	Other printing machinery	4 296	1.6
	Other products	487	29.3		Other products	182 304	66.6
	Total	1 665	100.0		Total	273 874	100.0

(Source: United Nations COMTRADE Database)

Table 11.3   EU region comparative product export profiles, 1970 and
             2009.

EU top global export products, 1970				EU top global export products, 2009			
SITC	Product description	Value, US$ m	As a % of total	SITC	Product description	Value, US$ m	As a % of total
73289	Other parts for motor vehicles	2 581	4.3	73289	Other parts for motor vehicles	111 217	5.6
85102	Footwear with soles of leather/ rubber	1 077	1.8	72499	Other tele- communications equipment	40 602	2.0
71931	Lifting and loading machinery	957	1.6	59999	Other chemical products and preparation	38 726	1.9
84144	Outer garments knitted, not elastic	929	1.6	54163	Bacterial products, sera, vaccines	38 366	1.9
65161	Yarn of continuous synthetic fibres	908	1.5	51285	Heterocyclic compounds, including nuclei	35 462	1.8
71842	Excavating, levelling, boring, etc.	861	1.4	71142	Jet and gas turbines for aircraft	30 570	1.5
67431	Plates under 3 mm uncoated not h.c.	823	1.4	86171	Medical instruments and appliances, etc.	29 768	1.5
24321	Lumber, sawn lengthwise, etc. conifer	756	1.3	82109	Furniture and parts thereof, n.e.s.	29 702	1.5
72499	Other tele- communications equipment	756	1.3	71992	Taps, cocks, valves & similar appliances	29 531	1.5
71992	Taps, cocks, valves & similar appliances	641	1.1	71842	Excavating, levelling, boring, etc.	27 979	1.4
	Other products	49 524	82.8		Other products	1 574 323	79.3
	Total	59 812	100.0		Total	1 986 247	100.0

(Source: United Nations COMTRADE Database)

that requires coherent policies for partnership between governments and the private sector. This is, however, unlikely to happen as long as governments intervene in the marketing of agriculture products, particularly staple foods that are subject to export bans.

The provision of infrastructure is key to market integration. One of the most important roles of governments is the provision of 'hard' infrastructure, such as roads, bridges, electricity generation plants and irrigation. It is, however, advisable that governments only provide the infrastructure that cannot be provided by the private sector in order not to crowd out the private sector. In the case of transboundary infrastructure, there is a need for governments to plan, programme and mobilise external funding, including the allocation of domestic resources for the implementation of the projects collectively. This would entail that infrastructure, economic planning and finance ministries work together on these regional projects, which is not the case at present.

Financial services

The liberalisation of the financial sector at both the national and regional levels has witnessed increased flows of cross-border invest- ments by commercial banks, including the emergence of African transnational commercial banks, which are now providing stiff com- petition to existing multinational banks from outside the continent. Among others, these banks include Ecobank, United Bank of Africa, Access Bank, First National Bank, Amalgamated Bank of South Africa and Kenya Commercial Bank. These banks are providing valuable services to their clients regarding business opportunities in the countries where they operate. Hence, for the first time, we are seeing cross-border investments being made by African multinational com- panies in different parts of the continent. This trend is not limited to African banks in that banks from Asia, India and China have also established their presence on the continent. These financial institutions are promoting regional integration in Africa and South- South trade and investments.

Proposed solutions for effective and mutually beneficial regional integration

A combination of factors, which, inter alia, includes political and economic reforms at both the national and global level, have created an enabling climate for the realisation of regional integration in Africa. In order to bring about intense and sustainable modernisation and structural transformation through regional integration the following measures are proposed:

- Intensification of political and constitutional reforms to enable effective participation in regional integration of governments, business, labour and civil society organisations.
- Empowerment of the AU and regional economic communities with supra-national authority over those aspects of regional integration that cannot be effectively and efficiently discharged by national governments.
- The development and strengthening of national and regional regulatory authorities to facilitate market-driven operations and prevent market failure, particularly of the financial sector.
- Facilitation of cross-border and foreign direct investment in setting up industries that can add value to Africa's abundant natural resources that are currently exported in either raw material or semi-processed form. National and regional development plans should provide specific targets against which progress in value addition, structural transformation and modernisation can be measured.
- Formulation and implementation at national and regional level of capacity building policies and programmes that facilitate and promote the speedy integration of the formal, informal and subsistence economies on the basis of market-driven complementarities and synergies.
- Development of human resources, including the overhaul of educational systems, to produce an educated cadre that has the requisite knowledge and skills for the economy.

Conclusion

Never before has Africa been in the position of being the last frontier in development. Africa's natural resources, including its relatively young population if properly harnessed, can provide the global economy with new sources of growth and continued prosperity, including global peace and security. For this to occur, there is a need to urgently speed up the integration of the African market, whose combined population and gross domestic product are 1.2 billion and US$1.4 billion respectively. The continent can only take advantage of the opportunities offered by the globalisation process and the global shift in economic power to emerging developing economies in other parts of the world, provided there is leadership with the vision that transcends national considerations and accepts that the world does not owe Africa anything, but rather that through its own efforts, Africa can join the league of nations as an equal partner.

SINDISO NDEMA NGWENYA is the Secretary General of the Common Market for Eastern and Southern Africa (COMESA).

References and suggested reading

Adedeji, A. (1993) 'Africa's Heritage of Participatory Democracy and Confederation' in *Africa Report* Vol. 38, p. 58.

Enright, M.J. and Scott, E. (2011) *The Greater Pearl River Delta*. 5th edition (Enright, Scott & Associates, Hong Kong).

Hirono, R. (2003) 'Chairman's summary', Initiative for Development in East Asia (IDEA), available at mofa.go.jp/policy/ada/region/e_asia/idea0308.

Hubbard, R.G. and Duggan, W. (2009) *The Aid Trap: The Hard Truths about Ending Poverty* (Columbia University Press, New York).

Keynes, J.M. (2007 [1936]). *The General Theory of Employment, Interest and Money* (Macmillan, London).

Kufuor, J. (2002) 'Ghana: The Limits of Self-Reliance' in *Financial Gazette*, 3 May, p. 5.

Mahbubani, K. (2008) *The New Asian Hemisphere: The Irresistible Shift of Global Power to the East* (Public Affairs, New York).

Nkrumah, K. (1961) *I Speak of Freedom: A Statement of African Ideology* (William Heinemann, London).

Schuman Declaration, 9 May 1950.

Te Velde, D.W. (2009) 'The Global Financial Crisis and Developing Countries: Synthesis of Findings of 10 Country Studies'. Overseas Development Institute (ODI) Working Paper 306, London.

Index

water 141–2
  health and poverty 142
  irrigation 208, 225–6, 275
  pollution 142
  resources 40, 208
  and soil erosion 217
water-borne diseases 141–2
wealth redistribution policy 8
welfare
  increase in expenditure 134–5
  programmes 8
  regimes in developed countries
    233–4
  transfers and government
    expenditure 175
Wellcome Trust 154
wildlife and national parks 220
  exploitation and poaching 220
World Bank 43–4, 158, 182, 224,
    235, 238–9
  Berg Report 235, 237, 241–2
  'Doing Business Survey 2010'
    170
  mission to African countries
    234–5
World Competitive Report
    129–30

World Economic Forum 170
World Health Assembly 156
World Health Organization (WHO)
    140–1, 143, 155, 158
  Framework Convention on
    Tobacco Control 163–4
World Trade Organization 245
WorldWideWorx SME survey 130

xenophobia 92
Xiaoping, Deng 260, 264

Zaire 191
Zambia 63, 163
Zanzibar 199
Zenawi, President Meles 199
Zille, Helen 77
Zimbabwe 9–10, 63, 148, 222,
    224–5
  destruction of food production
    145
  electoral violence 198, 199–200
  Great Dyke 65
  wars and political instability 143
Zuma, President Jacob 71–2, 83,
    91–2